organizational
evolution and
strategic management

SAGE STRATEGY SERIES
www.sagepub.co.uk/strategyseries

The objective of the *SAGE Strategy Series* is to publish significant contributions in the field of management in general, and strategy in particular. The books aim to make a scholarly and provocative contribution to the field of strategy, and are of a high intellectual standard, containing new contributions to the literature. We are especially interested in books which provide new insights into existing ideas, as well as those which challenge conventional thinking by linking together levels of analysis which were traditionally distinct.

A special feature of the series is that there is an active advisory board of strategy scholars from leading international business schools in Europe, USA and the Far East who endorse the series. We believe that the combination of the SAGE brand name and that of an active and strong board is a unique selling point for book buyers and other academics. The board is led by Professor Charles Baden-Fuller of City University Business School and the Rotterdam School of Management, and Richard Whittington of the Said Business School, University of Oxford.

Editors

Professor Charles Baden-Fuller, *City University Business School, London and Erasmus University, NL*
Professor Richard Whittington, *Said Business School, University of Oxford*

Editorial Board

Professor Frans van den Bosch, *Rotterdam School of Management, Erasmus University, NL*
Professor Robert Grant, *Georgetown University, USA*
Professor Tadao Kagono, *Japan Advanced Institute of Science and Technology*
Professor Gianni Lorenzoni, *University of Bologna, Italy*
Professor Leif Melin, *Jönköping International Business School, Sweden*
Professor Hans Pennings, *The Wharton School, University of Pennsylvania, USA*
Dr Martyn Pitt, *School of Business and Management, Brunel University, UK*
Professor Alan Rugman, *Kelly School of Business, Indiana University, USA*
Professor Joachim Schwalbach, *Humboldt-Universität zu Berlin, Germany*
Professor Jörg Sydow, *Freie Universität Berlin, Germany*

organizational evolution and strategic management

RODOLPHE DURAND

SAGE Publications
London • Thousand Oaks • New Delhi

© Rodolphe Durand 2006

First published 2006

SAGE Publications Ltd
1 Oliver's Yard
55 City Road
London EC1Y 1SP

SAGE Publications Inc.
2455 Teller Road
Thousand Oaks, California 91320

SAGE Publications India Pvt Ltd
B-42, Panchsheel Enclave
Post Box 4109
New Delhi 110 017

British Library Cataloguing in Publication data

A catalogue record for this book is available from the
British Library

ISBN-10 1-4129-0862-0   ISBN-13 978-1-4129-0862-7
ISBN-10 1-4129-0863-9   ISBN-13 978-1-4129-0863-4 (pbk)

Library of Congress Control Number: 2005932164

Typeset by C&M Digitals (P) Ltd., Chennai, India
Printed in India at Gopsons Papers Ltd, Noida
Printed on paper from sustainable resources

CONTENTS

LIST OF FIGURES

LIST OF TABLES

ACKNOWLEDGMENTS

Over the years, many people played a key role in orienting my ideas and research, and have participated directly or indirectly in the genesis of this book.

As far as international research is concerned, I owe Michael Lubatkin and Huggy Rao my progress in this domain. Both of them have taught me what academic research and discipline are, and their openness to foreign thoughts is an example to follow.

The decision to write this book has been supported by Richard Whittington, who encouraged me to develop my ideas in a more adequate format than articles. Kiren Shoman from Sage Publishers as well as Charles Baden-Fuller defended the project from the beginning to its completion. Douglas Miller, during a PDW session at the Academy of Management 2003, as well as Michael Lounsbury over conversations gave me confidence that this project could be of interest for organization and strategy fields. I thank them all for their trust and support.

Many of my French colleagues also deserve my deep acknowledgments. From HEC, Paris Jean-Pierre Detrie, Alain Dumont, Jean-Pierre Nioche and Bertrand Quélin accompanied me in the first years of postgraduate education. From EM-Lyon, Tugrul Atamer, Roland Calori, Pierre-Yves Gomez, and Philippe Monin shared their theoretical insights and friendship. From the Sorbonne, I attended professors classes led by Renaud Barbaras and Nicolas Grimaldi who showed me how to delve into the foundations of thought.

Discussions at workshops, conferences, and seminars were very constructive. Among others, my thanks go to R. Coeurderoy, M-L. Djelic, T. Kleiner, B. Kogut, J-A. Lamberg, J. McGuire, P. Murmann, A. Vas, and H. Volberda for sharing these moments.

The book has benefited from the professionalism of two proofreaders, Helen Ross and Paula Ross. They were very comprehensive with the linguistic traps unpurposefully present in the successive versions of the chapters. Finally, Julie Bayle-Cordier and Nancy Piacentini helped me to polish sections of the manuscript.

PREFACE

In this exciting book, Rodolphe Durand addresses fundamental issues in strategy and organization theory. Why do organizations evolve the way they do? How far can managers really shape organizational evolution? To what extent are organizations ultimately prisoners of their own environment? These are urgent questions in a world where firms seeem to rise and fall with increasing rapidity and where their chief executives claim such extravagant rewards for what are often fleeting successes.

Durand's wide-ranging and penetrating discussion matches the fundamental nature of the issues he raises. This book recognizes from the start the serious ontological and epistemological questions that underpin its issues and attacks them in a sustained and coherent fashion. As co-editors of the Sage Strategy series, Charles Baden-Fuller and I firmly believe that a book offers an important opportunity to go beyond the fragmented and cursory preliminary remarks scattered through the journal literature, and with this book Durand summons the intellectual rigor and breadth of vision to take full advantage.

This book is indeed animated by a broad view. It is characteristic of its range that it offers an authoritative discussion of historical and contemporary evolutionary theories in biology as a foundation for its critique of many contemporary approaches to evolutionary organization theory. Lamarck, Spencer, Darwin, Dawkins and Gould each find their place. It is equally characteristic of the book's ambition that Durand looks forward to when management scholars and scientists can equalize the balance of intellectual trade, with biologists and others looking to organization theory for *their* analogies.

As a corrective to standard Variation, Selection and Recruitment (VSR) models, Durand develops an Organizational Evolution and Strategy model that grants a substantial role to managers and organizations in shaping the environmental conditions for their continued evolution. Organizations make both selection-preserving and selection-transforming choices. Adaptation is distinguished from selection and co-evolution set in its context.

It is conventional to say that a book like this will inspire and guide doctoral students and researchers early in their careers. Certainly this book will so inspire and guide. Doctoral students will be drawn by the substance and wide-range of issues that the Organizational Evolution and Strategy model can address. They will also find critical help in the Checklist Appraisal Grid, allowing them to verify the status of the theories they are experimenting with.

However, I would say more. The substantive and systemic nature of Durand's discussion here will make this book valuable reading for established scholars of at least two further kinds. First, there are those who are busy already with empirical studies in the evolutionary tradition. The data and analytical demands of studies in this area can be all-absorbing. This book will help evolutionary researchers stand back, recall the bigger picture and see their place in the larger whole. As they see this larger whole, they will be able more effectively to plot the contributions of their individual studies to the advancement of this dynamic and increasingly-influential field.

But this book will be important for a second group of established researchers, amongst whom I would have counted myself. There are many who have been struck by the growing influence of evolutionary research, but have been anxious about the biological metaphors and environmental determinism that the conceptual language seems to imply. From outside, one wondered whether the success of evolutionary research was really a good thing. These anxious watchers-from-the-sidelines should be reassured by this book. They will be impressed by the gathering insights from an energetic discussion, but they will also find clear criteria by which to sort out the good from the glib. For strategy and organization researchers wishing to gain a comprehensive but critical view of where evolutionary research is going, Durand has provided an essential guide.

Richard Whittington
Oxford
July 2005

PART I POSITIONING THE QUESTIONS

The departure point of this book coincides with the onset of both the author's career as a researcher in the organization and strategy fields more than ten years ago and the technological telecommunication revolution of the 1990s. Why did we start using mobile phones at that time, rather than earlier or later? Why did that mobile phone have this form, size, features, and so on and not others? As surprising as it may seem, the search for answers to these innocent questions did not lead to an in-depth study of communication technologies, but to further questions concerning how companies crafted the industry. For instance, not only did Nokia surf on the industrial boom, but it also purposefully made choices that determined the penetration of mobile phones into households. Nokia combined technological capacities with marketing savviness and built a far-reaching advantage. Nokia even overcame the recession in the industry and reorganized itself to face the new challenges of technological convergence (mobile phones, cameras, personal digital assistants, digital jukeboxes). At that point, strategic questions arose rapidly regarding convergence of standards, market deregulation, internationalization of the communication industry, management of alliances, supply relationships, and technological advances; the organizations operating in the telecommunications industry and the people in charge of devising their strategies faced serious challenges regarding all of these dimensions. From a theoretical viewpoint, population ecology, evolutionary economics, and the resource-based view offered frameworks useful to the study of these issues, nested in a broader inquiry, summed up by a handful of questions. How do we think of organizational evolution? Why and how do organizations evolve, and what is the role of strategic management in this process? Is it really the organization that evolves? Are there not other elements in the external or internal environment of the organization that account for its evolution?

This book began from this anecdotal departure point. The time has now come to put into perspective the ideas that were developed partially in my early papers, all of which are concerned with performance, competitive advantage, and evolutionary models in organization science. More importantly, in the organization and strategic fields also, the time is ripe for a deeper dialogue, reflection, and appraisal of how we collectively refer to and use the evolutionary traditions brought about by nineteenth-and twentieth-century thinkers. This book endeavors to scrupulously follow the biological traditions, to present their arguments and limitations, and to show that the current approaches to organizational evolution enjoy a complex genealogy. It strives to bring to the foreground questions regarding the ontological and epistemological implications of our use of evolutionary models, and to propose a tentative model that enables us to reconcile intellectual lineages that give every appearance of being incommensurable.

The book consists of three parts. In Part 1, Positioning the Questions, Chapter 1 describes the difficulties and benefits of analyzing the problematic relationships between organizational evolution and strategic management. Chapter 1 also sketches the contents of the book's subsequent chapters. Chapter 2 addresses definitions, presents approaches that deal with organizational evolution and strategic management, and examines five conceptual puzzles applicable to both organizational evolution and strategic management. In the second part of the book, Building the Checklist Appraisal Grid of Evolutionary Models, three chapters discuss traditions in the area of biological evolution and current approaches to organizational evolution and end with the construction of a grid for evaluating evolutionary models to be applied to organizations. Finally, Part 3, The Organizational Evolution and Strategy Model, presents the Organizational Evolution and Strategy (OES) model and reflects upon its implications.

1 INTRODUCTION, CONTRIBUTIONS, AND OVERVIEW

Strategy researchers are particularly well positioned to conduct the complex, multidimensional, multilevel longitudinal studies that we suspect are necessary to fully understand the interactions between competence and competition. (Henderson and Mitchell, 1997: 12)

The philosopher must go further than the scientist. ... Philosophy is not only the turning of the mind homeward, the coincidence of human consciousness with the living principle whence it emanates, a contact with the creative effort: it is the study of becoming in general, it is true evolutionism and consequently the true continuation of science. (Bergson, 1911/1983: 369–70)

Organizational evolution embraces a full range of phenomena and may seem to be a protean theme whose determinants and consequences lie beyond anyone's reach. However, this book seeks to iron out some of the difficulties by presenting a documented account of existing approaches, discussing the contributions and limitations of these approaches, stepping back to study adjacent fields confronted with similar concerns, and suggesting additional propositions.

As a first stage in this 'journey', this chapter attempts to whet the reader's appetite. Next, this chapter presents the three major contributions of the book: first, a theoretical foundation for strategy compatible with evolutionary approaches, secondly, the Checklist Appraisal Grid for evolutionary models, and thirdly, the Organizational Evolution and Strategy (OES) model. Finally, the last section outlines more precisely the contents of this book.

1.1 WHY IS IT IMPORTANT TO REFLECT ON ORGANIZATIONAL EVOLUTION?

Writing a book implies respect for its readers, and part of the due respect concerns the explanation of the raison d'être of the book itself. Six reasons (at least) show why it is important to reflect on organizational evolution and study the sometimes thought antagonistic links between organizational evolution and strategic management.

First, reflecting on organizational evolution may give clues and help explain why economic factors change. Grandparents had and still have buying preferences and purchasing behavior different from those of their grandchildren. They do not shop in the same stores or use the same modes of payment, for instance. Start-ups endorse values and identities that stand out against long-standing market leaders. Reflecting on organizational evolution may contribute to our understanding of these contrasted traits, namely that it may explain why some companies do not pay attention to new customers' habits or new competitors' values while others quickly adopt and fashion these trends (for example, Barnett and McKendrick, 2004; Palmer, Pennings, and Zhou, 1993). Economic organizations are key players in social and cultural landscapes, and studying organizational evolution helps us to comprehend the evolution of the broader society.

Secondly, part of this book's intent is to resolve the incompatible alternatives: the inapplicable theorizing of academics vs. the non-validated recommendations of practitioners (Baldridge et al., 2004; Bennis and O'Toole, 2005). Over the last twenty years, organizational evolution has been a topic of interest for many different disciplinary fields. On the one hand, theoretical treatises abound, tackling the problem through narrow lenses. On the other hand, eclectic practical guides gloss over the determinants of organizational evolution and rush to common-sense principles in order to succeed in the endless and ruthless strife for (business) life. This book offers a simple but robust presentation of organizational evolution. It articulates the benefits and limitations of different advanced research perspectives, such as population ecology, evolutionary economics, and the dynamic RBV (Resource-Based View), among others. This book differs from excellent recent works on organizational evolution (Aldrich, 1999; Baum, 2002) in that it does not attempt to provide an exhaustive account of organizational evolution, in terms of research disciplinary subfields (power, networks, cognition, etc.) or of empirical works. It proposes a careful reflection upon the evolutionary tradition applied to a representation that connects organizational evolution to strategic management.

Third, a close examination of organizational evolution helps us discover the key mechanisms that affect the performance and survival odds of organizations. Understanding why and how firms change reveals the principal levers of action for decision-makers (Carroll, 1993). The association of such an apparently theoretical notion (organizational evolution) with a more practically oriented activity (strategic management) may reveal greater proximity than expected. Associating them provides a means to deal with a human agency's freedom within a context of both dynamic and constrained processes (Child, 1997; Hrebiniak and Joyce, 1985). Understanding organizational evolution, rationally or intuitively, is at the root of strategy and strategic management.

Fourth, beside the practical guidance of strategic management, this book encourages a more theoretical reflection on strategy, which has been left in disarray as schools of thought no longer seem to dialogue (Baldridge et al., 2004; Hinings and Greenwood, 2002). A sound theorizing of strategy and strategic management is needed. This book attempts to meet the requirement, and to avoid entrenchment into one school or the other. Our intuition is that behind the debate on the external vs. internal determinants of above-average performance lies an unresolved question: the nature of firm selection.

A fifth rationale for this book is to assess the real contributions of the recurring biological analogies in sociological, economic, and managerial literatures, whether academic or not. Biological analogies permeate [*se répand*] organizational analysis. Units under scrutiny become biological entities. A routine and a gene are alike, an organization is similar to an organism or a cell, and a population of organizations to a species. Observed patterns of development of living animals, whether social or not, are employed to describe economic activity and its variations, independently of the level of analysis. For instance, the terms 'industry life cycle', 'product life cycle', and 'capability life cycle' (Helfat and Peteraf, 2003) are supposed to adequately describe industrial sagas, product diffusions, and competence growth. While being informative at a macro level concerning possible evolutionary patterns, the life cycle analogy says little about the determinants of a specific organization's success or failure. Why does one firm successfully evolve through victorious product launches while its competitors fail in imitating or bypassing it? What role does strategic management deserve in the naturalistic logic of cycles? In the cycle analogy, firms follow a predetermined evolutionary path, and only the first movers seem able to hedge risks by positioning themselves at different stages of different product life cycles. While analogies play a role in scientific popularization, they do not necessarily contribute to a greater in-depth understanding of the phenomenon of organizational evolution. Analogies may even cloud scholars' and decision makers' judgments, offering illusory shortcuts where a stepwise analysis is in order. Certain notions (for example, genes, fit, adaptation) may increase the confusion. Defining organizational evolution precisely, exploring its underlying mechanisms, and disentangling its connections with strategic management are valuable efforts that can help to keep analogies in their rightful place.

Finally, this book is an effort to oppose the forces that constrain us to remain within our fields, bordered by disciplinary fences [*closures*]. While exposed to diverse sources of knowledge – such as organization theory, strategic management, sociology, philosophy, and artificial intelligence – this book's author certainly cannot pretend to be a specialist in every discipline. Nevertheless, there is a common thread connecting his forays into these disciplinary fields – the insistent question of the links between organizational evolution and competitive advantage. Our hope is, therefore, to encourage readers who are themselves involved in multi-disciplinary research to pursue their endeavors. [*efforts*]

1.2   CONTRIBUTIONS AND SUGGESTIONS

Three contributions form the nucleus of this book. The first relates strategy to an evolutionary thought of economic change. Strategy as an academic discipline has hesitated to define and position itself since its early days, when Weick (1979) insisted on managerial capacity for enactment while McKelvey (1982) and others stressed the fundamental importance of environmental constraints for organizations' survival. Strategic choice and environmental determinism may not be the two extremes of the continuum (Hrebiniak and Joyce, 1985), but still there is an urgent need to reconcile adaptationist and isomorphic tenets. Whereas tales of firm successes based on strategic management are widespread in business schools, the pivotal notion of selection dear to the Variation-Selection-Retention (VSR) framework (proposed by Campbell (Campbell, 1969; Baum and McKelvey, 1999)) leaves unanswered the question of the effect of human choices based on strategic intentions (Campbell, 1994). Hence, we must reconcile a conception of deliberate organizational changes with (seemingly) timeless natural selection principles. We need to explore whether or not selection criteria vary and can be influenced, thus connecting organization theory and strategy to praxis (Durand, 2001). Therefore, the major task boils down to conceiving of a non-teleological organizational evolution that integrates the agents' intentions and – perhaps independently of the latter – their actual actions.

l'ensemble

This book musters concepts, ideas, and models to bolster the underpinnings of strategy as a scientific discipline, overriding the sterile opposition between intention and selection. Therefore, this book aims, first, to provide a clear foundation for strategy and strategic management and to recast them in a general framework of organizational evolution. Strategy is not industrial economics, nor decision science, nor organizational sociology. Strategy is the necessary counterpart of organizational evolution. In this book, strategy is defined as an articulated theory of competitiveness that drives the choices of organizational members in favor of or against selection criteria that are present in their industry and organization. Strategic management is an applied set of practices guided by a theory of competitive action, namely, directing how to actualize potentialities from controlled resources and modes of exchange. These definitions are compatible with a clearer meaning of firm selection, and

mettre ensemble ⬅

bracket strategy and strategic management together with organizational evolution.

The second contribution of this book consists of the Checklist Appraisal Grid for evolutionary models. Table 1.1 presents an abridged version of the grid; the complete grid appears at the end of the second part of the book (see Table 5.3). The abridged version prefigures its four constituents: first, it tackles conceptual puzzles, such as time efficacy and level of analysis; secondly, it is logically cautious, for example, avoiding acceptance of biological analogies as scientific evidence; thirdly, it overcomes the limitations intrinsic to the VSR model, such as the immutability of the selection criteria; and fourthly, it meets the challenges raised in recent debates in the field of biology (for example, the formalization of evolution from the replicator-vehicle vs. replicator-interactor dyads). Based on study of extant literature from different perspectives (organization theory, strategy, biology, and philosophy), the grid enables researchers to evaluate the degree of validity of an evolutionary model, to anticipate stumbling blocks, and to reflect on the consequences of their theory, model, and advice.

obstacles

The Organizational Evolution and Strategy (OES) model is the third contribution of the book. It is an original attempt to overcome the many hurdles that keep us from reconciling environmental determinism and strategic intention. The third part of the book is devoted to its construction from a VSR core (Chapter 6) and the discussion of its implications (Chapter 7). The OES model is inspired by previous evolutionary representations (Baum and Rao, 2000; Volberda and Lewin, 2003) but differs in the units of analysis and the influential relationships among the units and across levels (Figure 1.1 gives an overview of the model). The OES model meets the 'Checklist Appraisal Grid' criteria: it answers the questions, is aware of the cautions, overrides the VSR limitations, and meets satisfactorily the recent challenges posed by biology. The OES model details the relationships that

Table 1.1.   A checklist appraisal grid of an evolutionary model (abridged)

	1	2	3
Conceptual puzzles about evolution (from Chapter 2)			
Is there a time efficacy in organizational evolution?			
Is there an ending/finality of organizational evolution?			
...			
Cautions (from Chapter 3)			
Decomposing levels of analysis			
Introducing population reasoning			
Avoiding finalism as scientific demonstration			
...			
VSR limitations (from Chapter 4)			
Immutability of selection criteria			
Conceptualization and integration of inter-relationships between entities			
...			
Challenges (from Chapter 5)			
Selection tautology (survival of the fittest)			
Level of analysis challenge: replicator-vehicle vs. replicator-interactor			
...			

1   The model responds very well to the issue
2   The model takes the issue into account
3   The model does not account for the issue

influence industry evolution, firm survival, and competitive advantage. Fourteen processes of interest, left unnamed in Figure 1.1, are presented and discussed in Chapters 6 and 7. Overall, the OES model allows us to revisit results of existing studies and paves the way for new research avenues. Three secondary contributions are also explored.

Chapters 3 and 5 supply, from a broad conceptual viewpoint, the substance of paradigmatic theories of biological evolution – and recent controversies useful for anyone interested in organizational evolution. These chapters, which are historically accurate and avoid attribution to Darwin of Spencer's or Lamarck's ideas, convey the conceptual milestones that help organizational theorists circumvent pitfalls and hazards when reflecting on organizational evolution and strategic management.

From an organizational theoretical viewpoint, in Chapter 4 the discussion and commentaries of the VSR framework (Baum and McKelvey, 1999; Campbell, 1969, 1990, 1994) and the co-evolutionary approach (Lewin and Volberda, 1999; Murmann, 2003) shed light on underlying assumptions of these conceptions. This is a much-needed endeavor to enable greater coherence in future research work.

From a practical viewpoint, two elements are worthy of mention: a taxonomy of evolutionary notions (Chapter 2, section 2.1), and the implications derived from the OES model (Chapter 7, Tables 7.1 and 7.2). The former underlines the imperceptible dimensions that we manipulate when using evolutionary notions, such as metamorphosis, improvement, or convergence. Concerning the latter element, the series of questions raised when evaluating selection pressures helps managers

Figure 1.1 The organizational evolution and strategy model

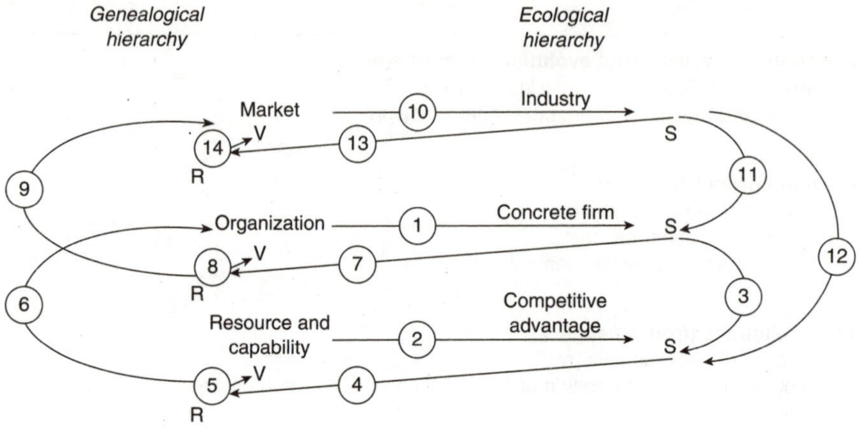

to represent the influences that constrain their discretionary power. Furthermore, these selection pressures embed themselves within the OES model. Clearly, uncovering the governing mechanisms of organizational evolution enhances the agents' capacity for action.

Finally, curious readers might be interested in unconventional arguments, such as:

- why evolution is caused and not a cause in itself (section 3.2),
- why we should abandon the association between firm and adaptation in the phrases 'firm X adapts' or 'the firm's adaptation' (sections 5.3 and 6.2),
- why the dynamic resource-based view is not tautological but merely takes 'objects' for 'properties' (sections 5.3. and 6.1),
- why we would be better off not applying Lamarckian, Darwinian, and Spencerian adjectives to qualify organizational processes (see section 4.3),
- why we should reserve the fit and fitness notions to very specific research contexts and methods (see sections 2.2 and 5.2).

Other iconoclastic ideas are left to the discovery (and hopefully the satisfaction) of the patient reader.

1.3 A LOOK AHEAD

This book consists of three parts, with a total of seven chapters. Chapter 2 completes this introduction, setting the stage for what follows by defining organization, organizational evolution, strategy, and strategic management. Chapter 2 also provides a taxonomy of sixteen common notions used to qualify evolution, showing the principles that underpin it. While the notions are not discussed extensively, this classification shows that fundamental differences exist, despite the use of a common vocabulary, between the terms associated with organizational evolution. Finally, Chapter 2 shows that organizational evolution and strategic management share five conceptual problems, which anyone involved in these fields must be aware of. They are the question of time efficacy, the possibility of applying unified evolutionary principles to various levels of analysis, the nature of selection in evolutionary frameworks, the compatibility of the consequences induced by organizational evolution and its causes, and reflections on the finality of evolutionary and strategic models.

Part 2, Building the Checklist Appraisal Grid of Evolutionary Models, is comprised of Chapters 3 to 5. Here, theses on both biological and organizational evolution are studied in order to build a 'grid' that will be useful in evaluating application of evolutionary models to organizations. Chapter 3 reviews extensively the three most often-cited evolutionary traditions: of Lamarck, Darwin, and Spencer. Going back to the original texts, Chapter 3 shows the key contributions of each tradition, and their usefulness to modern analyses that are applied to different entities. The rationale for this chapter is to clarify the conceptual bases of commonly used analyses of organizational evolution. Our academic literature rarely relates and integrates our references with the original evolutionary frameworks (Lamarckian, Darwinian, and Spencerian). Promoting organization studies as organization science requires that we not distort the ideas and logic we borrow from other fields (biology, economics, sociology, psychology, and so on) but rather deepen them so that one day the other fields will borrow from organization science. Therefore, this chapter is not so concerned about correcting the resultant misconceptions that may have occurred; rather, it poses the fundamental questions. What do we mean when we refer to past traditions? Do we need imports from them or not? Should these imports necessarily be accurate, or not?

Chapter 4 presents the Variation-Selection-Retention (VSR) model and considers whether it can become a paradigmatic framework for the study of organizational evolution. In particular, it considers how selection operates and fluctuates over time in the VSR model, and whether strategic management can be integrated within the framework. It shows that organizational evolution should be treated independently of the references to nineteenth-century biological traditions. Since the entities in evolution and the problems and issues at stake differ, and since biological thought and research have progressed, the use of qualifiers such as 'Lamarckian', 'Darwinian', or 'Spencerian' does not serve to advance organizational evolution; rather, it acts as an impediment. Sketchy references to nineteenth-century traditions blur notions, mistakenly attribute ideas to the original authors, and hinder development of independent thought regarding organizational evolution. Finally, Chapter 4 reviews and comments on the contributions of the co-evolutionary approach recently proposed by, among others, Lewin and Volberda (1999), Barnett (1997), Murmann (2003), and Henderson and Stern (2004).

Chapter 5 looks at contemporary arguments, developed in the mid-twentieth century by biologists and paleontologists, that refute the evolutionary synthesis. Four major cases are debated: first, the possibility of a unique paradigm accounting for micro and macro evolutionary phenomena; secondly the risk of tautological suppositions whenever extolling a selectionist logic; thirdly, the fallacy of considering every adaptation to be preordained and successful; and fourthly, concerns as to whether intermediary entities (such as the organism) are useful in any manner for understanding evolution in itself – since genetic explanations or environmental laws may suffice. In this chapter, we come to the conclusion that the criticism against adaptation hits home. Adaptation is not a causal power that determines and explains organizational evolution and competitive advantage. Other arguments, such as the selection tautology criticism and the ultra-selectionist view of genetic replication, however, are not accepted. Finally, at the end of Chapter 5 and in the conclusion of Part 2, we introduce the 'Checklist Appraisal Grid for evolutionary models'.

Part 3 presents the Organizational Evolution and Strategy (OES) model and looks ahead to some implications of our long journey. Chapter 6 develops, appraises, and refines the OES model, based on a two-fold hierarchy of entities (genealogical and ecological) and on three levels of analysis (market-industry, organization-firm, and resource and capability-competitive advantage). It describes the fourteen relationships that connect entities and levels in the OES model. Finally, Chapter 6 renders explicit the conditions under which the OES model applies.

Finally, Chapter 7 expands the discussion of the implications of the OES model and attempts to negate ideas that are often assumed. At the epistemological level, a final question is raised concerning the nature of causality in strategy research, and the political and moral implications of our conceptions of organizational evolution – whether or not in accordance with the OES model. At the theoretical level, propositions are made to further advance research in population ecology, evolutionary economics, dynamic RBV, and strategy research. At the empirical level, suggestions include the construction of panel data and the use of fixed- and random-effects models. Finally, a tentative questionnaire of practical interest closes the book.

Please note that this book has its own rhythm. Even-numbered chapters are dense and analytical. Odd-numbered chapters are considerably shorter; they present additional analyses supportive of the arguments (reflections on nineteenth-century evolutionary traditions, more contemporaneous debates in biology, and prolongations of the OES model) and are intended to be islands in the flow of organization and strategy references and arguments. Also, be aware that the cited references from organization and strategy literature support the arguments and illustrate ideas but do not pretend to be exhaustive. It is also possible that older references to Lamarck, Darwin, Spencer or others will be of interest to those – presumably a sparser readership – who would like to extend the reflection back to its intellectual origins. Finally, at the end of Chapters 2–6, a summary contains the major points of the chapter. Some times this is presented in tabular form and these boxes enable the reader who is pressed for time to retain the highlights and capture the flavor of the argument. There is a progressive integration of the blocks that will hopefully lead to unanticipated lessons for future research.

2 ORGANIZATIONAL EVOLUTION: PROBLEMS AND PROMISES

The evolution of evolution has sustained and supported a vision of evolutionary engineering. Evolutionary theories of history are invitations to intervention in history. (March, 1994: 49)

The field of research that is typically interested in organizational evolution is exceptionally vast. Institutional sociology, industrial economics, organizational ecology, and management theory, among others, have devoted hundreds of thousands of pages to the topics linked with organizational evolution. Evolution is a pervasive theme, simply because it characterizes the changes of the observable, and consequently exhibits constantly and ostentatiously the *explanandum*: that which has to be explained. Few people are interested in spending portions of their lifespan seeking to explain why things do not change. Economists speculate on deviance from market discipline (Schmalensee, 1985), while sociologists wonder about the isomorphic power of institutions (Carroll, 1993; DiMaggio and Powell, 1983). Organizational theorists may argue that companies follow a life cycle pattern, more or less, from their inception to growth and decline. Thus, alternative explanations surface to account for the diverse evolutionary forms that are observable in the exhilarating lives of many organizations. Specific triggers _déclencheurs_ would condition the way organizations grow and evolve (Haveman, 1992). For instance, size and age have been invoked and positively tested as giving birth to many liabilities that could undermine a firm's competitiveness and performance. _handicaps_ Liability of newness (Stinchcombe, 1965), liability of adolescence (Fichman and Levinthal, 1991), and liability of senescence (Ranger-Moore, 1997) are typical examples of similar dangers faced by organizations. Other authors, however, applaud the immense variety of evolutionary paths and even celebrate self-organizing phenomena that emerge from new ventures and within existing organizations (Gersick, 1991). They argue that the conditions for organizational emergence can be supplemented by organizational adaptability (Siggelkow, 2001). The direction of the evolution, nonetheless, is left open, which explains the great diversity in the evolutionary paths of different companies.

Before presenting an evaluation grid for these diverse evolutionary models applied to organizations, a task that Part 2 carries out, three preparatory steps are in order. First, this chapter opens with a section that defines as simply as possible organization, evolution, and organizational evolution. This section does not restrict the definition of organizational evolution to a single, narrow characterization; rather, it directs the reader to several notions akin to evolution that have been used in the literature, and proposes a taxonomy of these. Next, the second section of this chapter underscores three common pitfalls in the study of organizational evolution, namely succumbing to attractive analogies, to the seductive notion of fit, and to unnoticed restrictions of applicability. This section also raises questions and paradoxes related to organizational evolution itself, questions that anyone should ask when tackling the phenomenon. They involve methodological precautions as well as conceptual puzzles. The former deal with the distinction between variance and process approaches of organizational evolution. The latter grapple with time efficacy, the applicability of unified evolutionary principles at various levels of analysis, the under-characterized notion of selection in evolutionary frameworks, the compatibility of the consequences induced by organizational evolution and its causes, and the presence of a definite end to organizational evolution. Finally, the last section positions strategy and strategic management in the organizational evolution context, and discusses further contentious aspects of their relationships.

2.1 DEFINITIONS

This section presents definitions of organization, evolution, and organizational evolution. Regarding 'organization', it addresses several research traditions and seeks to offer operational definitions for them, independently of their profit or non-profit orientation. For 'evolution', we present a schematic description of biological evolution that connects two analytical levels: the genotypic and phenotypic spaces. Next, we tie both elements (organization and evolution) into 'organizational evolution' and, finally, using the basic who, what, why and how questions, offer a primary taxonomy of sixteen different evolutionary notions commonly applied to organization.

WHAT IS AN 'ORGANIZATION'?

Over the last decades, theoretical disputes about organizational evolution have coiled around crucial dimensions of organization definition, such as boundary maintenance, exchange characteristics, and isomorphic power of institutions. Indeed, depending on assumptions, organizations are socially constructed systems of human activity that are goal-oriented and boundary-maintaining (Aldrich, 1979, 1999). Organizations are efficient economic coordination modes that optimize exchange-specific characteristics (Williamson, 1985). Organizations belong to cultural, institutional, and social wholes and, as human collectives, are induced by the convergence of means and norms on exchange, technological prowess, and scientific ethos (Scott, 2001). From these perspectives, and in order to provide a manageable definition of organizations, we retain the five following fundamental theses:

First, organizations are social collectives that set goals and orientations; in this book, we dissociate individual motivations, beliefs, and ends from organizational goals and orientations. Personal, psychological, and philosophical considerations are subsumed under the organization's enounced goals and orientations. This does not deny the possible influence of individual ideas on an organization's orientations. We certainly stand with those who profess the importance of individual objectives for an organization's development. But we doubt the ultimate importance of these personal ends for the organization's evolution relative to other organizational and environmental determinants of performance and survival.

Secondly, organizations are collections of controlled resources, including human resources. The retention and protection of these resources determine the organization's boundaries. Firms constantly make choices impacting the resources, and they shape decisions to join or leave the organization. A consequence of this is the intrinsic and enduring heterogeneity of organizations.

Thirdly, organizations abide by few economic principles. On average, over the years, the sum of production, transaction, and coordination costs must be lower than the cumulated returns from activity. Disposable income and buyers' decision criteria impose drastic constraints on what organizations can viably offer. However, from this book's perspective, classical optimizing behavior and economizing principles are not necessary conditions for developing arguments and propositions about organizational evolution and strategic management. Some organizations will operate, survive, and evolve even in the absence of economic optimization. Since such organizations will probably be wasteful and ineffective, the general economic situation of the region hosting them will steadily lose ground vis-à-vis other regions. Therefore, while neither absent nor unrealistic, optimizing and economizing principles are limited to a particular subset of the general conditions of organizational evolution as presented in this book.

Fourthly, organizations interact with one another and develop exchange relationships of different kinds: supply, support, collaboration, consortium, franchise, and so forth. The transaction is one of the most widely available exchange relationships, and certainly one of the most significant if the organization is to survive as an unchanged entity. However, 'second-order' dimensions of organizational activity and inter-organizational relationships, for example, learning, cooperative association, and alliances, complement this transactional view and impact organizational evolution as well.

Finally, organizations develop relationships with institutions. A variety of actions exists that link together institutions and organizations: institutional emergence may trigger organizational entrepreneurship; ignoring institutional components can hamper organizational deployment; organizations may be creators or drivers of institutions. This diversity of possibilities feeds considerable debate, which this book barely touches on because of space limitations.

Taking into account these five elements just described, we now define organizations as:

purposive social collections of controlled resources, building exchange relations and interacting with other entities, and developing strategies for reaching objectives.

Figure 2.1   Four rules of transformation in biological evolution

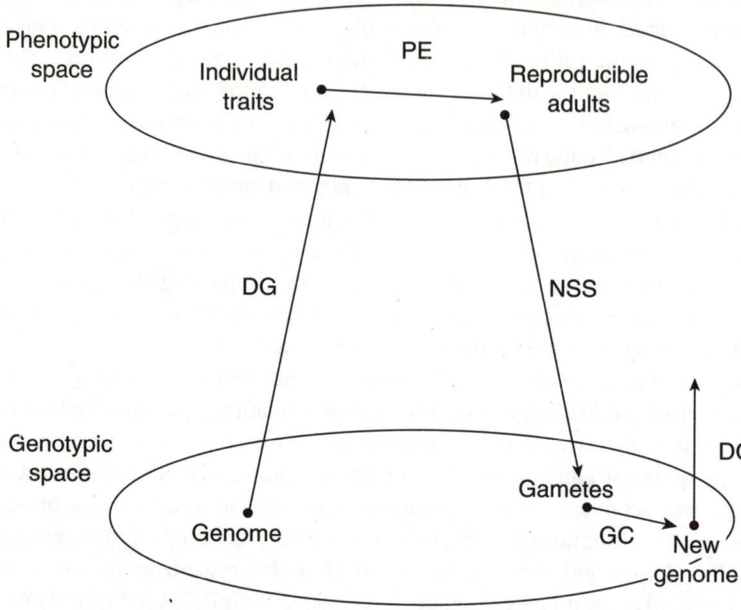

Definitions (adapted from Mayr 1991 and 2001)
Genotype: the set of genes of an individual; its genetic constitution.
Genome: the totality of genes carried by a single gamete.
Gamete: a male or female reproductive cell (e.g., spermatozoon or egg) that carries half of the organism's full set of chromosomes (in sexual reproduction).
Phenotype: the total of all observable features of an individual (including his/her anatomical, physiological, biochemical, and behavioral characteristics) resulting from the interaction between the genotype the individual inherited and the environment s/he encounters.

WHAT IS EVOLUTION?

The idea of evolution applies to an entity and characterizes a process of transformation. At this point, we simply define evolution as a series of identifiable events, events that may concern one or several entities, that may or may not alter their essential characteristics, and that may or may not proceed toward an anticipated stage or ending. We refer to an introductory description of evolution by the biologist Richard Lewontin (1974) and amended by the philosopher Elliot Sober (1984). According to them, four potential transformation rules lead to the phenomenon called biological evolution. Figure 2.1 displays them graphically.

Figure 2.1 presents the relations between the genotypic space that concerns the individuals' genetic constitution, and the phenotypic space where individuals' traits are expressed. Let us start with a genome. A first rule for transformation is expressed in developmental genetics (DG). DG encapsulates the laws for the passage from genes to phenotype. DG delves into the internal composition of the genome, the transformation of the information it contains into proteins, cells and organs, and the interactions with environmental factors that enhance or impair these developmental functions (nurturance, physical and chemical characteristics of the environment, and so forth). DG is, therefore, a first source of biological evolution.

We are now within the phenotypic space, where an individual exhibits particular traits and belongs to an ensemble of like individuals. A second rule for transformation is given by population ecology (PE). Population ecology describes the factors and interactions that intervene in the composition of cohorts of individuals. It includes the effects of environmental constraints (resource scarcity, carrying capacity) and of the selection of individuals as they mature and are likely to mate and reproduce. Examining the fluctuations over time of a population's characteristics (for example, birth, death, density, and speciation rates) is a second method of comprehending biological evolution.

A third rule of transformation connects the phenotypic space with the genotypic space. When an individual reproduces, half of that individual's genome is randomly transferred to the offspring via inter- and intra-chromosomal recombination (the other half coming from the other parent). Natural and sexual selection (NSS) fulfills this sorting and combinatory role. Hence, selection determines how individuals mate, and influences their fertility and the genetic recombination involved in sexual reproduction. In that context, evolution is driven by the law of selection, in part sexual selection (the choice of reproductive partners) and in part natural selection (that which governs the retention of genomic variations from one generation to the next).

A last series of laws, which plays a role in biological evolution, governs the genetic composition (GC) of the gamete pool resulting from reproduction. In this case, evolution is internal to individuals, and even located in their reproductive cells. The new genome that results from this complex pairing process is set for a new series of transformations, which will lead to its phenotypic expression first (DG) and then to other evolutionary processes (PE, NSS and GC).

Altogether, these four mechanisms establish the potential sources and different meanings of biological evolution. It may consist of genotype only (GC), phenotype only (PE), or include the passage from both levels (DG and NSS). In its broader sense, an evolutionary theory would integrate in one corpus the four transformation processes. This does not proceed without difficulties. The major obstacle to a unified theory of evolution deals with the possibility of representing genotypic and phenotypic phenomena in a common currency. Indeed, NSS assumes that phenotypic characteristics are causes of evolution while genotypic characteristics consist of effects. However, causal properties seem to be attributed to genotypes as well (for example, DG and GC), which complicates the causal processes at work in biological evolution.

This sketch of biological evolution complements the simple definition of evolution provided in the first lines of this sub-section. In particular, both the causal influences of transformational rules and the distinction of levels of analysis become salient. Therefore, we amend the definition:

> Evolution is a series of identifiable events causally linked together, which concern one or several entities at different levels of analysis that may or may not alter their essential characteristics, and may or may not proceed toward an anticipated ending.

WHAT IS ORGANIZATIONAL EVOLUTION?

parties (firms)

Available to us are two strands that represent a portion of what is meant by organizational evolution. First, organizations are purposive social collections of controlled resources, building exchange relations and interacting with other entities, and developing strategies for reaching objectives. Second, following from the preceding, biologically-inspired description, evolution is a series of identifiable events causally linked together, that concern one or several entities at different levels of analysis, that may or may not alter their essential characteristics, and that may or may not proceed toward an anticipated ending. A generic definition of organizational evolution could logically be:

> Organizational evolution is a series of identifiable events causally linked together, which involve at different levels of analysis one or more organizations (i.e., purposive social collections of controlled resources, building exchange relations and interacting with other entities, and developing strategies for reaching objectives), that may, but do not necessarily, alter their essential characteristics, and may or may not proceed toward an anticipated ending.

Organizational evolution, therefore, involves a variety of situations – such as smooth predetermined growth, a unit's collapse that has repercussions at the higher organization level, a switch in the organization's goals, and so on. Aldrich (1999), for example, distinguishes three major organizational transformations, each of which involves a break with existing routines that challenges the basis of organizational knowledge: a change in goals, in boundaries, and in activities. In order to differentiate between an encompassing and a restricted definition of organizational evolution, it is necessary to specify the representative types of organizational evolution and to gain access to its determinants.

From an extensive literature review, Van de Ven and Poole (1995) derive four ideal types of organizational development and change, the second type being properly 'evolution'.

First, 'life cycle' represents a linear and irreversible sequence of prescribed stages that unfold immanent potentials distinguishing the entity from its origin. The generative mechanisms leading to a life cycle evolution lie in the deterministic nature of an entity, proceeding from stage 1 to stage 2 and so forth.

Secondly, 'evolution' encompasses a cumulative and probabilistic sequence of variation, selection, and retention events. The generative forces conducive to evolution are the characteristics of a population of entities, such as the available resources necessary for its survival, its density (size), and the competition reigning within the population.

Thirdly, 'dialectic' concerns a recurrent and discontinuous sequence of confrontation, conflict, and synthesis between contradictory value-marked events. The repetition of localized oppositions animates and constitutes the generative forces of change and the terrain where divergent interests confront each other.

Fourthly, 'teleology' refers to a type of development where final causes manifest their influence under the form of goal setting, implementation, and fine-tuning of means to reach the desired end states. The generative forces driving this pattern include goal enactment, the search for consensus on the to-be-employed means, and a certain dose of cooperation between actors.

For Van de Ven and Poole (1995), evolutionary and dialectical theories operate on an aggregate of entities, while life cycle and teleology operate on a single entity. Evolution, like life cycle, responds to a prescribed (but distinct) mode of change, while for teleology and dialectic theories, the mode of change is constructive. 'A prescribed mode of change channels the development of entities in a prespecified direction, typically of maintaining and incrementally adapting their form in a definite, calculable way. A constructive mode of change generates unprecedented, novel forms that, in retrospect, are often discontinuous and unpredictable departures from the past' (Poole et al., 2000: 68). Van de Ven and Poole situate the prescribed and constructive modes of change, or 'motors', as these authors call them, either within a single entity or between entities. They next classify the existing and possible theories of organizational evolution into a two-motor-, tri-motor, and even a quad-motor theory wherein all the 'motors' will operate concurrently. For instance, population ecology (Hannan and Freeman, 1977, 1989) corresponds to evolution, namely, the case of a prescribed motor between entities where competitive selection operates among entities. Adaptation-selection models conjugate the prescribed motor between entities, with a prescribed motor within entities as an immanent program (Aldrich, 1979).

The clear merits of Van de Ven, Poole, and colleagues are twofold. They have laid down the principal components of evolutionary theories and have articulated them. From their work, we see that organizational evolution concerns a broad array of phenomena that answer the following four questions:

1 Does the evolution apply to a single entity or to multiple entities ('who')?
2 Does the evolution entail an alteration of the involved entity(ies) ('what')?
3 Does the evolution contain a teleological determination (namely, a prespecified orientation, an announced goal, or a predefined ending) ('why')?
4 Does the evolution imply relationships between entities, or not ('how')?

Depending on the answers to these four questions, we suggest, describe, and position sixteen types of evolution processes (see Figure 2.2).

A PRIMARY TAXONOMY

We begin the analysis with the eight evolutionary notions that do not involve relationships between entities (namely, that respond negatively to the fourth question, 'Does evolution imply relationships between entities?'). Then, let us compare the two different evolutionary notions, *change* and *metamorphosis*, using commonsense responses to the 'who', 'what', and 'why' questions. Change is an alteration of an entity that does not necessarily assume a pre-ordained result. Technological change represents an alteration of a function as performed by a set of employed techniques (Nelson, 1995; Tushman and Anderson, 1986). Some companies initiate or absorb technological changes and as a result change themselves with no guarantees of success (Amburgey et al., 1993). Other typical changes are replacements of top management team members, acquisitions, and diversifications. In contrast, metamorphosis involves one entity that alters into a new form that is largely predetermined. A classical example of metamorphosis in the international strategy literature deals with the transformation of a small company into a multimarket, multi-unit organization (Vermeulen and Barkema, 2002). Thus we see that, while change and metamorphosis concern a single entity ('who'), that is altered ('what'), they differ on the 'why' question. In turn, a *sequence* corresponds to a situation where the entity is not assumed to bear any alteration and for which no predetermination exists in the evolutionary process. For instance, growth corresponds to a sequence of quantitative increases of an entity. An absence of alteration but an end-driven process of transformation corresponds to an entity's *improvement*. The entity remains the same and the goal has been reached.

When different entities evolve, other outcomes are possible. An alteration without a predefined end describes a *mutation*. A mutation necessitates several entities to be effective – at least a mutative entity and its receptacle. For instance, the mutation of a component – for example, the sudden opposition of British Airways' employees to the drastic cost reduction plan in the late 1990s – triggers a variation on some dimensions for the entity hosting the component – the airline company until the replacement of its CEO. While a sequence figures a series of events at a sole entity level, mutation suggests consequences at upper levels of analysis and requires a comparison vis-à-vis rivalling entities. The conjunction of an alteration in part or all of the entities with a given, positive orientation creates a situation of *progress*. In this case, progress at the multi-entity level parallels metamorphosis that applies at a single-entity level. For example, over the last ten years the reorganization at Bang & Olufsen according to a redefined identity and the creation of a new structure (alteration) involving several parties (such as retailers and clients, namely, other entities involved) succeeded in achieving goals (teleology) that can be considered as progress.

Entities may also experience a process of evolution that does not alter them in their form and structure and has no pre-assigned orientation. In such cases, we can talk of a *development*, and later call it harmonious or unbalanced. A development model displays a process of immanent change, namely, a process in which existing potentials unfold over time, more or less promptly, such as in the case of loose cooperative agreements that have their stages of development (Van den Bosch et al., 1999). Finally, an absence of alteration of the entities evolving according to a given orientation characterizes a situation of *adjustment* between the entities. The entities adjust to each other's generation or to larger environmental conditions. While improvement applies to single units, adjustment is characterized by a consistent, oriented series of events affecting several entities.

The eight previous evolution cases comprise evolution cases within the focal entity, either considered in isolation or with other parties involved. All the new cases imply 'between entities' relationships (namely, that evolution does imply causal relationships between entities). First, *transformation* relates to a single entity undergoing an alteration without predefined orientation that influences its relationships with other entities. For example, the recruitment of professional statisticians in a few small private banks has led to the transformation of these organizations and of their relationships with clients and set up the creation of a mutual fund industry (Lounsbury, 2004). Having provided a localized, dense, social and institutionally embedded service, each private mutual fund now had to transform its private banking offering into a range of professional and diversified services for more demanding clients coming from broader spheres. Looking at the finance industry at large and the relationships between sectors (mutual fund, retail banking, private banking, and so on), the professionalization phenomenon could be dubbed a *recombination* rather than a transformation, as it involves different types of entities.

Second, an important category of between-entities evolution concerns cases combining alteration and teleology. At a single-entity level, this evolution is often referred to as adaptation; when involving multiple entities, it is called a fit. *Adaptation* ties an entity's faced challenge to its altering actions and (beneficial) result. For instance, Brown and Eisenhardt (1998) studied adaptation and performance in twelve computing firms and showed that a large number of interactions between the heads of businesses in a company enables them to constitute a structured team that competes efficiently in the market place. Depending on situations (for example, an attack on the low end product line or an urgent need for innovation), these emergent cohesive teams help the entity to adapt and succeed in its objectives (namely, defense of the product line, launch of successful innovations). *Fit* connects the acting organizations to their environment. Fit is a relative measure, namely, relative to the organizational competitors' fit. To keep all the odds on its side and not risk environmental misfit, the organization must develop a balanced strategy of change. The exemplary research by Deephouse (1999: 149) concludes that 'moderate amounts of strategic similarity increase performance' between rival firms. In his research, the relationship with the environment rests upon a calculated difference between a firm's investment and the industry's average investments. In this study as in many others, there is a certain autonomy between an industry landscape and a firm's relative strategic positioning over time, characteristic of the notion of variable fit between entities and their environment (Levinthal, 1995).

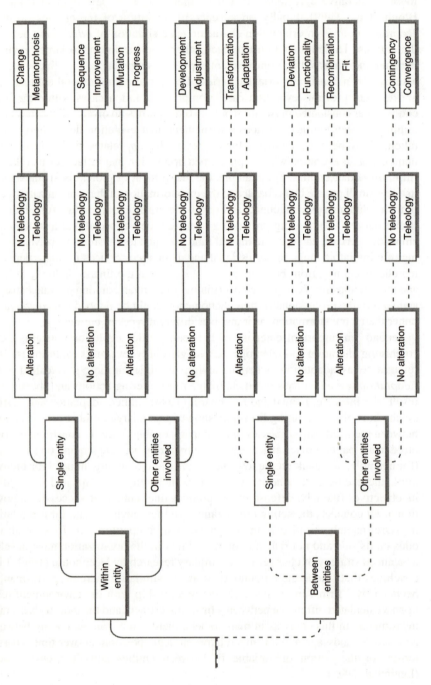

Figure 2.2 Evolutionary notions applied to organizations

Thirdly, when entities do not face major alterations, and no particular ends are involved, comparison of an entity's evolution (respectively, different entities' evolutions) with other similar entities is a deviation (respectively a contingency). *Deviation* does not presuppose a specific end or target for the series of events undergone by an entity. It results from a comparison of trends and trajectories between a single entity and a set of other comparable entities. *Contingency* results from a series of events that affect different entities and their relationships, and leads to an unassigned alignment between involved entities (Donaldson, 2001).

Finally, when entities do not face major alterations but follow a pre-set orientation, a single entity's evolution (or different entities' evolutions) vis-à-vis others demonstrates its functionality (or convergence). *Functionality* presupposes that the entity fulfils its predetermined role and deploys its effectiveness in relation to its environment. Organizational capabilities have been conceptualized accordingly in the literature, where they fulfill a given role depending on contextual factors (for example, governance, learning, or incentives). For instance, Gulati (1999) shows that a firm's alliance capability plays a function in a firm's decision to enter new alliances, based on certain types of network resources. *Convergence* indicates a predefined and smooth junction of entities' characteristics and behavior via continual interactions. Tushman and Romanelli's (1985) idea of punctuated equilibrium is a good example of different companies' behaviors entering into phases of convergence followed by disruptive transformation phases, resulting in typical patterns of industry evolution.

This brief description of sixteen types of evolution, depicted in Figure 2.2, illustrates the variety of meanings attached to the term. It also suggests that a unified theory of evolution is difficult to attain for constitutive reasons: the presence of teleology in evolutionary processes, relations between levels of analysis (for example, genotype and phenotype), and prevalent causality (at a level or between levels) complicate the analysis. This explains why additional characteristics must be added to the general categories represented in Figure 2.2. For instance, authors distinguish between radical and incremental changes (Greenwood and Hinings, 1996), gradual and punctuated development (Tushman and Romanelli, 1994), and reactive or proactive adjustments (Siggelkow, 2001). In addition, as an organization is a purposive social collection of controlled resources, one amongst many of its potential objectives can be the voluntary transformation of environmental characteristics for the organization's sake (Durand and McGuire, 2005). This type of strategy increases the degree of complexity in the study of organizational evolution, leading to what has been called 'co-evolution effects' (Lewin and Volberda, 1999). Moreover, many other categories have been added to the evolutionary picture, such as learning, recombination, entrepreneurship, and corporate venturing. Finally, many disciplines, including economics, political science, sociology, and psychology, contribute their approaches to the field of organizational evolution. Although their perspectives offer individual concepts and notions that shed light in specific cases, they, unwittingly, cloud the organizational evolution field as well.

2.2 THE DIFFICULT STUDY OF ORGANIZATIONAL EVOLUTION

Beyond this formal description of typical cases of organizational evolution, one has to take into account at least three corollary elements when studying organizational evolution that raise further issues and debate. First, we present three classical organizational evolution frameworks and show that while driving out interesting features of organizational evolution, the frameworks suffer nonetheless from severe shortcomings. Secondly, methodological difficulties arise, too. Organizational evolution rarely occurs in isolation; instead, it is related either to many possible independent variables (variance approach) or to other processes (process approach). Finally, some interesting conceptual debates and paradoxes surface when the hurried researcher (unconsciously or not) fails to signal one or another dimension of the to-be-explained evolutionary phenomenon. Among these conceptual puzzles, time effects, determination of accurate levels of analysis, and efficiency of selection are noteworthy.

CLASSICAL PITFALLS: ATTRACTIVE ANALOGIES, SEDUCTIVE FIT, AND APPLICABILITY DOMAIN

Let us focus on three evolutionary frameworks – among many more – that have been consistently applied to evolving organizations. They all have contributed interesting insights into evolutionary phenomena, but each suffers from some shortcomings that confirm how difficult it is to study organizational evolution. In order to uncover important pieces of these phenomena, it seems inevitable that other aspects will be eclipsed. Simplifying assumptions of punctuated equilibrium descriptive models, unmentioned assumptions of fit used in adaptationist frameworks, and empirical simplifications of population ecology provide enlightening insights into organizational evolution but concurrently may raise doubts about the generalizability of many current research findings.

Punctuated equilibrium and attractive analogies for organizational evolution

Teleological models of organizational evolution (for example, metamorphosis, life cycle, functionality, and convergence models) suppose that organizations evolve through a series of alternating, differentiated periods. Among these models, the punctuated equilibrium model has been widely recognized and applauded. Using this model, Tushman and Romanelli (1985, 1994) propose that organizations

> progress through *convergent* periods punctuated by *reorientations* which demark and set bearings for the next convergent period. Where middle-level management interpolates structures and systems during convergent periods, executive leadership mediates between internal and institutional forces for inertia and

competitive forces for fundamental change. It is executive leadership which initiates, shapes, and directs strategic reorientations. (Tushman and Romanelli, 1994: 1141)

Gradually, organizations converge on a common definition of industry characteristics. During the convergence period, competitive selection increasingly aligns organizational behavior, structure, and resources. Convergent periods display incremental and interdependent change activities and decisions that tend to reinforce consistency with strategic orientation. These periods are interrupted by infrequent and intense periods of internal reconfigurations of organizations according to new visions, missions, and goals. These brutal reorientations engage the organization in simultaneous shifts in strategy, distribution of power, structure and control systems (Tushman and Romanelli, 1994). The cumulativeness of former periods generates an organization's history, which provides the context within which current and future periods of change occur. Tushman and Rosenkopf (1996) show that the combination of CEO succession with executive team changes triggers discontinuous changes (while succession without executive team changes enhances incremental changes). This results in a punctuated equilibrium and provides pace to organizational evolution. As noted above, Van de Ven and Poole (1995) qualify the punctuated equilibrium model as a dual-motor theory, since it combines a constructive motor within the entity (the organization) and a prescribed motor between entities (at the population level).

In this representation of organizational evolution, the two mechanisms that play a role within organizations are mutually exclusive. Either the firm follows the prevailing business methods in times of convergence, or it reconfigures itself rapidly to be competitive in the next phase of convergence. A blind spot in this model concerns the determinants of the sudden reorientation stage at the firm level assuming that a change in executive leadership drives organizational reorientation (Sastry, 1997). But what drives top executive succession? Why do organizations alter their forms, structures, and controls? Is it done for reasons of efficiency or to establish power (Westphal and Zajac, 1994)? Furthermore, at the industry level, an unanswered problem concerns the overwhelming convergent phenomenon. Why does a punctuated equilibrium result from that process? Many other outcomes could derive from the various changes that are happening: segmentations, industry dilution, anomy, and so on. The punctuated equilibrium framework remains more descriptive than predictive. The very notion of punctuated equilibrium resembles an 'as if' notion that works analogically. Gersick (1991) offers an enlightening example of how apparently similar patterns seem to follow a punctuated equilibrium model. However, although the punctuated equilibrium model may correctly describe certain dynamic phenomena, it may not adequately explain organizational evolution. Therefore, a first pitfall of the study of organizational evolution is to take for granted probable patterns of events, 'as if' they were causally linked.

Adaptationist models and the strange beauty of fit

According to Figure 2.2, adaptationist models concern cases where entities are altered, interact, and contain a dose of teleology. This type of evolution is called 'adaptation' for a single entity, and 'fit' when different entities are involved. More specifically, adaptationist models emphasize organizational changes and moving equilibrium among intra-organization constitutive components and also vis-à-vis the threats and opportunities present in the environment (Levinthal, 1997). Therefore, the organizational adaptation model implies a changing environment, such as a technological competition (Tushman and Anderson, 1986), an industry formation (Levinthal and Myatt, 1994), or an institutional evolution (Fox-Wolgramm et al., 1998). Fit has cohabited with organizational evolution and strategy for decades. Chandler (1962) demonstrated the importance of strategy-structure fit, while Lawrence and Lorsch (1967) showed the determinant role played by the fit between the structure and the environment of firms for their success. Since then, the notion of fit has been used to the extent that Porter (1996) identified strategy as the search for fit.

Thinking of strategy as fit involves at least three important assumptions. First, the notion of fit is closely related to the underlying assumption that environmental conditions are given, and organizational fit may or may not coincide with these conditions. The basic argument assumes: the greater the fit, the better the performance. Recently, Siggelkow (2001) offered a conception of organizational fit that distinguishes external fit (the appropriateness of a set of choices given environmental conditions) from internal fit (the consistency among organizational choices). The limitations of this typology lie in the fact that, again, the 'environmental change' comes first, demoting the firm's behavior to a reactive mode.

Secondly, to keep the odds in its favor and not risk misfit, the organization must develop a balanced strategy of change, as illustrated for instance in Deephouse's (1999) study. One of the principal assumptions of this strategic balance theory is that 'other determinants of competition, legitimacy, and performance are assumed constant in order to focus on the role of strategic similarity' (p. 149). We agree that to give evidence of an effect (in this case, how a strategic change fits, namely, translates into performance advantage vis-à-vis competitors) some conditions must be held constant, but these ceteris paribus postulations are nevertheless quite limiting.

Finally, fit evokes a multiplicity of associations between entities. As such, the concept remains loosely defined. For instance, Venkataraman (1989) distinguishes six different types of fit depending on first, the degree of specificity of the functional form of the fit-based relationship and secondly, the choice of whether or not to anchor the fit-based relationship on specific criteria. Included in fit are: profile-deviation, mediation, moderation, gestalts, covariation and matching. For instance, fit as 'matching' implies that the match between strategy and structure enhances administrative efficiency (Chandler, 1962), but requires its own metrics and specific criteria. It is evident that the variety of meanings of fit can obfuscate the validity of the adaptationist arguments and results.

To summarize, the adaptationist models of strategy hinge on fit, an ex post test applied to an organizational alteration and intended to validate its conformity with environmental conditions. The 'adaptation fallacy' is to attribute a priori to any organizational alteration a high degree of functionality if not optimality (Hodgson, 1993). Indeed, such a fit attribution postulates: first, the nature of the environment (whether stable or turbulent, for instance); secondly, the nature of a firm as reactive; thirdly, a substantial independence between organizational changes and the environment; and fourthly, ad hoc definitions of fit and specific relationships between 'fitting' entities. These assumptions, when left unmentioned, constitute the seductive pitfall of adaptation and fit theories.

Ecological models and specific conditions of applicability

Ecological models emphasize organizational alterations across populations as the result of an environmental selection process (for example, see PE in Figure 2.1). Studying organizational evolution at the population level, Carroll, Freeman, and Hannan have given different explanations for observable patterns of populations' evolutions (Hannan and Freeman, 1977, 1984, 1989; Carroll, 1985; Carroll and Hannan, 2000). For instance, the density of organizations, namely, the number of firms in a given population, typically follows a concave pattern of growth and decline over time. This may be due to several causes, according to population ecologists. The exploitation of rare environmental resources leads to the proliferation of organizations that flock to the resource reservoirs and exit the population as the reservoir is depleted. Macro-inertial factors such as cultural roots, technological stability, or historical constraints may prevent old and established organizations from following newer trends in organizing work and processes, technological know-how or institutional coherence, causing a population's degeneration over time. Finally, organizations compete against each other for a critical determinant of survival: legitimacy. Selective replacement does not allow organizations to define their own characteristics, but supposes that environmental selection differentially attributes alignment functions depending on the organizational forms. A growing number of organizations legitimize the population until a point where intra-population competition offsets the benefits of legitimacy, resulting in a reduced population density. Empirical works on large populations of organizations have focused primarily on the last argument, showing interesting results at least as far as population growth is concerned but less so for population decline (Carroll and Hannan, 1989; Hannan et al., 1995).

However, one of the reasons that density of organizational populations follows a typical shape and time path – initial slow growth, subsequent explosive growth, and stabilization (Hannan and Carroll, 1992) – could be due not to population determinants, but rather to definitional characteristics and specific conditions that artificially homogenize organizations into populations. Let us explain this point. Under which conditions can pre-World War One labor unions be compared to current labor unions? How and why is a nineteenth-century brewer comparable to the contemporary around-the-corner craft-beer producer? What are the theoretical and empirical impacts of limiting the definition of populations to delimited areas (such as daycare centers in Toronto (Baum and Singh, 1994a) or Manhattan hotels (Baum and Mezias, 1992)) or of considering a vast geographical space (such as Argentinean newspapers (Delacroix and Carroll, 1983) or the American savings and loan industry (Haveman, 1993))? By specific conditions, we mean the conditions under which the conceptual and legal definitions of a daycare center, a newspaper, or a credit union remain valid over time and across definite spatial regions. In addition, specific conditions cover the reasons that justify the coding choices used to keep in or select out organizations as like or unlike the population's other constituencies. Carroll and Hannan (2000) spend chapters warning against methodological traps when embracing data collection and coding. Nevertheless, the consequences of the particular definitions of organizations and populations (internal characteristics and relevant spatial domain, for instance) on the generalizability and validity of the results remain underdeveloped in population ecology. Left unnoticed, these specific restrictions of applicability may induce us to over-generalize the findings of population ecology studies.

METHODOLOGICAL PROBLEMS RAISED BY ORGANIZATIONAL EVOLUTION

The lack of a clear definition of evolution – or, rather, its encompassing nature – is a problem that has bedevilled the development of a unitary theory of organizational evolution. In addition, it has induced another shortcoming. Whereas definition is unfocused and observation is delicate, methods used to test hypotheses have resorted to traditional variance approaches, dear to many other aspects of organizational science but perhaps imperfectly adapted to evolutionary processes.

From a methodological perspective, many studies about organizational change and evolution have established comparisons and variance analysis among entities. Yet, variance analyses suffer from some shortcomings when applied to dynamic patterns and processes. Variance approaches provide general and valid explanations when the associations between variables apply uniformly across a broad range of situations. Variance approaches relate a dependent variable to independent variables using several strict assumptions. Variance approaches presuppose that the world is made of fixed entities with varying attributes and that a change in a variable is a change in its attributes but not a deep alteration of the entity. An independent variable influences the dependent variable based on an efficient causality: a cause produces an effect. In variance approaches, the underlying causal mechanisms that generate a result are supposed to operate continuously. Attributes cannot have several meanings over the course of time, for temporality is simple and linear. Lastly, for variance approaches, final causality where orientation shapes the process is not a valid generative mechanism.

Some authors argue that by nature, evolutionary phenomena (and in particular organizational evolution) conform inadequately to these underlying conditions required for a correct application of variance approaches. This encourages Poole, Van de Ven and colleagues (Poole et al., 2000; Van de Ven and Poole, 1995) to suggest a process explanation rather than a variance explanation of organizational evolution. These authors, like many others in historical studies, sociology, and developmental psychology, defend a process approach wherein entities may alter over time. The unit of analysis in process approaches is a central subject that situates itself at the intersection of events that are occurring and those it provokes.

Various types of causality may be involved, including efficient causality, final causality, … . In the case of final causality, in particular, a central subject may conceive a goal that influences its behavior. Here, the process approach could be adapted to teleological evolutionary notions such as improvement, metamorphosis, adjustment or progress (Figure 2.2). This approach offers a general and valid explanation that emphasizes a particular and coherent arrangement between the acting entities, unlike, for example, the variance approach that emphasizes a uniform cross-context validity. The malleability of explanatory arrangements combined with a temporal sequence of independent variables (the acting entities, their traits and properties, and so on) further distinguish the process approach from the variance approach. Finally, proximate effects and longer-range consequences cohabit in a process approach.

As a consequence, evolution as a series of interrelated events at different levels of analysis raises not only the problem of the theoretical focus used to observe and explain it, but also the very habit of using particular methodological lenses, including variance approaches and process approaches. Evolution follows rules of transformation that may be theorized either as a succession of input/output variations or as an enveloping sequence of events, depending on the presence and persistence of various subjects and agencies.

CONCEPTUAL PROBLEMS RAISED BY ORGANIZATIONAL EVOLUTION

Beyond the theoretical and methodological difficulties, several noteworthy conceptual problems and paradoxes about organizational evolution deserve mention. We will meet them again at various points in this book, and we will attempt to solve some of them in the third part of the book. They are briefly described below.

Time: what influence does time exert on organizational evolution? First, one may understand this question as a speculation about time efficacy. A key assumption of evolutionary thinking is the dependence of present and future states on prior history, known as 'path dependency' (Dosi and Nelson, 1994). When we probe deeply into teleological aspects of evolution, however, final states might also condition the occurrence of stages and paths. In a sense, this introduces a dependence of current states on future history (Lovas and Ghoshal, 2000). A second interpretation of the time question concerns the observed time and the influence of the window of observation and the perceptions of time on the interpretation of evolutionary phenomena (Huy, 2001). Again, does it make any sense to lump together nineteenth-century and contemporaneous specimens of a population so as to exhibit expected curves representative of demographic patterns? How many periods are necessary or sufficient in simulations in order to uncover hypothesized results? Mitchell and James (2001) comment on the implications of how we theorize and measure 'when the events occur'. They underline several causes for false associations, incorrect effect attribution, and over- and under-estimation, using techniques such as meta-analysis and structural equation modeling. How these time effects act and interact constitutes a central problem for organizational evolution and strategic management, not only from a methodological standpoint but also from a conceptual one.

Level: an important dimension for typifying evolution is the matter of the single entity versus different entities to which it applies (see Figure 2.2 and examples of punctuated equilibrium and population ecology approaches). A corollary problem of this distinction hinges on the identification of the correct level of analysis at which evolution operates (Figure 2.1). There is a debate amongst organizational specialists to determine the dominant influence of relevant levels of analysis where selection forces operate (Durand, 2001). Is it the organization itself that evolves as an entity? The resources it controls? The population in which it is embedded? Many possibilities crisscross their causal arrows, to such an extent that Baum (1999) considers that complexity theory rivals evolutionary models for the explanation of co-evolutionary phenomena. Hence, that thorny question of levels of analysis could undercut the establishment and development of evolutionary theory as applicable to organizations.

Selection: Another intriguing question concerns the core notion of selection. As a pivotal mechanism in evolutionary frameworks, selection seems to be continuously operative – it never stops measuring 'fit' or rejecting maladaptive forms. In most evolutionary models, selection appears as essentially ahistorical (Bruderer and Singh, 1996; Dobrev and Carroll, 2003). Where there is no pre-assumed teleology, there is a selection force that logically justifies trait retention and form survival. However, this raises an important issue: What is the importance of human volition and discretion in evolutionary paths in history, economics, and strategic management? For at least half a century, since the Alchian (1950)-Penrose (1952) debate, this question has gnawed at theories that look at the economic foundations of firm success through an evolutionary lens.[1] Broadly speaking, selection needs to be specified on its own, with respect to its causes, forms, and effects, for it connects intimately with the possibility and meaning of human agency, namely strategic (at the organizational level) and economic intervention (at the industry level).

Cause and consequence: As a *cause*, what effect does organizational evolution produce? Put differently, scholars consider whether organizational evolution is beneficial or harmful to firms. Their responses usually hinge on the relative congruence of any organizational change with environmental conditions, namely, fit, alignment, or balance (Porter, 1996; Powell, 1992; Deephouse, 1999). Adaptation theory is based on recognition of early weak signals that firms must interpret and integrate, whereas population ecology and neo-institutional frameworks are based upon fidelity to strong signals of conformity (Polos et al., 2002; Greenwood and Hinings, 1996; Dacin et al., 2002). Therefore, depending on the theory one utilizes, opposing courses of action are possible, legitimate, and arguable: on the one side, extreme versatility to adapt and strong innovativeness; on the other, indifference to feeble environmental signals and strong conformity (Kraatz and Zajac, 1996). Theoretical inconsistency and practical indecisiveness result from this paradoxical situation.

As a *consequence*, organizational evolution stems from heterogeneous sources. Environmental shifts, technological races, multipoint competition, and global trends influence the path, rhythm, and form of a firm's evolution. Internal factors also play a prominent role in organizational evolution (Szulanski, 1996). Organizational inertia drastically constrains organizational evolution, while learning opens free spaces for action. Top executives' perceptions may either catalyze or stifle middle managers' initiatives; organizational attention may either structure decision processes or bias resource investment (Ocasio, 1997; Durand, 2003), with diverse organizational evolution effects. The variety of factors potentially influencing organizational evolution is thus another conceptual challenge.

End of evolution: for some philosophers there is no ending of human history, because history is circular (Nietzsche, 1885). Others have announced the end of history for religious, spiritual, esthetic, or ethical reasons (Fukuyama, 1993). Few of them postulate that a metaphysical entity, let us call it 'spirit', realizes itself via human activity (even unknowingly and even despite individuals (Hegel, 1807)). For evolutionists who follow this line of thought, evolution goes hand-in-hand with a tendency toward improvement and progress (Nelson, 1990). An underlying happiness overlays every aspect of evolution, and strategic management grafts itself onto that promise of a better future (Lovas and Ghoshal, 2000). For other evolutionists, evolution passes through organizations and realizes itself quasi-independently of the forms and attributes it endorses (Hannan and Freeman, 1989; Polos et al., 2002). To them, the presence of a definite end would be the end of evolution. If there is an identifiable ending of organizational evolution (increase in efficiency, economic progress of humankind, inevitable trend toward a pre-revolutionary zero-profit global economy), how can we imagine that it proceeds through the very actions of organizations and their members? If there is no identifiable ending of organizational evolution, can evolutionary models offer more than a lackluster description of patterns and forms of organizations' transformations and recombinations? Are we not between a rock and a hard place if we wish to represent at an upper level of consciousness the deep meaning of organizational evolution?

2.3   WHERE DOES STRATEGIC MANAGEMENT FIT IN?

The preceding section illustrated the theoretical, methodological, and conceptual difficulties of the study of organizational evolution. It closed with a question about the role left for intentionality. Indeed, in this chapter we have already mentioned that organizational selection challenges both the theoretical validity of strategic management (its effectiveness) and its applicability to concrete cases. In addition, strategic management presumes that human agency significantly influences how things evolve, an assumption which is not shared by all evolutionists. In this section, we first define strategy and strategic management, and then demonstrate that both notions face the same five conceptual problems that organizational evolution faces.

Table 2.1   Some definitions of strategy

Strategy is concerned with drafting the plan of war and shaping the individual campaigns, and within these, deciding on the individual engagements. (Von Clausewitz, 1976: 177)

Strategy is the determination of basic long-term goals and objectives of an enterprise, and the adoption of courses of action and the allocation necessary for carrying out these goals. (Chandler, 1962)

Objectives represent the ends that the firm is seeking to attain, while the strategy is the means to these ends. (Ansoff, 1987: 104)

A firm's strategy is its theory of how to compete successfully. Some theories of how to compete successfully are better than others, and the study of strategy is the study of alternative theories of how to compete in different competitive contexts. (Barney, 2001: 22)

A strategy is an integrated and coordinated set of commitments and actions designed to exploit core competencies and gain a competitive advantage. (Hitt et al., 2003: 144).

STRATEGY AND STRATEGIC MANAGEMENT

Table 2.1 lists several definitions of a firm's strategy. The literature on this subject, formulated in several major textbooks (Barney, 2002; Grant, 2005; Hitt et al., 2005), presents the factors that drive industry and firm performance, and the means to escape the 'regression towards the mean' phenomenon. Regression towards the mean expresses the statistical probability that firms that outperform the competition in one time-period tend to converge to their industry mean in the next period, as do under-performers (Greve, 1999). For us, strategy is a theory about competitiveness that helps organizational members select among available resource utilizations and exchange modes. The distinction between strategy content (namely, the organization's objectives and means that constitute its theory of competitiveness) and strategy process (namely, how to implement the organization's commitments and decisions) hints at the difference between strategy and strategic management. Strategy provides the framework within which effective practices take place. Strategic management is the set of concerted concrete actions that actualize (or not) the theorized competitive potentialities resulting from the combination of resources and modes of exchange.

In the traditional strategic corpus, strategy is about deciding and acting on levers to maximize performance ratios, such as returns on investments, assets, and equity. Increasing numerators using better price-quantity mixes and reducing denominators via outsourcing, for instance, constitute emblematic techniques. Remaining competitive is at the heart of an organization's strategy, its way to avoid regression toward the mean and to 'bias' the odds in favor of the organization – so as to deliver consistently above-average performance. Thus, firms compete to gain access to specific assets and to provide superior satisfaction to their stakeholders and, in particular, to their shareholders. The rationales for delimiting the areas of organizational commitment are, principally, to make economies of scale and economies of scope (Chandler, 1990). Efficiencies derived from volumes and learning enable an organization to keep ahead of its rivals by accumulating economizing effects, developing market presence, and accruing profits. Economies derived from cross-utilization of existing resources and competencies provide cost, time, and deftness advantages in the achievement of announced goals. Generating and reaching configurations in which economies of scale and economies of scope are defensible is the purpose of a firm's strategy. Strategies differ at different levels of organization, and scholars like to distinguish among the diverse approaches and sub-natures of strategy (Whittington, 2001). For example, corporate strategy encompasses the major challenges of the overall organization (including degree of diversification, new product search, sharing of competencies, and geographic synergies) while business level strategy is devoted to one line of business.

In order to fine-tune the distinction between strategy and strategic management, we use an analogy (which we dislike as scientific evidence, but approve of as a didactic method). We adjust the simple model of biological evolution (see Figure 2.1) to our context. Let us assume a collection of resources in a resource space (that some would readily equate with a market for resources). We have defined an organization as a 'purposive social collection of controlled resources, building exchange relations and interacting with other entities, and developing strategies for reaching objectives'. Hence, a strategy (S) is an effective proposition that orients and transforms a set of dispersed resources into a combination of resources that adhere to a logic of action. It is a transformation rule that concentrates elements from the resource space around a formulated theory of action. Strategic management (SM), on the other hand, is the mechanism that transforms a collection of resources into a concrete organization that belongs to an organizational space. SM actualizes the potentialities contained in the resources (their services (Penrose, 1959)), their combination, and their modes of exchange.

Once we are in the organizational space, wherein organizations compete, some mechanisms determine whether organizations survive or not. For reasons of simplicity, we continue to use PE (population ecology) as a label for this mechanism involved in organizational evolution. Indeed, the conservation of the resources, and of their properties (such as their uniqueness, non-imitability, and non-substitutability (Barney, 1991)), obeys another series of rules, which we call ES (Economic Selection). Economic selection attributes economic value to the remaining resources owned by all the surviving organizations. It refers, for instance, to the economies of scale and scope mentioned earlier. Depending on their characteristics, some resources now have a higher value inside the organization that owns them than they do outside, while others are worth more outside their organization (Peteraf, 1993; Peteraf and Barney, 2003). Therefore, the result of ES is an ensemble of resources in the resource space, which are deemed to be controlled by surviving organizations or recombined in new ones. A process of resource reallocation ensues when organizations exchange, sell, and acquire resources, in order to attain an enunciated goal. This last process can be incorporated into strategy (S), which precedes another round of SM, PE, and ES.

Of course, the analogy between the transformation rules of Figure 2.3 and Figure 2.1 falls short for many reasons. First, since resources are not genes, developmental genetics is an inadequate metaphor for strategic management. Secondly, economic selection has only a distant resemblance to natural and sexual

Figure 2.3 Is strategy a transformation rule for organizational evolution?

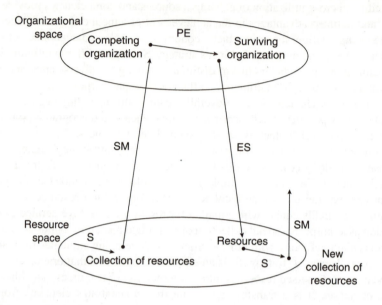

selection. Finally, strategy and genetic composition do not obey the same laws and principles. Despite these shortcomings, Figure 2.3 fixes important determinants of organizational evolution (properties of resources, collection of resources and organizational competitiveness, and ecological and economic selection influences) and joins – albeit loosely – strategy, strategic management, and organizational evolution within a common framework.

A CLOSER ENCOUNTER BETWEEN ORGANIZATIONAL EVOLUTION AND STRATEGIC MANAGEMENT

We have mentioned five conceptual puzzles raised by organizational evolution (time, level of analysis, selection, cause-consequence, and end). Strategy and strategic management face comparable conceptual problems, a further indication that both require a theoretical basis and analysis in conjunction with organizational evolution.

Time: time efficacy affects organizational evolution, not only in terms of path-dependency and teleological determinations but also in terms of the diverse perceptions and representations of events that occur in an organizational history. As March (1994) pointed out in the quotation at the beginning of this chapter, the accounting of history has given way to strenuous attempts to engineer history itself. The theorization of organizational action (namely, strategy) and the subsequent commitments and practical implications (namely, strategic management) represent these attempts – and frequent accomplishments. Seizing a window of opportunity, establishing time-management, and focusing on economies of time are ways to express how and why time counts. The underlying question that strategy and strategic management confront is the reality of their time efficacy in organizational evolution. Do they really drive events? Is there a decoupling between the theory (strategic discourse), action (strategic implementation), and a purported organizational evolution?

Level of analysis: a fundamental indeterminacy for strategy is the accurate assessment of the level of action that determines organizational evolution. Do environmental trends influence survival or does a shift in inner organizational arrangements prevail over more distant influences? Without a clear understanding of how organizational evolution works at every level of analysis (infra-organization, organization, and supra-organization), neither strategy nor strategic management can effectively theorize and influence action. In a nutshell, what are the real impacts of strategy and strategic management at the various levels of analysis involved in an organization's becoming?

Selection: strategy selects resources, market places, and actions. Strategy *is* selection. Nevertheless, strategic choices are bounded, constrained, circumscribed by the exogenous forces and factors that select organizational forms, traits, and behavior. This raises some questions. Is a strategy freely elected? Are strategic management techniques, recipes, and practices unreservedly selected? Organizations are selectors but they may also be selected. Can strategy and strategic management effectively influence the selection criteria that cull out certain organizations and retain others? Could strategic management fashion selection criteria so as to eliminate undesired competition? Maybe such arguments imply that naturalistic notions of organizational evolution (for example, life cycle and metamorphosis) would be erroneous depictions of the evolutionary phenomenon.

Causes and consequences: as causes, strategy and strategic management would determine organizational evolution. Depending on its theory of competitiveness, an organization implements strategic actions that shape its boundaries and transform its exchange relationships (Williamson, 1999). As consequences, strategy and strategic management are reactions vis-à-vis environmental modifications and their rivals' changes (Henderson and Mitchell, 1997). How can we reconcile these circular relationships in a sound and scientific manner? Is strategy a transformation rule for organizational evolution (see Figure 2.3)? Do strategy and strategic management hold a special causal power that informs organizations, or are they simply a set of discourses and practices that are subject to the vicissitudes of any discourse and practice (Donaldson, 2003; Durand, 2002; Powell, 2001)?

End of evolution: a strategy involves a goal and an orientation for an organization. This is independent of the fact that organizational evolution may or may not have a prescribed end (teleology). One paradox ensues: in case of an end to organizational evolution, what is the role of strategy and the effect of strategic management? Independently of the assigned goals and objectives, organizational evolution would tend to its proper end, which annihilates in great part strategy's role and strategic management's efficiency – but, coincidentally, it legitimizes the emphasis on contingency that has existed since the inception of strategy as a field (Donaldson, 2001). If there is no end to organizational evolution, strategy and strategic management perform an influential task in orienting organizational evolution. But what are the rationales for having one strategy succeed over another? Is intentionality simply efficacious, enabling strategists to modify organizations according to their visions and desires? Is strategic management a mere corollary of strategy, actualization of potentialities that ensues naturally according to a theory of organized action? Are there not selection factors that – independently of the ascribed visions and missions – determine the retained organization's resources, traits, and … strategists?

2.4 CONCLUSION

This chapter has provided definitions of an organization, organizational evolution, strategy, and strategic management. Beyond the definitions, the chapter presents a preliminary representation of evolution as a conjunction of transformation rules intra and across levels, which raises further questions as to how to determine causal influences in evolutionary models and whether or not to compare biological with organizational evolution.

A taxonomy of sixteen common notions helps disaggregate four structural dimensions of organizational evolution, based on the following questions.

1 Does the evolution apply to a single entity or to multiple entities ('who')?
2 Does the evolution entail an alteration of the involved entity or entities ('what')?
3 Does the evolution contain a teleological determination ('why')?
4 Does the evolution imply relationships between entities, or not ('how')?

This typology is helpful in positioning assertions and frameworks related to organizational evolution. It shows the fundamental differences that precede the usual terms associated – too often, loosely – with evolution.

This chapter has also stressed the difficulty in achieving a full understanding of what organizational evolution represents, since every highlighted side darkens another aspect of the evolutionary phenomenon. Punctuated equilibrium and convergence theories describe events more than they predict them. Adaptationist models rely heavily on fit, a practical but elusive concept. Ecological models homogenize organizations despite their historical and geographical (if not strategic) differences; nevertheless, they offer convincing macro-descriptive patterns of population evolution. Organizational evolution connects an organization with a changing environment and the present time with adjacent temporalities (the past via inertia, and the future via goals and promises). This raises problems in choosing the appropriate methods for analyzing evolution's content (by variance approaches) or process (by process approaches). Organizational evolution is a challenging concept from a methodological standpoint as well as from a theoretical one.

Finally, noteworthy conceptual puzzles common to both organizational evolution and strategy include: time efficacy, the applicability of unified evolutionary principles at various levels of analysis, the under-characterized notion of selection, the compatibility of the consequences induced by organizational evolution and the causes inducing it, and the presence of a definite end for organizational evolution. These conceptual difficulties associate organizational evolution with strategic management, underlining their interdependence and the need for theoretical integration of these phenomena.

2.5 SUMMARY

DEFINITIONS

Organizations are purposive social collections of controlled resources, building exchange relations and interacting with other entities, and developing strategies for reaching objectives.

Organizational evolution is a series of identifiable events causally linked together, that involve at different levels of analysis one or more organizations that may, but do not necessarily, alter their essential characteristics, and may or may not proceed toward an anticipated ending.

Strategy is a theory about competitiveness that helps organizational members select among available resource utilization and exchange modes.

Strategic management is a set of concerted concrete actions that actualize (or not) the theorized competitive potentialities resulting from the combination of resources and modes of exchange.

Positioning evolutionary notions: a useful taxonomy				
Evolution	Who	What	Why	How
Change	Single entity	Alteration	No teleology	Within entities
Metamorphosis	Single entity	Alteration	Teleology	Within entities
Sequence	Single entity	No alteration	No teleology	Within entities
Improvement	Single entity	No alteration	Teleology	Within entities
Mutation	Different entities	Alteration	No teleology	Within entities
Progress	Different entities	Alteration	Teleology	Within entities
Development	Different entities	No alteration	No teleology	Within entities
Adjustment	Different entities	No alteration	Teleology	Within entities
Transformation	Single entity	Alteration	No teleology	Between entities
Adaptation	Single entity	Alteration	Teleology	Between entities
Deviation	Single entity	No alteration	No teleology	Between entities
Functionality	Single entity	No alteration	Teleology	Between entities
Recombination	Different entities	Alteration	No teleology	Between entities
Fit	Different entities	Alteration	Teleology	Between entities
Contingency	Different entities	No alteration	No teleology	Between entities
Convergence	Different entities	No alteration	Teleology	Between entities

Conceptual puzzles about organizational evolution

	Organizational evolution	Strategy/strategic management
Time efficacy	Is there a time efficacy (final cause) in organizational evolution?	What is S/SM time efficacy? Does it drive real events (decoupling between discourse and action)?
Level of analysis	At which level of analysis does evolution operate?	Does S/SM have a real influence on organizational becoming?
Selection criteria	Are selection criteria specified in their form, effects, and durability?	Does S/SM have an influence on the selection criteria?
Cause and consequence	Can evolution be, concurrently, a cause and a consequence?	Is S/SM a cause of organizational evolution or a later consequence?
End of evolution	Is there an ending/finality to organizational evolution?	Paradox of S/SM role and efficiency. Influence of intentionality?

NOTES

1   Alchian (1950) hypothesized a world where luck would provide companies with profits guaranteeing their survival. The repetition of successive draws is compatible with the idea that some companies will survive, based on their alignment with environmental conditions and independently of their economic and strategic choices. Penrose (1952) criticized the radicalism of this argument as she refused to apply biological constructs to companies. She highlighted the importance of human rationality (and its limitations) and motivation in a firm's behavior, growth potential, and survival odds. Selection would not be a pure and blind mechanism that haphazardly distributes profits.

PART 2   BUILDING THE CHECKLIST APPRAISAL GRID FOR EVOLUTIONARY MODELS

Previously, we emphasized several predicaments of the research on organizational evolution and strategic management (definitional, theoretical, methodological, and conceptual). Organizational evolution is confronted with time issues, level-of-analysis problems, the thorny conceptualization of selection, the cause-and-consequence positioning dilemma, and questions about the finality of organizational evolution. Strategy and strategic management intersect with organizational evolution at these same problematic places.

This second part of the book offers a detour from direct responses to these questions and problems. We submit that the study of the origins of the evolutionary paradigm may prove useful and enriching, and so we invite the reader to take a closer look at how the ideas of evolution emerged and developed in nineteenth-century Europe (Chapter 3). Then, in Chapter 4, we offer perspectives on three approaches of organizational evolution (population ecology, evolutionary economics, and the dynamic resource-based view), explaining their merits and potential; in this chapter, we also critique the VSR model and review co-evolutionary theses used in organization and strategy studies. Finally, we explore recent debates in biology and philosophy that are pertinent to our field and propose what constitutes the core contribution of this part of the book, the Checklist Appraisal Grid for evolutionary models (Chapter 5).

It is also necessary to confess to a concealed objective in this second part of the book. Our hidden agenda attempts to respond to three serious shortcomings present in many current studies concerned with organizational evolution.

First, most of the knowledge accumulated by organizational scientists is presented in articles where the theoretical developments are often short and extremely focused. That leaves scant space for alternate visions, and entices authors to utilize accepted conceptions of evolution, and to avoid questioning their fundamentals and prerequisites. Original models such as Lamarckism and Darwinism get distorted or are cited incoherently. In order to overcome this tendency, we attempt to reposition the dominant evolutionary theories and to examine their arguments, ideas, and propositions. At stake, more than historical accuracy, is the ability of organization and management science to build a body of knowledge that is as free as possible from inaccurate attributions and logical and conceptual errors.

Secondly, specialization in research creates parallelism in research avenues. Evolution is a transversal theme common to biology, organizational science, sociology, artificial intelligence, and certain aspects of physics. Some research crossover is needed to build a dialogue, compare paths, and make objective appraisals about results. Organizational scientists focus insufficiently on this. This lack of crossover and dialogue is detrimental to the advancement of the field. Thus, another goal is to try to create a bridge to related fields in a coherent, objective, and fruitful manner.

Thirdly, most of us think that the dominant model for organizational evolution, the Variation-Selection-Retention (VSR) model, could become a paradigm of socio-cultural and organizational evolution (Baum and McKelvey, 1999). Its advantages are simplicity, parsimony, and communicability. The VSR model is anchored in a Darwinian tradition, which the public is familiar with and can summarize in a few precepts (simplicity). After Freud and the Freudian vulgate as displayed in magazines, people can no longer look at their children the same way as before (guilt permeates parenthood). After Darwin and the Darwinian vulgate spread over the pages of the business press, everyone is ready to tell a story about the birth and demise of an organization. Based on a Darwinian interpretation of socio-cultural evolution, but also on the graft of hypotheses alien to the original Darwinism, the VSR model deconstructs organizational reality into manageable sub-elements and three intelligible processes (parsimony): supposedly blind variations, selection, and retention. Communicability flows from simplicity and parsimony, rendering the VSR model seductive and efficient. Behind the scenes, however, the VSR model ignores constitutive elements that, unmentioned, could limit future research on the relationships between organizational evolution and strategic management. Notably, a critique of the would-be paradigm's basic assumptions is in order.

These three issues – lack of in-depth discussion of evolutionary traditions, lack of cross-fertilization among disciplines, and the need for an evaluation of the VSR model – motivated this second part of the book. More precisely, Chapter 3 presents an inquiry into the origin of three evolutionary traditions in biology that have been used extensively in the organizational science realm, consciously or not, properly or not. Lamarck's, Darwin's, and Spencer's major intellectual contributions are detailed. We describe not only what these authors said but also what many of us incorrectly attribute to them. The objective of the chapter is to avoid turning back to our old ways, both theoretical and methodological.

Chapter 4 presents the VSR model of socio-cultural evolution (Campbell, 1960; Baum and McKelvey, 1999). It puts into perspective three commonly used evolutionary approaches employed in the organization and strategy literature: population ecology, evolutionary economics, and dynamic RBV. This chapter conducts two comparisons on these evolutionary approaches. One regards the genealogy of these three approaches vis-à-vis the nineteenth-century Lamarckian, Darwinian, and Spencerian traditions. The other exemplifies how these approaches insert themselves into the VSR model. Finally, Chapter 4 reviews the recent contributions of the co-evolutionary approach. The important conclusions of this chapter concern: first, the interrelated genealogy of the three organizational evolution approaches, secondly, their respective specific appropriations of the VSR model, and thirdly, the questionable status of the VSR model, as a valid paradigm or an overly flexible framework.

Chapter 5 presents more radical and philosophical considerations about the nature of heredity and selection in evolutionary frameworks. During the mid-twentieth century, a corpus integrating Darwinian insights with paleontological and genetic research evidence emerged. It took the form of what has been called 'evolutionary synthesis' (Mayr, 1982). However, since the 1970s, at least four vivid debates have emerged among biologists that question the merits of the evolutionary synthesis. They concern four 'cases': the case against micro-macro continuity, the case against selection, the case against adaptation, and the case against the organism. However, these debates have not greatly affected organizational theory, which remains focused on populationist explanations inherited from evolutionary synthesis and the VSR model presented in Chapter 4. Following the four cases, this chapter concludes with the 'Checklist Appraisal Grid for evolutionary models'. The connection between organizational evolution and strategic management now has a firmer basis, but it still awaits a fuller formulation in the last part of the book.

3 · EVOLUTIONARY THEORIES IN RETROSPECT

You appear to me to suppose that external conditions modify machinery, as if by transferring a flourmill into a forest you could make it into a sawmill. (Huxley, in letter to H. Spencer, cited in Peel, 1971: 146)

In Chapter 3, we detour from our final destination. We describe and put into perspective the emergence in the nineteenth century of several conceptions of evolution, applied to biology and to society at large. Our contention is that many of the problems faced by contemporary organizational theorists and strategists look similar to the issues faced by the evolutionists of the nineteenth century, Jean-Baptiste de Lamarck, Charles Darwin, and Herbert Spencer. An examination into the past works of these three thinkers supplies a robust footing for the modern theories of organizational evolution.

In the first section we capture the essence of the arguments of Lamarck and Darwin, the figureheads of two important streams of evolutionary thought, who theorized the evolution of individuals and of species. Lamarck supports transformism while Darwin subscribes to descent with modifications based on natural selection. In the second section, we turn to the works of the first declared 'synthetic evolutionist', Herbert Spencer, and discuss five of his major errors, which are of great interest to scholars who study organizational evolution. Lastly, we suggest the useful contributions of this literature review for our contemporary work on organizational evolution and strategic management.

3.1 WINNOWING THE EVIDENCE: TRUE AND FALSE ASCRIPTIONS TO LAMARCK AND DARWIN

Two models of evolution coexisted in the nineteenth century and are still in use today in social and organizational sciences. Lamarck suggested that evolution proceeds through the inheritance of environmentally induced variations. For him, individual alterations spring from both a natural tendency of organisms to adhere to their living conditions and a transmission of acquired characteristics from one generation to the next. Darwin assumed that evolution ensues from a selection of favorable variations carried by individuals. He introduced rivalry at an intra-species level and inheritance as the pivotal factors ensuring gradual preservation of the favorable variations in successive generations of individuals.

LAMARCK

Jean-Baptiste de Monet, Chevalier de Lamarck (1744–1829) was a French botanist and naturalist. After the French Revolution he became a professor at the Museum d'Histoire Naturelle in Paris. While once seduced by 'fixism', namely, the assumption that species are fixed and that observable specimens derive from fixed types, Lamarck came to defend a different view – called 'transformism' by many scholars – in his major opus, *Zoological Philosophy*.

What Lamarck says

For Lamarck, life depends on the organization of matter, and not on the matter itself. Only 'l'ordre des choses' (the order of things) distinguishes the animated from the inert. Movement, for instance, results from a specific organization whereby organic fluids act, combine themselves, and animate certain parts of the body. Therefore, a central, natural, organic force organizes beings, from simple forms (the lowest rungs on the ladder of development) to more elaborated forms. 'The evolutionary progression continually begins anew, with spontaneous generation constantly replenishing the store of primitive organisms. Within a lineage, lower rungs on the evolutionary ladder are vacated, and higher rungs are eventually occupied' (Sober, 1984: 148). This incoercible force expresses itself in the form of 'permanent flows' (blood and others), 'nervous fluids' (that transmit move-ment), and 'crystallization of matter' (such as tissue formation). It animates living beings and accounts for the presence of a hierarchy of living organisms. Noteworthily, superior animals, because of their sensitivity, perception, and will, can access and manipulate that fundamental cause of fluids' excitability, move-ment, and action.

But this force that leads to internal movements and organic formation encoun-ters surrounding conditions and environmental constraints. Indeed, species are not hierarchized in a continuous order; rather branches appear in the chain of being. The second force, and certainly the predominant one, that accounts for these rami-fications is the habituation acquired by living beings in relation to the particular circumstances of their surrounding life conditions. This force of habit thwarts the natural internal force that would otherwise give a linear and progressive hierar-chy to living beings. Modification of behavior and prolonged habit cause indi-viduals of living species to exercise some functions and organs more than others when environmental circumstances require such exercise. Frequently used organs develop and strengthen, while unused ones wither away. For Lamarck, environment imposes needs and requirements on species. Individuals react to these needs and requirements, and, because of the first force, more nervous fluids will reinforce the organs and more complex tissue organization will result. Hence:

> First Law: In every animal which has not passed the limits of its development, a more frequent and continuous use of any organ gradually strengthens, develops, and enlarges that organ, and gives it a power proportional to the length of time it has been so used; while the permanent disuse of any organ imperceptibly weakens and deteriorates it, and progressively diminishes its functional capability, until it finally disappears. (Lamarck, 1809/1914: 113)

Superior organisms are able to internalize the cause of excitability of their 'subtle and expansive' fluids. External pressures in that case do not play a direct influence, but rather a catalytic effect which – via sentiments, consciousness, and will – triggers active efforts to modify behavior and habits. When these modifications appear in great number in a localized population, reproduction mechanisms perpetuate the acquired manifestations. The second law of Lamarckian evolution states that acquired characteristics are passed down from one generation to its offspring:

> Second Law: All the acquisitions or losses wrought by nature on individuals, through the influence of the environment in which their race has long been placed, and hence through the influence of the predominant use or permanent disuse of any organ; all these are preserved by reproduction to the new individuals which arise, provided that the acquired modifications are common to both sexes, or at least to the individuals which produce the young. (Lamarck, 1809/1914: 113)

What is commonly remembered of Lamarckism is a reduced version of these two laws: the function creates the organ and the inheritance of acquired traits. This is certainly a reductionist version of Lamarck's ideas. It concentrates on the final results of his works and neuters very important premises: an *ordre des choses* bestows life; a hierarchy exists among beings; environmental circumstances distort linear development of species; a supposed internal irritability of fluids supplies movements and actions; and superiorly organized animals internalize a capacity to influence the causes of that internal irritability. For Lamarck, individuals' behavioral adjustments to their environment explain organic change, which diffuses under conditions of heritability and sufficient frequency among species mates.

What Lamarck does not say

Because they forget these important premises, or because they neglect the original texts, many scholars and respected authors perpetuate old errors and commit new ones. Our conviction is that only a clear understanding of what an author said enables followers to develop further ideas. Committing and reiterating errors confuses and holds back ideas. For instance, despite the fact that his *Zoological Philosophy* is an important treatise, a landmark in the study of evolution, Lamarck is not the 'inventor' of transformism. Other naturalists defended this thesis before him and adorned it afterwards (Canguilhem, 1998; Grimoult, 2001). Three common, less anecdotal misunderstandings deserve mention.

First, Lamarck never assumed that all individuals or species have a tendency to become more complex. For Lamarck, there are degrees of organic complexity in the different living species – from unicellulars to humans – but the supposed linearity in living beings' complexity is unobservable. He argues that an internal force causes fluids, nerves, and matter to coalesce into functions and organs. Contrary environmental forces oblige beings to develop new functions and organs, leading to the observable variety of species. Observable complexity is the result of a succession of species, each deviating from their original theoretical trajectory due to the material circumstances they encounter, and based on their intrinsic propensity to feel and modify their behavior. Neither species nor individuals, however, tend to become more complex.

Secondly, Lamarck does not assume that individuals have a willpower enabling them to prompt morphological changes. For him, there is a connection between the degree of evolution of a living being and the capacity of this being to orientate some of its behavior and habits. However, there is no direct connection between that capacity and morphological generation.

Thirdly, Lamarck does not use the term 'adaptation' in his *Zoological Philosophy*. In his first and second Laws, he formulates the idea of a correspondence between environmental conditions and species' characteristics. His idea is that of repeated use and disuse of a function; and there is necessarily a long time before behaviors become habits, habits create organs, and organs transfer to the species (under the restricting condition of biparental acquisition of traits). 'Adaptation' is a term that arose subsequent to the time at which Lamarck studied and wrote, and it imperfectly accounts for Lamarck's ideas. Indeed, adaptation is more often the process by which individuals (not species) alter their characteristics in response to changing environmental conditions. It is a rather end-oriented and rapid phenomenon that does not involve any particular theory of inheritance (see Chapter 2, Figure 2.2). Many of these characteristics do not correspond to Lamarck's ideas, and it is a misnomer to refer to his conception as 'adaptationist'.

Therefore, when we attribute to Lamarck the idea that organizations have a tendency to complexity, a self-reflective capacity leading to structural adjustments (like double-loop learning for instance), and an adaptability based on a direct correspondence between environmental conditions and organizational characteristics, we are simply wrong. Besides, we miss the essence of Lamarckism and limit our capacity to conceive of organizational evolution on bases other than the hackneyed mnemonic slogans: 'the function creates the organ' and 'there is inheritance of acquired traits'. Lamarck cannot to be presented as anti-Darwin, since both he and Darwin belong to different generations and different scientific traditions.

DARWIN

Charles Darwin (1809–82) studied theology at Cambridge University before embarking on a five-year journey on HMS *Beagle* to study the geology and nature of Latin American coasts and islands. He collected thousands of specimens and kept a journal in which he repeatedly questioned whether or not current knowledge could adequately account for his observations. It was only twenty years after his return, and eight years spent on developing a taxonomy of barnacles, that he produced an abstract version of his fundamental treatise, *The Origin of Species* (1859). He was pressed to produce such a reduced version by the concomitant appearance of A. Wallace's essay, which presented ideas that were very similar to his own thesis.

What Darwin says

Darwin had many sources of inspiration, one of the most significant being Malthus. Malthus's work induced Darwin to reflect differently from his predecessors on species and populations. Malthus theorized the mechanistic, numeric progression of populations and the necessary constraints entailed by an exponential growth, in particular on food supply. Darwin's major variation was to integrate the idea of competition within a population rather than maintaining it at the level of one species against another species.

Ernst Mayr (1991) gives a circumstantiated account of the genesis of Darwin's evolutionary thought. Darwin's theoretical building blocks consist of four elements: first, the recognition of common descent: existing beings descend from a common ancestor; secondly, diversity of species: there exists a great diversity among living beings because of the multiplication of variations that thrives according to surrounding conditions; thirdly, gradualism: variations impose themselves at the level of a population over time and can lead to different observable species; species do not originate from a sudden modification of a single individual (a theory known as 'saltationism'); and fourthly, natural selection: variations that represent a survival or reproductive advantage remain present in the population while unfavorable variations are not selected.

Opposition to Darwin's ideas was virulent, nurtured by fervent believers in creationism (the creation of all living species by God), in fixism (species do not vary), and in saltationism (species appear anew in their entirety from a single individual). The original opponents were joined later by partisans of essentialism (for whom categories and concepts are pure and definitive) and by defenders of the idea that humans occupy the peak position in the chain of beings. However, Darwin's explanatory system does not depend upon the existence of God, nor on a final cause. It is an open-ended phenomenon, which conjoins reasoning at a population-level, environmental conditioning, and an indirectly observed explanatory power (natural selection). For Darwin, individuals and populations evolve over time, and human beings very likely share a common ancestor with certain species of monkeys.

Darwin did not offer direct evidence of natural selection. Rather, he argued a theory of descent with modifications by natural selection and justified his hypotheses derived from the theory by two means (see Gayon, 2003). First, natural selection is considered to be a law, deduced from very likely premises, which were partially observable: struggle for existence (a consequence of uneven rates of reproduction and food supply), inheritance of individual peculiarities, and existence of variations impacting survival or fertility. Secondly, analogical evidence, for example, artificial selection introduced by man in agriculture, gives credit to the hypothesis of natural selection. In Darwin's writings, natural selection is, therefore, not a principle but rather a complex fact with some significant explanatory power.

A great benefit of Darwin for the next generations of researchers has been the stabilization of the levels of analysis: inheritable characteristics, individuals, and populations ('varieties' or 'races' in Darwin's own words). Favorable variations are selected, rather than individuals per se. Species are not fixed but evolutive categories. Moreover, Darwin assumes that a relative advantage is sufficient for selection to operate, and thereby avoids the finalized or theological reference to absolute perfection:

> Natural selection tends only to make each organic being as perfect as, or slightly more perfect than, the other inhabitants of the same country with which it has to struggle for existence. And we see that this is the degree of perfection attained under nature [...] Natural selection will not necessarily produce absolute perfection; nor as far as we can judge from our limited faculties can absolute perfection be everywhere found. (Darwin, 1859: 201–6)

Darwin (1859) defines natural selection as 'the preservation of favorable and the rejection of injurious variations'. This definition raises obvious concerns because the terms 'favorable' and 'injurious' reveal judgments on variations, which cannot be done ex ante. The nature of the variation depends on many factors, in particular those related to the environment. While Darwinian evolution does not intersect with Lamarck's transformism, it is noteworthy to mention that Darwin was not a pure 'selectionist' and that he repeatedly referred to environmental influences on individual variations (Mayr, 1991: 109; Gould and Lewontin, 1979). Some of Darwin's followers make selection prevail over any other cause (Weismann, 1883) and deny the influence of Lamarck's theories as triggers for variations. Heritability of variations for Darwin is a prerequisite for their selection. He also believed that parents' traits merge themselves in the offspring, a process of 'blending inheritance' contradicted by yet-to-come genetic research. Indeed, Darwin was unaware of Mendel's contemporaneous discovery of genetic inheritance mechanisms and of facts later established that show that inheritance is 'hard', namely, based on genetic material peculiarities – rebutting the 'soft' inheritance thesis of acquired characteristics.

Darwin's theoretical triptych (variation, inheritance, and natural selection) relies extensively on the central panel: inheritance. Artificial selection shows that purposeful variations affecting individuals, their reproducibility, and their survival odds, are preserved for generations. Individual differences from the average of the population are gradually fixed by individuals and alter overall the population's characteristics. Reversion and atavism raise serious concerns regarding this theory. Since inheritance is a precondition for selection to operate, is inheritance a stronger force than selection? Darwin rejects the possibility that artificially selected animals, reverting to a state of nature, would regress toward a prior form, and argues that animals would retain domestically inherited traits. Furthermore, variation and heredity are the premises of natural selection, but remain largely unexplained by Darwin. Langton (1979) and Gayon (2003) insist on the inductive nature of Darwin's proposition and that, from Darwin's inductive generalizations, no hypothetical deductive theory of inheritance really ensues.

What Darwin does not say

As with Lamarck's ideas, it is not uncommon to distort Darwin's theses. Three typical simplifications, in our view, entail important consequences for the study of organizations. First, Darwin's theory is neither evolution nor evolutionism: it is the theory of descent with modifications due to the influence of natural selection. Darwin did not use the term 'evolution' until the sixth edition of the *Origin of Species*, mostly in reaction to Spencer's influential systematic philosophy of evolutionism. Again, for Darwin, diversity of life results from a gradual process of selection, with ramifications. The ex post observable result of selection of inheritable variations constitutes an evolution. But evolution is not a causal mechanism in Darwin's theory.

Secondly, Darwin's theory cannot be reduced to the VSR model. Instead, it corresponds to a Variation, Inheritance, and natural Selection (VIS) triptych. Natural selection relies extensively on inheritance. Only favorable inheritable variations are selected. Selection is not the sorting of individuals but a bias in survival probabilities of an individual endowed with favorable variations that can be passed on to future generations. Therefore, Darwin's theory joins two interpretations, which are compatible – even though not obviously so. On the one hand, natural selection is a causal mechanism that leads to population diversity and diversification. On the other, Darwin's theory of inheritance explains the observable changes in individuals' characteristics over the generations. As Mayr (1982) suggests, there is an inversion in the operating order between Lamarckism and Darwinism. Whereas Lamarckism suggests that environmental conditions trigger an organism's variations passed on by inheritance, Darwinism stipulates that individual inheritable variations precede environmental selection. Therefore, retention is an appendage that was later introduced by social and organizational theorists. For Darwin, 'retention' is integrated within the inheritability property. As such, retention is a sine qua non condition for selection, since inheritance is a prerequisite if a favorable variation is to diffuse in a population.

Thirdly, Darwin applied his theory to animal species rather than to human societies and organizations (Bowler, 2003). While Darwin disliked applying his theory to human societies, Galton and other post-Darwinians, such as Weismann and Pearson (the mathematician who formalized the use of correlation and regression coefficients), defended racism and eugenics on supposedly Darwinian assumptions. Francis Galton (1822–1911), grandson of Erasmus Darwin, and cousin of Charles, developed a theory of heredity and eugenics that stated that children of exceptional parents, although perhaps less exceptional than their parents, would not revert to the 'meaner' characteristics of the population. Whereas inheritance is the pivotal mechanism by which Darwin defended the gradualism of his theory, Galton radically subsumes selection to heredity. Selection of variation has its reverting force, regression, that attracts individual variation to the mean of the population to which one belongs. While for Darwin populations undergo gradual changes in characteristics, for Galton there is neither displacement of a population's mean characteristic (Darwinism) nor an inheritance of acquired traits (Lamarckism). For Galton, selection cannot form species or races, for they exist intrinsically. This obviously contradicts Darwin's conception that 'the number and diversity of inherited deviations of structure, both those of slight and those of considerable physiological importance, is endless' (Darwin, 1859: 12).

In his later work, Darwin (1871) became more philosopher than scientist, and dealt with human societies, explicitly affirming that morality and ethics, while not necessarily benefiting any individuals in particular, provide a tribe or a group with a collective advantage over other tribes in its chances of surviving and reproducing. Anthropology was the only area in which Darwin strayed from his idea of variation-based selection. He conceded that when moral sentiments and culture play an important part for a species, the fundamental role of selection (of well-endowed individuals) is raised to a higher level: the group's well-being and advantages. In that case, inheritance of individual variations is to be counterbalanced by cultural and institutional factors, a very temperate assumption when compared to the ideas of social Darwinists such as Galton.

Overall, Darwin did not explain why a particular species thrives in a particular setting. His theory, later labeled 'theory of evolution,' put forward an explanatory mechanism, natural selection, which is supposed to be operative for any species in any environment. As Darwin repeatedly commented, *Origin of Species* was 'one long argument' rather than an exhaustive treatise. While Lamarck's theory is developmental, both at the individual and species levels, Darwin's theory is not. Darwin's theory does not account for the transformation of species from an aggregation of individual specificities. That individuals change, in Darwin's perspective, does not explain per se the changes in species. Rather, internal variations selected at a population level due to their relative benefits steadily build up the new contours of a population's characteristics. For Darwin, selection encompasses two phenomena, a diffusion by replacement and a fluctuation of average individual characteristics. Selection alone does not drive evolution. 'Selection implies evolution only when no evolutionary force counteracts it and *the trait being selected is heritable*' (Sober, 1984: 151). Thus, there is no necessary direction in Darwin's evolutionary theory, nor are there ascribed, preordained characteristics vital to survival. On that basis, Mayr (1991) agrees with Gillespie (1979) that what Darwin claims in the *Origin* to be merely 'one long argument' is, in fact, one long argument against creationism.

3.2 FIVE CURRENT LESSONS DERIVED FROM SPENCER'S EVOLUTIONISM

Today, organization science is approximately the same age as when Durkheim founded the bases of sociology in the early years of the twentieth century. The slight difference being that one century later, we should not commit the same mistakes once made by our predecessors. The virtues of taking a historical and trans-disciplinary approach are manifold, but the strongest of all is to prevent current research from winding up in dead ends. The case of Spencer is interesting for three reasons. First, he mixed biological and sociological studies and grafted his intuitions onto a unified but erroneous framework. Secondly, he was contemporaneous with the emergence of Darwinism and the scientific study of societies. Thirdly, his influence on public policy and industrial evolution permeated the UK and the USA for decades after his death. Spencer's works offer at least five memorable lessons in our effort to theorize on organizational evolution. We should first separate the description from the explanation of evolution; secondly, dispense ourselves with finalist explanations; thirdly, avoid the use of biological analogies; fourthly, be consistent; and fifthly, define the nature of causality present in our theories. Finally, Spencerism is positioned relative to Lamarckism and Darwinism.

FIVE (UNINTENDED) CONTRIBUTIONS OF HERBERT SPENCER'S EVOLUTIONISM

Herbert Spencer (1820–1903) pursued during the entirety of his life a sole objective: developing a comprehensive understanding of the evolution of organized systems. Spencer sought evidence of the influence of a fundamental principle in the manifold observable manifestations offered by his environment: bugs, flowers, human society, stars, and so on. In more than forty years of production, he never taught at a university, and it was only in the last years of his life that he was able to live from the revenues of his writings, coming from both the UK and the USA. Nowadays, Spencer is barely considered worth mentioning as a contributor in many of the fields he examined: astronomy, geology, psychology, and, to a lesser degree, biology. Mayr, in his opus, *The Growth of Biological Thought* (1982) mentions Spencer only to downplay his influence, stating for instance that Spencer's theory of evolution is obviously vacuous and the consequent principles derived from his ideas dangerous. Hence, 'it would be quite justifiable to ignore Spencer totally in a history of biological ideas because his positive contributions were nil' (Mayr, 1982: 386). While this statement might be fair as far as biological ideas are concerned, Peel's (1971) viewpoint is more balanced: the enduring debt we owe to Spencer about evolution theory is important, but for the very reason that he failed in his ambition to establish evolutionism. Even more, serious consideration of Spencer's evolutionary theory is necessary and helps to base evolutionary theories more solidly. In particular, the five elements listed below remind us of the pitfalls of any inquiry on organizational evolution and strategic management.

Separating law and cause of evolution: Spencer is the founder of evolutionism. At the heart of his system of thought, evolution is all-pervasive and enduring. The all-embracing Spencerian theory of evolution accounts for astronomic, geologic, organic, embryologic, psychological and social phenomena (Spencer, 1857, 1862, 1883, 1892). His *First Principles* announce what evolution is:

> Evolution is an integration of matter and concomitant dissipation of motion; during which the matter passes from an indefinite, incoherent homogeneity to a definite, coherent heterogeneity; and during which the retained motion undergoes a parallel transformation. (Spencer, 1862: 396)

In this abstract definition, evolution distinguishes between the simple and complex organization of individual components. Integration of matter extends the size of units, but evolution is not the simple aggregation of matter. A move towards differentiation characterizes evolution. Differentiation shows the aptness of units to fulfill a particular function, and goes hand in hand with specialization. Each component fulfills a function, deemed desirable and necessary due to the environmental conditions. Equilibration of components stems from successive adaptations of the entity to its environment. Spencer notes in his autobiography (in an irony he does not seem to perceive) that his own thought followed the principle of evolution, and thus reached a climax at that moment. When equilibration appears unreachable, the counterforce of evolution, dissolution occurs, and organizations fall apart. Adaptation consists of battles successfully waged against the dissipative power of a disaggregating force. Spencer's evolution is intrinsically a gradual process, whereby individual members adapt to the whole, and the whole to its environment. Adaptation, and thus evolution, leads to heterogeneity, since the homogeneous is unstable, and perpetually under attack from external shifts and internal incongruence.

The first lesson derived from the study of Spencer's works is that at that stage of elaboration, Spencer's evolutionism reached the point where the law and the cause of evolution were separated. In his earlier works, he fuses at least three distinct ideas. First, evolution is what fuels any process of change. It is an insuperable force. Secondly, evolution is the observable manifestation resulting from the encounter of force with matter. Finally, evolution is the natural and well-oriented principle that leads parts to harmonize with the whole. Spencer gives us a clearer distinction between the law (an account of a pattern that can become prescriptive) and the cause (for him, an insuperable force) of evolution. For Spencer, *the law of evolution* is descriptive and expresses a move from homogeneity to heterogeneity, while *the cause of evolution* is its very principle of action due to the instability of the homogeneous, the multiplication of effects from a same cause, and the transmission of acquired characteristics from one generation to the next.

Finalism: more than a decade before stating his *First Principles*, Spencer's *Social Statics* (1850) elaborated on the evolution of contemporaneous relationships between individuals and society. Spencer studied how a society attains happiness, and he addressed the problem of evil in society:

> All evil results from the non-adaptation of constitution to conditions [...] No matter what the special nature of the evil, it is invariably referable to the one generic cause – want of congruity between the faculties and their sphere of action. Equally true is it that evil perpetually tends to disappear. (Spencer, 1892: 27)

Thus, adaptation tends asymptotically towards perfection, namely a perfect congruence between agency and surrounding conditions.

Later in his life, in his *Principles of Sociology* (during the 1870s) cognizant of the social interdependence of human actions in society, Spencer suggested that justice should be the greatest value of individuals. By not altering others' spheres of activity in one's own affairs and pursuit of happiness, one enables everyone to attain a higher level of adaptation and happiness. Spencer continued on the same line of reasoning and inferred a dull post-Kantian maxim of moral actions, a transcendent moral imperative respectful of others in all conditions of action, which he terms the liberty of each limited by the like liberties of all; a further consequence being that the individual's claims become sacred in society, implying a subordination of whatever may limit them. As individuals tend toward perfect fit and superior individuation, they become mutually dependent on those who are like them. Adaptation is that tendency toward a still incompletely realizable but accessible perfection.

> Progress is not an accident but a necessity. [...] As surely as the tree becomes bulky when it stands alone, and slender if one of a group; as surely as a blacksmith's arm grows large, and the skin of a labourer's hand thick; as surely as a passion grows by indulgence and diminishes when restrained; as surely as a disregarded conscience becomes inert, and one that is obeyed active; as surely as there is any meaning in such terms as habit, custom, practice; – so surely must the human faculties be moulded into complete fitness for the social state; so surely must evil and immorality disappear; so surely must man become perfect. (Spencer, 1892: 31)

As we observed in Chapter 2, the question of teleology is inherent to evolution. Spencer presents many instances of evidence of obtruded finalism, namely, a tendency to pose the end as the causal principle of changes. This finalism is a necessary condition of his theory, as nicely expressed by Wiltshire:

> If evolution is not toward a greater and more unmixed good, unthinkable consequences follow. Either men are doomed to eternal misery, or else they have a duty as rational beings to struggle against evolution, which would nullify Spencer's social conclusions. Regression and 're-barbarisation' cannot be dismissed as transient manifestations of rhythmic dissolution, but must be accepted as unalterable facts of the human condition. (Wiltshire, 1971: 208)

In this respect, however, Spencer is almost a caricature of flawed reasoning and logic. Attributing to an end (progress, fit, or evil) a causal power dismisses the validity of the analysis from the start.

Limits of biological analogies: the quote from Spencer (two paragraphs above) illustrates another problem: his recurrent use of biological analogies and other metaphors to support his line of arguments. In terms of methods, Spencer admits the metaphorical and analogical nature of comparisons when likening organizations to organisms. Further, he asserts that there is obvious correspondence between organisms and organizations. Analogies become arguments.

> Like other organisms, the social organism has to pass in the course of its development though temporary forms, in which sundry of its functions are fulfilled by

appliances destined to disappear as fast as the ultimate appliances become efficient. Associated humanity has larval appendages analogous to those of individual creatures. (Spencer, 1892: 237)

A century later, this quote presents perhaps a metaphorical interest, but certainly not a scientific validity. In our current research, we have to avoid these comparisons. The burden of the proof is on the researchers, who cannot satisfy themselves with mere parallels and associations. Hence, we should develop proper means of definition, description, and independent modeling (or as independent as possible) of basic analogies and metaphors.

Inconsistencies: in the nineteenth century, a brutal confrontation took place between theological and scientific explanations of the presence and disappearance of living beings. The core of Spencer's scientific creed was the rejection of any miraculous intervention in natural causation. Causes explain past phenomena and prolong their effects in the present. There is a causal continuity, unbreakable in Spencer's thought. Notably, after the publication of *Principles of Psychology* and, more precisely, between 1855 and 1859, Spencer modified his evolutionary conception to account more clearly for causal permanence. He believed in the fundamental necessity of change to produce heterogeneity. Therefore, in the unfolding of his system, Spencer introduced a supreme causal principle, the persistence of force, as the legitimization of the 'fundamental necessity' of change. That principle, observable in its effects, is unknowable in its causes and by nature indemonstrable. Peel (1971) emphasizes that at the crux of evolution, besides the homogeneous-heterogeneous transformation, is the 'unknowable force'. Morality and happiness, once the end points of evolution, have been replaced by a mysterious force that pushes its effects forward in every material and elementary particle. 'Mystery is at the evolution's origin what was happiness at the evolution's end' (Durand, 2000: 78).

The fourth lesson from Spencer's works consists in keeping coherence and consistency in an explanatory model. Spencer noted that naivety tainted the irrepressible march to happiness that he had endorsed (Spencer, 1850). He therefore tempered the use of adaptation as a teleological mechanism driving evolution. In his efforts to scientifically demonstrate that causes and effects interact and explain the gradual passage from homogeneity to heterogeneity, he introduced a major inconsistency. Under the guise of ousting naïve teleology, he smuggled it in by the back door with the 'unknowable force'. This is the foible that debunks his whole system of thought. His agnostic conception is now based on a fundamental principle, unknowable, unconditioned, and indemonstrable, that animates every movement towards change in a pursuit of constant adaptation. Peel (1971) insists on this metaphysical root of evolution, in sheer contradiction to the agnostic theory of evolution that Spencer defended.

Causal indeterminacy: the 'fundamental necessity' in the chain of causes and effects, originating in the 'unknowable force', leads to specialized forms of heterogeneity. In order to account for dissolution, the victory of disaggregating forces, Spencer redefined causality. He developed the idea of a 'fruitful causality' according to which 'every active force produces more than one change – every cause produces more than one effect'. In so doing, his conception of causality becomes confused. Every cause produces more than one effect and the absence of a cause also produces more than one effect. Thus, dissolution in its different forms can be explained by insufficient incorporation of new matter, an inappropriate motion, or the weakness of a cohesive principle. Indeed, with such a malleable conception of causality, Spencer chose different determinant factors at will. In later sociological works, this causal indeterminacy blemishes his theory. 'Character, shaped by inheritance, determines institutions. Institutions, the systematized face of environment, shape character. Spencer admits a mutuality of influence, but his ascription of determinacy shifts with context' (Wiltshire, 1971: 213). What we should learn from this fifth lesson is the great need for clarity when we talk about causality in our models. When and why are causal relationships effective? Can these relationships be inverted? What is the permanence of these concepts and their relationships?

SPENCER IN PERSPECTIVE

While not wishing to linger on Spencer, it remains worthwhile to put his work into perspective. Attribution mistakes could be avoided in the future and intriguing parallels surface when contrasting Spencer's principles to those of Lamarck and Darwin.

Spencer and Lamarck: false immanence and true Lamarckian history

We commented earlier on how finalism had changed form in Spencer's metaphysics, passing from a pure teleology (aiming at progress and happiness) to the unfolding of an unconditioned force. Due to the dwelling presence of the 'unknowable force' in Spencer's articles and books, critics have denounced his 'immanentism', namely, the inclusion of a supreme immanent cause able to explain each and every change from within the unit of change. Haines (1988), however, argues convincingly that Spencer's evolutionary theory is not immanent, as people who merely browse through his works claim. Spencer's concept of progress is teleological not because its biological foundation assumes immanence, but rather because it incorporates the utilitarian *telos* of human happiness (Haines, 1988: 1207). Changes that an instable organism undergoes depend on shifting environmental conditions (Lamarckian hypothesis) rather than on a preordained series of events (immanent or epigenetic conception of change). Spencer's evolutionism therefore would correspond more to a Lamarckian culturized biology or biologized history than to a theory of immanent change.

In his biological studies, Spencer stoutly defends the direct influence of the environment on organisms, and the transmission of acquired traits to future generations. This Lamarckian principle accounts for a large part of observable evolutionary phenomena. In his sociological studies, too, the exercise and actualization of man's latent intrinsic capabilities (superior to those of any other animal) develop more or less rapidly depending on favorable circumstances and on the asymptotic tendency of adaptation to move towards perfection. This tendency is inherently rooted in vitality, echoing Lamarck's natural internal force present in living beings. There is a parallel between the Lamarckian *ordre des choses* and the 'unknowable force' beating at the heart of Spencer's evolutionism. In fact, the functional differentiation, the observable complexity, and the resulting increasing diversity – the three interdependent Spencerian sub-theories of social evolution underscored by Perrin (1976) – belong to the Lamarckian realm.

A valid reason for Spencer's reliance on Lamarckism is his overly ambitious desire to unify biological, psychological, and sociological observable phenomena. Social and cultural evolutions retain essences of the past: knowledge, morality, institutions. Had he rejected Lamarck's biological principles, Spencer would have been at odds with his own Lamarckian sociology. Therefore, Spencer preferred repeated pleading for biological Lamarckism to the collapse of his entire and presumably all-coherent theoretical edifice. The abandoning of Lamarckism 'would have driven a wedge between biological and sociocultural or "superorganic" evolution, and so nullified the major premises of the entire Synthetic Philosophy' (Peel, 1971: 143).

Spencer and Darwin: two misunderstandings

Let us state bluntly the two points of difference between Spencerian and Darwinian theses. First, Darwin is the father of the natural selection theory of evolution (but not the father of evolutionism); Spencer is the author of a synthetic philosophy of change called 'evolutionism' (although he was unable to understand and integrate Darwinian selection in his system). Secondly, Darwin did not initiate social Darwinism; Spencer did.

Spencer misunderstood Darwin's conception of natural selection in two ways. First, Spencer claimed to have anticipated Darwin's ideas in his essay on population (Spencer, 1852). However, in this essay, the adaptation mechanism at play is definitely Lamarckian: in the face of population pressures or resource shortages, animals must adjust to the existing conditions, with the successful survivors passing their traits on to their offspring. Darwin argued differently: variations and differentiation exist at a population level; some of these are to be selected. Spencer maintained a view of evolution at an individual level, an organism transmitting its traits to the next generation. Secondly, Darwin used selection in his framework as a way to explain the limitation of the number of descendants of a population. He did not suppose a hierarchy between the forms of life, and even less amongst human societies. There is no real perfection, nor an end of ideal adaptation. Darwinian selection is not teleological. Darwinian selection rewards relative advantage and not perfect adaptation. Relative adaptation to the extant conditions enhances survival, and the stronger the species, the more it will bring about diversity and variations. Therefore, Spencerian selection misses the essence of Darwin's idea of selection. On the one hand, Spencerian selection is not a real principle of evolution – unlike Darwinian selection – but only a consequence of a Lamarckian adaptation. On the other hand, Spencerian selection assumes a tangentially perfect match between an individual and its environment, whereas Darwinian selection does not postulate any such fundamental hypothesis.

Spencer was himself the source of some confusion between his ideas and Darwin's. In the late 1860s, when Spencer's theses were losing ground to Darwin's natural selection hypotheses, he attempted to replace the abstract Darwinian natural selection principle with another soon-to-be-popular expression: 'survival of the fittest'. As Malthus had argued, pressures of population create competition, and competition favors the well endowed. For Spencer, the theoretical equality that exists amongst individuals is, in reality, a competitive equality. Theoretically, individuals have equal claims to make use of their liberty, but they actually improve themselves in their concrete actions. Theoretical equal advantages are the starting condition of social evolution, but are actualized in uneven distribution of natural abilities. Undeniable endowment differences exist that perpetuate over generations, and instill a stepwise progression toward adaptation – at the expense, regrettably but necessarily, of the 'unfit'. When this is not the case, the signs of maladaptive accomplishment (such as pain, unhappiness, and discomfort) develop in societies. Therefore, men should rise and move against intrusive policy makers who, instead of favoring the natural adaptation process, hamper it by maintaining the unfit.

Society advances where its fittest members are allowed to assert their fitness with the least hindrance, and where the least fitted are not artificially prevented from dying out. (Spencer, 1892: 81)

However, survival of the fittest does not imply the war of all against all but, tangentially, the arrival at a threshold where cooperation, fueled by moral sentiment and proper behavior, supersedes ruthless competition. This last, conciliating part of Spencer's argument has not been retained by history. However, the former part of the argument, the survival of the fittest, has nurtured a current in sociological studies – particularly vehement during the last decades of the nineteenth century and the first third of the twentieth century – that seemed to justify ruthless capitalism, racialism, and eugenics (Hofstader, 1959). This 'Social Darwinism' was based on Spencer's extreme ideas, Galton's restricted definition of species and inheritance, and Pearson's mathematical and statistical developments.

3.3   CONCLUSION

Figure 3.1 represents the major components of three of the most influential nineteenth-century evolutionary conceptions. It helps us to configure the different articulations of their structure and argumentation. Notably, Figure 3.1 demonstrates two of the Darwinian specificities: populational analysis and the variation-inheritance-selection triptych. It also stresses the importation of key Lamarckian transformism elements into Spencerian evolutionism. Finally, it banishes notions alien to all three evolutionary conceptions, which were introduced later by Galton among others: fixism and regression toward the mean.

The three models did not share a common destiny. Lamarckism has been repudiated in biology. Spencerism inspired a vivid current of literature, particularly in American sociology and economics. However, Darwin's theory has experienced many inflections and an unprecedented echo in the last 150 years. This has not been an immediate or a steady process. Bowler (2003) calls the 1875–1925 period the 'eclipse of Darwinism'. During that period, rival theories flourished. Selectionism, neo-Lamarckism, orthogenesis, neo-Darwinism, and Mendelianism developed alternative hypotheses to account for the flow of findings and evidence brought forth by naturalists, paleontologists, and geneticists. One of the greatest evolutionary biologists, Ernst Mayr, reminds us in each of his books what happened during the 1930s and 40s – namely, the 'second Darwinian revolution, also called the "evolutionary synthesis"'.

During that period, Mayr argues, naturalists and geneticists reached a consensus on several issues. Fundamentally, they overcome their divergence at the level of analysis that matters most: intra-populational variations for geneticists, and species and geographic variations for naturalists (comprising taxonomists and paleontologists). They became more attuned to each other's theses, and succeeded in bridging micro-evolutionary with macro-evolutionary processes. Mayr (1942) himself played a role in the so-called 'synthesis' by showing that mutation – once supposedly able to generate phylogenic changes or even species changes – simply provided random variations at the genetic level. Natural selection was consecrated as the driving force operating on abundant and available variations. Natural selection operates at the genetic level, but indirectly via the survival of individuals who transmit the favorable genetic materials. Inheritable favorable variations are selected, not individuals. Selection is not the sorting of individuals but a bias in survival probabilities of an individual endowed with favorable variations.

Thus, the second Darwinian revolution occurred when Lamarckism was abandoned. Evolutionary synthesis rejected 'sports', namely, drastic changes, as uncommon and more deleterious than favorable. Gradualism gained favor. Naturalists brought to the fore population thinking and new methods that could be applied successfully by geneticists. They introduced population-wide distributed genetic variations that were not simple taxonomic expressions of a mutation vis-à-vis wild types (a reasoning drawn from the Mendelian tradition). Several authors have commented on the true nature and amplitude of the evolutionary synthesis (see Bowler, 2003: 326). For many researchers, evolutionary synthesis helped construct a general evolutionary worldview that, in the aftermath of World War Two atrocities, did not condemn humanity to despair but instead strove to scientifically root a philosophy of hope.

Figure 3.1. Principal components of three nineteenth-century evolutionary models

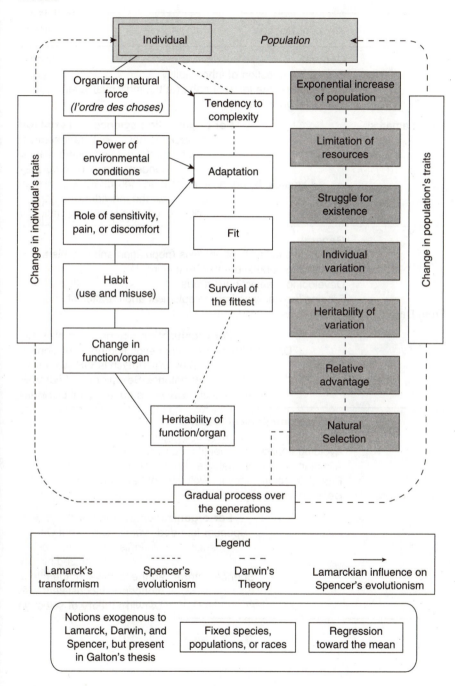

3.4 SUMMARY

	Key contributions
From Lamarck	**General** Posing the question of inheritability Reflection on the force of habit (at the individual level) Theorization of transformism <div align="right">**For organization science and strategy** Lamarck did not 'invent' transformism Lamarck did not suppose a natural tendency toward complexity Lamarck did not assume that an individual's willpower is able to alter the individual's organism Lamarck's conception is not adaptationist</div>
From Darwin	**General** Decomposing levels of analysis (population and organism) Introducing population-wide reasoning Developing a selectionist model Freeing the analysis from teleological and creationist conceptions <div align="right">**For organization science and strategy** Darwin's theory is neither evolution nor evolutionism Darwin's triptych is VIS (Variation- Inheritance-Selection) and not VSR Darwin is not a Social Darwinist</div>
From Spencer	**Five methodological lessons** Separating law and cause of evolution Avoiding finalism as scientific demonstration Avoiding biological analogies as evidence Providing consistency in evolutionary frameworks Defining causality <div align="right">**For organization science and strategy** Spencer founded evolutionism – not Darwin Spencer's evolutionism is a 'Lamarckian' biologized history Spencer introduced the 'survival of the fittest' concept – inconsistent with Darwin's theory of selection</div>

4 EVOLUTIONARY MODELS IN ORGANIZATIONAL THEORY

Whereas for the numerous small firms in the parallel ecologies, bankruptcy can probably be assumed to be selecting for competence ... , for the large heterogeneous conglomerates, subfirms may be protected from the bankruptcies they deserve. (Campbell, 1994: 34)

This chapter brings to the fore three crucial issues: first, the overlooked assumptions and epistemological status of the Variation-Selection-Retention (VSR) model; secondly, the complex genealogy of evolutionary ideas within three classical evolutionary research streams; and thirdly, the contributions and limits of the coevolutionary approach. This chapter is pivotal to the construction of the Checklist Appraisal Grid for evolutionary models.

First, noting that organizational theory integrates sociological perspectives in the study of organizational evolution, the chapter begins with the VSR model of socio-cultural evolution proposed by Campbell (1960, 1969), which has been widely described and utilized in organizational evolution and strategic management literature. The first section provides a critique of the VSR model that shows that important assumptions of the model must be acknowledged.

The second section reviews three major streams of evolutionary research: population ecology (Hannan and Freeman, 1989), evolutionary economics (Nelson and Winter, 1982), and the dynamic resource-based view of the firm (Teece et al., 1997).

The third section shows that none of these classical perspectives on organizational evolution derive, untainted, from Lamarck, Darwin, and Spencer – and therefore we ought not to refer to them so blithely. The VSR model itself results from a composite descent of the ideas of biological evolution that the nineteenth century has bequeathed to us.

In the fourth section, the three contemporaneous evolutionary approaches are contrasted to the VSR model. Critical remarks are introduced that concern the possibility of the VSR model attaining the status of a 'paradigm' for social, cultural, and organizational evolution. These findings require us to consider organizational evolution as a particular object of study and to overcome what we call 'the VSR challenges'. Such challenges concern, for instance, the difficulty of characterizing selection in the VSR model, and the unlikely integration of strategic management within this model.

Finally, the last section reviews the co-evolutionary approach. An immoderate use of this approach, which integrates many different layers of influences (institutional, cultural, economic, social, and so on), incurs the risk of diluting its contributions, resulting in an ungraspable dynamic whole. However, on the positive side, important conclusions may be obtained: for example, selection does not necessarily select strong competitors; organizational competitiveness relates to a firm's effect on its rivals' survival; and, therefore, competition determines evolution, according to the degree of each organization's competitiveness.

4.1   CAMPBELL'S VSR MODEL

Donald Campbell died in 1996 and left many major contributions to the fields of social science and epistemology (Brewer and Collins, 1981; Baum and McKelvey, 1999). His influence was unprecedented in such areas as the natural selection model of knowing, the multi-trait/multi-method perspective, and the theorization of contextualized perception and conception. This chapter focuses on the Variation-Selection-Retention (VSR) model, also referred to as the (B)VSR ('B' standing for blind variation). The first stage of this evolutionary model is variation, implying multiplicity of elements. Technological variation, for instance, is characterized by multiple standards, techniques, and processes. The second stage is selection, a process that results in success or failure (Campbell, 1960; Aldrich, 1979; Baum and Singh, 1994b; Baum and McKelvey, 1999). The last stage is retention, which indicates that organizations are able to identify the selected variations and reproduce them in order to increase their likelihood of survival (Weick, 1979; Winter, 1995; Aldrich and Kenworthy, 1999).

Campbell argues that the (B)VSR model is the sole useful explanation of socio-cultural evolution and, notably, that it provides the observable (and remarkable) 'fit' between social systems and their environments. Campbell (1969: 70) acknowledges the danger of biological analogies, saying: 'It is the variation-and-selective-retention process which seems appropriately borrowed from biological evolution, rather than analogues to the course of biological evolution'. He then adds: ' ... This section offers an analogy between natural selection in biological evolution and the selective propagation of cultural forms. ... The analogy to cultural cumulations will not be from organic evolution per se, but rather from a general model for adaptive fit or quasi-teleological processes for which organic evolution is but one instance' (Campbell, 1969: 73). Thus Campbell avoids the trap of associations between biological and sociological or organizational entities. What matters is the cumulative process of selective retention in society rather than the correspondence between entities (a routine is not a gene, a resource portfolio not a genotype, and so forth).

Campbell attempts to revive socio-evolutionary theory, brushing aside the socio-evolutionary theorists' inclination toward socio-Darwinism. Campbell delineates three necessary and sufficient conditions if an 'inevitable' better fit with the selective system is to occur: First, numerous variations, secondly, consistency in selection criteria over time, and thirdly, a mechanism for retention of the selected variants that deterministically lead to an improved fit. This simple triptych supplies sufficient evidence of the 'improbable and marvelous' adaptation of living organisms to their environment, says Campbell. Based on the same three conditions (although not on the same biological entities), a socio-cultural evolutionary or learning process is also 'inevitable' – epitomizing a first step towards an evolutionary epistemology and social construction of scientific progression.

In social systems, blind variations are of three types: among social units, among events within a social unit, and among the members of a social unit. According to the (B)VSR process, some deliberate variations might be more successful if they could be pre-selected, whereas others might suffer from path-dependent cognitive or social conditioning (Romanelli, 1999). However, for Campbell, deliberate or intelligent variations do not generally supersede blind or haphazard variations. While variation operates at a component level, the second stage, selection, operates at macro-levels (conserving complete social organizations). These include a diffusion of variations between social groups, a selective propagation of temporal variations, an imitation of individual practices, a selective promotion to leadership and educational roles, and 'rational selection' (based on economic principles).

A tortuous question arises regarding the consistency of the selection criteria over time, namely, their degree of persistence and the strength of conformity they convey. Moreover, determining selection criteria from the observation of current organizations or organisms contains the seeds of circular inference, and ruins the possibility of examining their very nature (Campbell, 1960, 1969). Furthermore, the multiplicity and embeddedness of selection systems complicate this analysis (Campbell, 1974). Finally, retention mechanisms, as social artifacts that coerce learning and behavior, represent – at the same time – a guarantee of knowledge preservation and the accumulation of selected variations within and across groups. However, the rigidity of retention mechanisms instills inertia, restricts individuals, and causes rejection of traditional mores. Thus, individual hedonistic impulses alter social institutions' selective forces and affect retention systems.

Unlike theories of biological evolution, socio-cultural VSR theory accounts for convergent evolutionary paths. Ordinary inventions result from cumulative knowledge that is connected synchronously by independent individuals. Campbell touts the deterministic discovery of evolutionary theory, independent of key individuals such as Darwin and, presumably, himself. Campbell prefers the mechanistic and disembodied format of VSR evolution to either the necessary accomplishment of any 'Spirit of the Time' or to the hagiographic and emblematic figures of scientific genius or Schumpeterian entrepreneurs – or managerial icons. He writes, 'Too often, in contemporary social science, analysis stops when it is traced back to individual motives, as though these were the prime mover, the uncaused beginning of causal sequences' (Campbell, 1969: 81).

Beyond the recognition of the good fortune of the (B)VSR theory of socio-cultural evolution, extensively applied to the world of organizations, three components of Campbellian evolutionism, seldom spelled out, deserve mention. First, as evidenced by the last quote, much of Campbell's thinking hinges on his view of human nature engaged in a tension between altruistic and egoistic attitudes – not to use the term 'interest'. Campbell argues 'that the culturally evolved moral norms are predominantly preaching against the very sort of personality that biological individuals would produce – tendencies for selfish and nepotistic cheating on social contract, free-riding and freeloading on the altruistic products of others, etc.' (Campbell, 1994: 26). In a plea for advancement in research, Campbell seems to violate his own elementary methodological caution against biological analogies and comparisons by advocating for a better comprehension of human nature. He says, for example: 'The use of evolutionary theory in management science should ... pay attention to the human nature produced by biological evolution, especially by the genetic competition among the cooperators so conspicuously absent in the ultrasocial insects and the naked mole rats' (Campbell, 1994: 38). It is therefore intriguing to note how much human nature matters *in fine* for Campbell and evolutionists (Baum and McKelvey, 1999). Indeed, evolutionists seek the real mechanisms that can account for organizational evolution and study how human activity may achieve it, yet they ignore human nature and use rudimentary cognitive and behavioral approximations in their models and theories (Hendrick, 1999). Human nature is a blind spot in evolutionary models, and the study of evolving populations often serves as a haven against engagement with human – too human – power, ethics, and desires.

Secondly, Campbell refers to the VSR evolution as a quasi-teleological process inexorably leading to adapted fit. He comments on the inevitability of biological adaptation and, analogously, of socio-cultural adaptation. A corollary and inevitable phenomenon appears in Campbell's propositions: one by one, every viable mode of living must be tested as variations propagate from one mode to a close other (Campbell, 1969). A consequence of the niche-filling process is that evolutionary theorizing must not be unilinear but must capture its 'multi-dimensional opportunism'. The accumulation of selected variations enables the complexity of the overall evolving system to grow. Attributing positive value to steadily increasing complexity, Campbell deduces that a certain form of progress results from socio-cultural evolution.

Finally, Campbell reiterates the equal value of blind and deliberate variations (Campbell, 1990, 1994). Why does he insist on blind variations as the most (and sufficient) plausible version of variations? Because blind variations surpass human individuals and agencies; namely, they are better than 'the rational social science of the ruling elite' (Campbell, 1969: 74). Campbell contends that a group-level efficiency may supersede individual human interventions, saying: 'We must reject the methodological individualism as an a priori assumption, make the issue an empirical one, and take the position that groups, human social organizations *might be* ontologically real, with laws not derivable from individual psychology' (Campbell, 1994: 4). There are political underpinnings to Campbell's evolution theory and Campbellian realism. We will return to this point in the last chapter of this book.

Before giving a critical appraisal of the (B)VSR evolutionary framework (section 4.4), let us first present three streams of literature that are inspired by or derived from the VSR model and that apply to organizations. (See section 4.2

for their presentation, and section 4.3 for their positioning relative to biological traditions.)

4.2   THREE APPROACHES OF ORGANIZATIONAL EVOLUTION

Organizational evolutionary approaches vary according to whether they emphasize exogenous, intrinsic, or combined conditions in organizations. Population ecology deals chiefly with the exogenous conditions of organizational evolution, whereas research on dynamic capabilities concentrates on determinants internal to the organization. Evolutionary economics occupies an intermediate position, since some of its research concerns feature exogenous factors while others (such as routines) are at the root of an intrinsic definition of the firm.[1] In this chapter, the contributions of population ecology to organizational evolution are presented first, followed by evolutionary economics, and finally by the dynamic resource-based view of the firm.

POPULATION ECOLOGY

The population ecology of organizations, according to its proponents, describes and explains the diversity of organizational forms (Hannan and Freeman, 1989). It examines the sources of variability in organizations, as well as the reasons for their similarities. For Hannan and Freeman (1984), a population of firms is a collection of organizations sharing a common dependency on their material and social environment and on the resources they can obtain. Hannan and Freeman (1977, 1989) indicate that their conception favors the Darwinian hypothesis of change and selection over the Lamarckian conception. For them, the Lamarckian process implies that human actors and firms learn and incorporate learning into their behavioral repertoires. According to the Darwinian competitive process, 'if there is a *rationality* in play, it is the rationality of natural selection' (Hannan and Freeman, 1977).

Hannan and Freeman (1989), and Carroll and Hannan (2000) rely on the compatibility of three explanations of organizational evolution when studied at the population level. First, the availability of essential environmental resources is limited. Therefore, the organizations of a given population exploit the corresponding resources until they almost exhaust the carrying capacity of the environment. Secondly, organizational forms embody historically specific conditions, which imprint them so much that their longevity is jeopardized as historical conditions (and technologies) change. The third explanation is social phenomena, which explain the upsurge and contraction of population density. On the one hand, an increase in the number of organizations constituting a population creates legitimacy for the population; on the other hand, proliferation triggers competition, leading to contraction of the population's size.

Environmental capacity

Echoing Malthusian and Darwinian assumptions, population ecologists identify the carrying capacity of the competitive environment as a first construct that influences organizational evolution (Brittain, 1994). The carrying capacity is the number of firms or firm populations that can prosper in a given state of the environment. Indeed, the carrying capacity of the environment affects both the degree of population selection and the odds of a firm's selection. The carrying capacity depends mainly on institutional rules, laws and other regulations (Baum and Oliver, 1991), and on the availability of environmental resources (Wholey and Brittain, 1989). Every modification of institutional variables (for example, abrogation of a law, change of standards) and every change in the availability of external resources (caused by deregulation, the discovery of a new raw material or technology, of different means of communication or production, and so on) modifies the carrying capacity of the environment and defines its evolution (Tushman and Anderson, 1986; Barnett and Hansen, 1996). Therefore, organizational evolution varies in rhythm and intensity depending on variations in carrying capacity due to political, legal, or economic events. For instance, new technological advances (for example, ADSL in telecommunications) broaden the carrying capacity of the environment until the carrying capacity for Internet operators is supposedly attained. In other words, a firm's evolution depends upon the initial state of the carrying capacity, upon how some related events modify it, and, eventually, upon the firm's ability to seize an upcoming opportunity. For ecologists, however, a firm belongs to an organizational form, and a firm's evolution depends not on its uniqueness but on its ability to spawn in a niche and to constitute an organizational form with other organizations of its kind.

Organizational inertia

Secondly, in addition to the nature of the environmental carrying capacity, an organization's ability to seize opportunities depends on organizational inertia. Early on, Hannan and Freeman (1977) focused on the role played by inertia in organizational evolution. Organizations are subject to inertial forces such as sunk costs, incomplete information, internal political constraints, and their own history. Inertia results from the structured processes that enable an organization to account for what it does and what it pursues (accountability) and also to achieve low variance in performing a task (reliability). Inertia results also from the structured patterns of action and communication between an organization's members. Cultural values, cognitive frames, and collective representations shape and condition the collective reactivity of the organization (Polos et al., 2002). They also condition the manner and the outcome of collective decisions, independently of threatening stimuli. Inertia is often equated with a resistance factor, hampering implementation of required changes. In ecological models, however, inertia can be a consequence of selection rather than a cause or precondition of selection.

Hannan and Freeman (1984) relate structural inertia to societal and, especially, economic institutions. When the carrying capacity of the environment changes, organizational forms occupy the available space and exploit external resources. In return for their acceptance by economic actors (such as customers, workers, and shareholders), firms must be financially and socially accountable for their actions and reliable as regards their products and services. These two fundamental conditions render structural inertia necessary as a first step in the establishment of both firms and, through imitation and propagation, firm populations. Hence, Hannan and Freeman deduce their 'first theorem': 'Selection within populations of organizations in modern societies favors organizations whose structures have high inertia' (Hannan and Freeman, 1984: 155). Inertia provides coherence, replicability, and reliability within a firm. Furthermore, inertia gives confidence to the firm's stakeholders regarding its ability to prosper and survive. Structural inertia is thus a necessary consequence of selection in a competitive environment with a given carrying capacity. The liability-of-newness phenomenon (the above-average demise rate of young firms) finds an explanation in this requirement. The Internet economy is a good illustration of it, since many e-companies failed because they were unable to be reliable and accountable.

However, there is a threshold to the beneficial relationship that can exist between inertia and firm survival. As just mentioned, to a certain extent a high organizational inertia reduces the selective pressure on a firm. But even if inertia restrains an organization from disordered ventures and over-diversification, when a radical transformation of environmental carrying capacity occurs, an entire population of organizations may disappear due to their structural inflexibility (Tushman and Romanelli, 1994). Inertia may cause organizational rigidities that can prove fatal when new competitors unexpectedly appear (Carroll and Hannan, 1989; Kelly and Amburgey, 1991). Although inertia is required in order to survive, excessive inertia can hamper a firm's development and may reduce a firm's nimbleness. Indeed, structural inertia affects the amount of time a firm needs for both learning and reacting (Rumelt, 1995). Therefore, any firm must reach a threshold of inertia to survive. This threshold differs according to the considered populations. However, once the threshold has been reached, relative inertia determines the level of selective pressures on populations, forms, and firms.

Strategy and population dynamics

Another important consequence derives from the concept of structural inertia. Inertial organizations cannot easily (at minimal cost) modify their strategic orientation. Ecology theorists define two principal strategies that firms may adopt: specialist and generalist (Carroll, 1985). The odds of survival are different according to the generic strategy retained by the firms and the characteristics of the competitive environment. To decide whether to adopt a generalist or a specialist strategy, firms must carefully consider the nature of rivalry, since greater or lesser proximity in the competitors' form affects a firm's selection (Kelly and Amburgey, 1991). A great difference in the forms indicates that the firm's populations are specialists in one type of environment but lose efficiency in another: for each population of specialist firms, the strategy, structure, and technology are adapted to one single part of the competitive environment. However, if the forms are similar, firm populations can compete more efficiently, and the pressures for selection will become harsher (Freeman and Hannan, 1983).

Selection pressures at the organization level correspond to the cost of a sub-optimal strategy to environmental conditions at a point in time, namely, the cost of being a generalist (as opposed to a specialist) in a competitive situation favoring the specialist. Both the similarity of the firms competing in an environment and the variability of the environment affect this cost, and consequently influence selection pressures. When the environment is uncertain, with rapid changes initiated by adaptive firms, the environment is said to be fine-grained. In cases where the changing states of the environment are slow and where reorganizations of companies are rare, the environment is coarse-grained (Hannan and Freeman, 1989). The specialist prospers when the environment is fine-grained, undergoing variations in the environment but surviving, on average, because the periods of fluctuation are close together. But if the environment becomes coarse-grained, the specialist will not be able to endure the continuous selective pressure on generic resources, because it has counted on specific resources; the specialist thus becomes sub-optimal (Miner et al., 1990), and the generalist firm becomes more competitive through resource diversification. Thus, organizational selection is increased by the misfit between the 'grain' of the environment and the 'chosen' strategy relative to competitors' strategy 'choice' (Baum and Singh, 1994a). It has to be clear that 'choice' in this context is at its minimal value, and 'attribute' or 'predefinition' could be used interchangeably.

In their empirical studies, population ecologists find convergent patterns of population deployment. Density of organizational populations follows a typical shape and time path: initial slow growth, subsequent explosive growth, and stabilization (Hannan and Carroll, 1992; Carroll and Hannan, 2000). Population ecologists argue that legitimization increases at a decreasing rate according to the number of competitors (namely density), while competition increases at an increasing rate. In the low range of density, founding rates are high and mortality rates rather low. At higher ranges, competition dominates and founding rates decline whereas mortality rates rise. They assert that large and dominant organizations cannot influence selection pressures and entry rates in their industry.

Remarks

While interesting, this theory and the corroborating empirical results suffer from some limitations. Population ecologists assume that legitimization of an organizational population increases with its density at a decreasing rate. But why? Restricting conditions must apply for this assumption to be true. For instance, when institutions modify the carrying capacity of the environment through a legislative process (for example, the Glass-Steagal Act, the Sarbanes-Oxley Law), the possibility of an organizational population's formation is already legitimate. Legitimization may precede the organizational founding, and may even be preselected by organizations carving out new legitimate niches through the legislative process. However, individual founders must not have prior strategic resources that bias legitimization *ab ovo* in the ecological accounts. Cannot iPod by Apple and Steve Jobs legitimate the industry instantly, based on prior reputation and status?

Does legitimization really increase after further entries? Maybe competition only increases the pressure, the more so as followers enter and exit, until an oligopoly (for example, Apple, Microsoft, and one or two other companies) controls the industry. In that latter case, competition within organizational populations would not increase with its density at an increasing rate as hypothesized by ecologists, but would decrease at an increasing rate after the formation of the oligopoly.

Zucker (1989) criticized the bedrock principle of population ecology because population ecologists seldom directly measure and test legitimacy and competition. They content themselves with data on founding, disbanding, and density. However, while competition is arguably a population-level dimension, legitimization of a population is less solidly anchored at a given level (McKendrick and Carroll, 2001). Even more, legitimization could better apply at an organizational level than at a population level. In other words, the effect of an organization's legitimacy can supersede the effect of its belonging to a legitimate organizational form (Rao et al., 2003). Furthermore, it is not impossible to theorize that competition applies also at an organizational level or at the level of dyadic relationships (Baum and Korn, 1999). By this, we mean that the degree of competition within a population results from the agglomeration of entity-based or relation-based competitive intensity, rather than being a pure population-level property. Again, individually defined competitive relations would override the population effect of competition (Gimeno and Woo, 1999). Finally, organizational ecology and demography remain quite silent about how both organizational forms and subforms emerge and organizations evolve. They combine and derive functions that say barely anything about a population constituent's evolution. This follows from their choice of relevant levels of analyses, but results in naïve confessions, such as: 'The reformulated model shifts the research problem from explaining the renewal to predicting the emergence of new organizational subforms. Unfortunately, we lack the necessary theory' (Carroll and Hannan, 2000: 238).

EVOLUTIONARY ECONOMICS

Evolutionary economics provides a liaison between the ecology determinants of organizational evolution, which are out of a firm's immediate control (carrying capacity, strategic misalignment, and organizational inertia), and more manageable determinants of organizational evolution, presented by the dynamic resource-based view of the firm. Referring to Figure 2.3, population ecology (PE) belongs solely to the organizational space, while evolutionary economics is one principal component of what we have called economic selection (ES). The dynamic resource-based view organizes its concepts and mechanisms in the resource space and constitutes a building block of strategy (S). Evolutionary economics (Nelson and Winter, 1982) introduces technology and time as the driving forces of the evolution of organizations and industries – echoing the conclusions of population ecology regarding the misfit between the nature of the environment and a firm's strategy. Evolutionary economics also provides concepts, such as routine, that are fundamental in explaining how firms build and replicate practices in order to escape from selective zones in the environment (Zott, 2003).

Technological change and trajectories

Technological evolution is the principal factor underlying the ongoing process of economic change and variety, according to the evolutionary approach. Yet technological evolution is not a random process. It follows modes of development that depend on technological opportunities, knowledge, and beliefs at a given point in time (Arthur, 1989). A technological 'trajectory' describes the technical and learning structures underlying technological evolution (Rosenberg, 1976). Nelson and Winter (1977) refer to natural trajectories and technological systems, and Dosi (1988) to a 'technological paradigm' (in reference to the Kuhnian structure of scientific revolutions). A good illustration of this phenomenon – where technical mastery, knowledge, and beliefs converge – is the development in the nineteenth century of the gasoline automobile rather than the electric car – a development that will be reexamined in the twenty-first century.

This path-dependent view of technology evolution is not neutral regarding organizational evolution (Dosi and Nelson, 1994; Silverberg et al., 1988). At the beginning of a technological trajectory, selection pressure is higher for organizations that strive to impose a new standard than for less innovative organizations. After a while, sticking to their old technological trajectory, passive firms may bear a higher selection pressure than innovators (Tegarden et al., 1999). Convergence toward a dominant design is a critical contingency that accounts for varying selective pressures. At the beginning of a trajectory, firms concentrate on product innovation. At the end of a first stage (the 'era of ferment'), the product's essential characteristics are established; this composite of required properties forms the 'dominant design' of the product (Abernathy and Utterback, 1978; Anderson and Tushman, 1990). Once a dominant design has emerged, the competitors direct their attention to fine distinctions likely to be valued by consumers, and they no longer consider fundamental changes to the general architecture of the product (Tushman and Anderson, 1986). The production techniques become more specialized, and more specific. Thus, an organization benefits from introducing a major variation only if it succeeds in establishing its design. The case of the medical imaging sector (Mitchell, 1991) and the famous example of VHS cassettes illustrate the benefits of establishing the dominant design. Suarez and Utterback (1995) demonstrate the relevance of technological evolution in their explanations of structural transformations in six industrial sectors and of firms' survival probabilities. According to this study, early entry (which allows the pioneer to impose its technological design) or late entry (after the uncertainty about the dominant design has largely been removed) relative to the appearance of the dominant design increases the probability of firm survival.

Applying these results to organizational evolution, one can infer that technological trends at the industry level and organizational characteristics (such as promising variations, routines) do not pressure firms identically – if they have contributed to the establishment of a dominant design or if they have recognized the appearance of a new dominant design early enough and have exploited it

(Tegarden et al., 1999; Durand and Coeurderoy, 2001). This differentiated result of economic and technological conditions on firms is deeply rooted in the evolutionary conception of the firm. For evolutionary economists, the conception of an evolutionary firm rests essentially on the definition of organizational routines (Nelson and Winter, 1982). The organization's memory and the realization of its know-how characterize routines (Cohen and Bacdayan, 1994). Routines define a collection of organizational interactions, codified or not, and solutions to concrete problems. A firm that has 'memorized' the development of a technological trajectory and is able to manage the diffusion of a dominant design clearly has an internal advantage over its competitors. This amounts to temporarily reducing the pressures of firm selection. (See the time compression diseconomies in Dierickx and Cool, 1989.) For this reason, pioneers, by increasing their selection hazard in the short term, strive to increase it for their competitors in the long term.

Organizational routines and trajectories

Nelson and Winter (1982) distinguish three principal types of routines: operational routines are executed mechanically, like a computer program; generic routines are the foundations for improvement of firm processes through incremental change; search routines concern new combinations of factors and result in true innovation and radical changes, laying the foundation for long-term improvement in performance. Search routines set the stage for the emergence of radical innovations, which defines the Schumpeterian inspiration of this conception of economic change.

For evolutionists, organizational evolution means that the different routines which constitute a firm evolve distinctly through the triptych of variation-selection-retention (Miner, 1994). Thus, strategic reflections on the internal characteristics of knowledge, rules, and procedures within a firm are necessary in order to evaluate the degree to which a firm is restrained by its past history. Paralleling the notion of a technological trajectory, evolutionists extend the properties of path dependency at the firm level (Szulanski, 1996); hence, they define the 'organizational trajectory' as an internal selection mechanism (Campbell, 1974; Henderson and Stern, 2004).

The organizational trajectory characterizes the effects over time of a firm's routines. An organization is engaged in certain actions that are irreversible or have strong momentum. The combination of these pre-existing routines restricts the future development of the firm. By the same token, stakeholders' behavior may limit the evolution of an organizational trajectory. For example, customers may demand firms not to weaken their original product by radically modifying it (Iansiti and Khanna, 1995). In addition, an organizational trajectory is strictly dependent on the presence of search routines. These routines evolve according to the individual qualifications of the firm's employees (Nelson and Winter, 1982) and the dynamics between firms and competing technologies (Tushman and Rosenkopf, 1992). As a result, an organization must utilize search routines in order to implement its future strategy and to escape from the adverse influence of its organizational trajectory (Moorman and Miner, 1998). Levinthal and March (1993), building on the exploration/exploitation distinction, contend that the long-term viability of a firm depends on its ability to engage in sufficient exploration. Thus, all things being equal, the breakdown between search routines and other routines has an impact on an individual organization's evolution relative to its competitors (Lewin et al., 1999).

THE DYNAMIC RESOURCE-BASED VIEW

Evolutionary economics models the causes enabling mutations to occur within an organization, the diffusion processes at the routine or technological level, and the resulting industrial configurations, but it does not fully elucidate the source of competitive advantage (Foss and Eriksen, 1995). Distinguishing between the types of routines does not provide an adequate assessment of a firm's competitive potential. The Resource-Based View of the firm (RBV) and, specifically, the stream of dynamic resources strive to make up for this shortcoming (Montgomery, 1995).

Resources

The RBV concentrates its analysis on the capacity of firms to liberate rents and to bet on their specificities in order to withstand competition (Barney, 2002). Inspired by Penrose (1959), the RBV proposes that firms' idiosyncratic differences underpin their likelihood of succeeding. Penrose offers the hypothesis that a firm's maintenance of performance over time depends on the economies of growth that are intrinsic to that firm. Qualitative differences between resources that underlay production explain firm heterogeneity (Penrose, 1959). Thus, a firm can be considered a unique bundle of resources, and its cost position may be more a function of its resource portfolio than of its market position (Wernerfelt, 1984). Barney (1991), Grant (1991), and Peteraf (1993) develop the valuable criteria that provide the opportunity for rent appropriation. In the RBV, Ricardian rents, along with monopoly and quasi rents, play the key role in driving profitability. Because of their low mobility and scarcity, producers use idiosyncratic resources with variable competitive and rent-generating power (Peteraf and Barney, 2003).

Although the notion of barriers is inherited from models in industrial economics, Wernerfelt develops the concept of 'resource position barriers'. He says, ' ... an entry barrier without a resource position barrier leaves the firm vulnerable to diversifying entrants, whereas a resource position barrier without an entry barrier leaves the firm unable to exploit the barrier (1984: 173). From his point of view, resources protect the firm's appropriation of monopoly and quasi rents against rival strategic moves. In explaining firm performance, proponents of the RBV have developed an analysis that increasingly, over the years, has defended the dominance of firm effects over industry effects (Rumelt, 1991). In a key article, Dierickx and Cool (1989) distinguish between the stocks of assets and the flows of investments that enable firms to build competitive advantage from the inside. They suggest four major mechanisms behind the sustainability of a firm's privileged asset position: time compression diseconomies, asset mass efficiencies, interconnectedness of asset stocks, and causal ambiguity. These four mechanisms keep competitors from imitating the firm's production efficiency.

The RBV interprets differences in firm profitability as reflections of differences in the streams of rents accruing to firms, which in turn are affected by differences in the control and management of strategic resources (Amit and Shoemaker, 1993; Winter, 1995). The RBV postulates that a firm's competitive advantage results from capturing the value of an asset that is temporarily under-valued by the players in an industry (Makadok, 1999). Hence, a firm benefits from asymmetrical information. In a sense, a firm is in a position of arbitrage (Makadok and Barney, 2001). The worthy strategy consists of betting on rent-earning resources before the competitors perceive the potential value of the asset in question or when they cannot imitate the firm that is building a competitive advantage (Zott, 2003).

A firm's strategic moves are often reinterpreted from the resource-based viewpoint: acquisition means controlling new bundles of resources, diversifying implies preserving the relatedness of the resource portfolio, and so on. Other studies emphasize the role played by resources in creating business success. For example, McGrath et al. (1995) define 'competence' in operational terms. They relate the 'comprehension' of the team and the 'deftness' of task execution to the degree to which a firm can reliably meet or exceed objectives. As a matter of fact, the ability to uncover resources and resource potentials is crucial (Makadok, 1999), and organizational effects may compromise the exercise of a firm's capabilities (for example, its forecasting ability) (Durand, 2003).

Dynamic capabilities

A sub-branch of the RBV, called the 'dynamic capabilities approach', has advanced the process of internal analysis, subsuming the dynamic principles of evolutionary economics under the administrative efficiency of the organization. According to the dynamic capabilities approach,

> competitive advantage comes from dynamic resources rooted in the most profitable routines within the firm, embedded in the organizational process and conditioned by their history. Because of the imperfection of markets, or more precisely of the non-transferability of tangible assets, like the securities, the identity of the organizational experience, these aptitudes cannot be bought; they must be built. (Teece and Pisano, 1994: 553)

Thus, the development of new aptitudes is the result of localized learning processes, depending on the past experience of the firm (Teece et al., 1997; Helfat and Peteraf, 2003; Winter, 2003).

Therefore, the progress of a technology is no longer seen as a mere trajectory along a natural path; instead, it is viewed as the consequence of specific evolutions in the architecture of the technological system, evolutions initiated and led by firms (Henderson and Clark, 1990). The assembly of several technologies with their own evolution at different levels of the system may render obsolete some technological trajectories while preserving others – as well as the underlying technological resources and capabilities (Eisenhardt and Martin, 2000). Whereas evolutionary economics traditionally presents radical innovation as a rupture of a technological trajectory, the dynamic capabilities perspective regards radical innovation as a firm's deliberate intent to destroy a rival's competencies and to modify a rival's ability to evaluate technological performance (Iansiti and Khanna, 1995; Rosenbloom and Christensen, 1994).

A way for an organization to preserve control and mastery of its own evolution consists of modifying the competitors' perception and displacing the locus of economic selection towards new capabilities or resources. The emergence of new bundles of resources underpinning success modifies competitors' perceptions and behavior (Moran and Ghoshal, 1999). Competitors must imitate, replicate, or substitute assets, processes that diminish the intrinsic value of the successful firm's resources and capabilities (Barney, 1991; Barnett and Hansen 1996). Therefore, a change in the bundle of valuable and dynamic resources required to be competitive displaces the selective pressures from a firm to its competitors (Gimeno and Woo, 1999). Playing with the different services provided by the resources and potential externalities enables a firm to strategically conduct its organizational evolution (Bonardi and Durand, 2003).

This approach entails a redefinition of routines. Evolutionary economics has long been content to view routines as technical, structural, and mechanical organizational attributes (Nelson and Winter, 1982). However, following their encounter with strategists and organizational theorists during the mid-1990s (Montgomery, 1995), evolutionary economists agreed on a definition of routine that illustrates their convergence: 'A routine is an executable *capability* for repeated performance in some context that has been *learned* by an organization in response to *selective pressures*' (Cohen et al., 1996: 683). Notably, in this definition, the implementation of the routine in response to selective pressures epitomizes the reactive, behavioral, and mechanistic nature of routines. However, as a capability, a routine is embedded in social and cognitive settings and, therefore, its contents may convey effect and identity (Pentland and Reuter, 1994; Feldman, 2000). Therefore, an organizational evolution may bring about consequences for the routines not only in terms of behavioral patterns but also in terms of discrepancies between identity and projected images, acquired knowledge and extant learning capacity, current know-how and desirable abilities. This is why Pentland and Reuter (1994) qualify routines as 'effortful accomplishments'.

The dynamics of capability and of resource-building and exploitation impinge on soft and subtle characteristics of the organization that possesses or controls them. Idiosyncrasy overlays not only economic attributes of resources (inimitability, non-transferability, non-substitutability, and so forth) but also cognitive dimensions, social processes, and representations. For strategy formulation and strategic management, firms have to choose not only the markets and businesses they compete in; they must also think of resources and dynamic capabilities as a way to alleviate or exacerbate selection pressures.

Consequences

The consequences of considering that the source of organizational evolution and variety in industry stems from firms' heterogeneity are critical. First, the search for the determinants of organizational evolution moves upwards in the chain of determinants. Efforts in this direction parallel the requirements once formulated by Porter (1991). However, Porter's level of analysis, namely industry analysis, is inappropriate for resolving that organizational question and is resistant to dynamic extensions (Foss, 1996). The upshot of his analysis is that two longitudinal factors explain a firm's success: initial conditions and managerial choices. These fall very short indeed in contributing even modestly to the task. What are initial conditions? When can we say that a condition is initial? Do firms have diverse initial conditions, and if so, how can we reconcile these particularities in one analysis at the industry level? What are managerial choices? Are all organizational choices deliberate and purposeful? What are the implications of idiosyncratic managerial choices for industry analysis that lies on the prerequisite of firm similarity? These are a few of the many questions that undermine the basis of what Porter (1991) proposed.

Yet, RBV advocates do not bring many more satisfactory elements to the debate about the origins of an organization's uniqueness (Foss and Knudsen, 2003). The contingent association of causal powers within an organized social system would give to that system a differential rent profile that insightful or rather 'hindsightful' managers could exploit and sublimate. It seems however that these stipulations on contingency might characterize a regression of ideas back to pre-scientific considerations about luck and chance.

Nonetheless, the dynamic RBV has an opportunity to enrich our understanding of organizational evolution. First, the conception of dynamic capabilities and routines under their cognition and identity facets should be prolonged. Determinants of individual and organizational identity, extended versions of individual and organizational capitals (such as social capital), and institutional constraints (norms, values, and symbols) may help characterize an organization's idiosyncratic characteristics better than notions like luck that mask but do not reduce our ignorance. Second, another consequence of delving into organizational intricacies bears on the asymmetrical causality that this postulate introduces into the analyses. Whereas an analysis that takes place in the organizational space (see Figure 2.3) can explain organizational evolution without paying too much attention to organizational individualistic traits, an analysis that begins with the postulate of organizational heterogeneity entails a supplementary obligation: to formalize the principles of organizational evolution as a phenomenon influenced by both intrinsic determinants (heterogeneity) and extrinsic determinants (namely, population- and industry-wide factors.) Thus, such a study involves making assumptions or taking positions with regard to the possibility of parallel evolutions, interactions, or even mutual effects between extra- and intra-organizational determinants. Logically, the integration of these possible relationships clears the ground for co-evolutionary ideas and arguments (Levinthal and Myatt, 1994; Barnett and Hansen, 1996) that will be commented upon in section 4.5.

4.3 COMPARING EVOLUTIONARY TRADITIONS

Drawing on the preceding presentation, the three evolutionary approaches are compared with the Lamarckian, Spencerian, and Darwinian traditions as handed down from the nineteenth century. The VSR model is also analyzed using that lens. Finally, from these analyses important implications derive for future studies on organizational evolution.

COMPOSITE DESCENTS

Examples abound that describe organizational change in Darwinian or Lamarckian terms. For instance, in their history of Health Care Organizations in the Twin Cities, Van de Ven and Grazman (1999) present the debate in these terms: 'Organizational scholars who follow a Darwinian view of evolution (e.g., Hannan and Freeman, 1977, 1989; McKelvey, 1982) argue that traits are inherited through intergenerational processes, whereas most organizational scholars who follow a Lamarckian view (e.g., Burgelman, 1991; Nelson and Winter, 1982; Singh and Lumsden, 1990) argue that traits also can be acquired within a generation through learning and imitation' (Van de Ven and Grazman, 1999: 186). In this section, we wonder if such characterizations are accurate, and we carefully trace back the lineages of the current organizational approaches to earlier evolutionary traditions. Figure 4.1 traces the components of each evolutionary tradition in biology from the nineteenth century and illustrates the genealogy of extant approaches of organizational evolution.

Genealogy of population ecology, evolutionary economics, and dynamic RBV

In Figure 4.1, horizontal lines represent the three evolutionary approaches: population ecology, evolutionary economics, and the dynamic RBV. Vertical traits cross the horizontal lines, and intersections contain a symbol imprinted with a letter. Each symbol corresponds to a component of a biological tradition from the nineteenth century: squares refer to Darwinism, circles to Lamarckism, and triangles to Spencerism. The components of these biological traditions are those presented in Chapter 3, and reproduced in Figure 3.1. The letters in the middle of the symbols stand for 'Yes' or 'No', with a capital *Y* indicating a strong acceptance of the component by the evolutionary approaches, a capital *N* indicating strong rejection, and a lower-case *y* or *n* indicating a moderate position. Figure 4.1 is only a generic representation of the evolutionary approach's genealogy and cannot pretend to encompass every author's subtleties.

Figure 4.1 highlights how intertwined the organizational evolution approaches are. Certainly, population ecology is firmly anchored in one of the three biological traditions, the number of capital Ys attached to Darwinism being the greatest of all three approaches. However, the idea of relative advantage – depending on an individual, gradual, and heritable variation, transmitted to offspring and later to a wider population – seems absent from population ecologists' discourse. Environmental resources, political conditions, and institutional movements account for an organizational form's formation and development better than imitation,

Figure 4.1 A comparison of evolutionary perspectives and biological perspectives

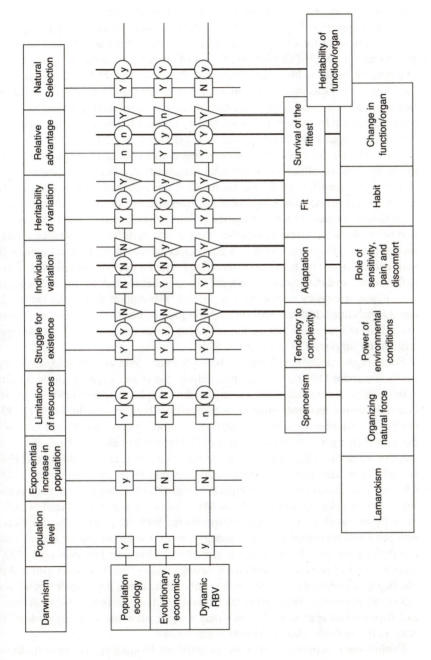

vicarious learning force, or economic diffusion do – even though the latter mechanisms play a crucial role in an organizational form's development.

Furthermore, imports from Spencerism blur the picture. Population ecologists do not adopt the adaptation tenet of Spencerism. But, for instance, the notion of 'fit' (namely, adequate linkage between the environmental resources and the nature of the organizational form) is closer to a Spencerian view of teleological adaptation than to the unspecified Darwinian process of descent. Accordingly, either because of greater fit or due to historical efficiency, 'the survival of the fittest' concept translates Spencer's ideas into organizational forms better than Darwin's. As a matter of fact, certain ideas (see Figure 3.1, which mentions purity and regression toward the means), rejected by Darwin but developed by militant followers such as Galton, are reflected in organizational ecologists' works (Polos et al., 2002).

Greve (1999), for example, describes how a core change in the market position of an organization affects organizational performance. After core changes, performance will regress toward the market mean. A quasi-natural selection law – at best a revived echo of Alchian's argument for independence of the results of managerial actions (Alchian, 1950) – readjusts individual performance within the population of competitors. Greve shows that change affects differently the probability of success, depending on a company's past performance. Inertial effects tend to prevail, and changes in a firm's core specificity entail a decline in performance back to the market mean. Cautiously enough, Greve indicates that 'to derive this hypothesis, it was necessary to use the simplifying assumption that organizations had equal capabilities. If their capabilities differ greatly, each organization will regress towards its unique mean and the hypothesis of regression towards the market mean will not be supported' (Greve, 1999: 594).

Some organizational ecologists, echoing Spencer, tend to use analogies as arguments. Freeman (1990), for example, defines the object of study in these terms: 'Competition among individual starlings is not completely ignored to be sure, but it generally seems less interesting than competition between starlings and grackles' (1990: 21). Another example of questionable lineage concerns the use of images from the early ages of population genetics that have fallen almost entirely into oblivion. For instance, in the early decades of the twentieth century Haldane and Fisher defended the idea that gene pools could be conceived as independent entities wherein mutations occurred randomly. While justifiable in logical and mathematical terms, this 'beanbag genetics', as Ernst Mayr dubbed it, was contradicted as early as 1911 by the work of Castle using experiments with rat populations. Interactions between genes are important and 'beanbag genetics' has lost its interest and relevance, except for some specific modeling (Crow, 2001). However, Freeman states that, in order to conduct population analysis, a 'species analog' must be developed and that 'the bag of variables that co-vary as a result of differential net mortality is what we call an organizational form' (1990: 9). However, although it is out-of-date in biology and disproved by applied studies, one may wonder what this 'beanbag ecology' can bring to the analysis when applied to organizations.

Evolutionary economics also mixes different biological evolution traditions. Selective mechanisms of organizational and industry evolution belong to the

Darwinian realm, while adaptation possibilities via innovation and imitation relate very much to Spencerism. While population ecology does not enthusiastically welcome the so-called Lamarckian influences (except for the importance of environmental conditions and perhaps a softened version of the heritability of functions applied to organizations), evolutionary economists utilize 'Lamarckian' ideas generously.[2] In particular, the role of habit, embedded in routines, as well as the intrinsic capacity of organizations to alter certain functions and to replicate the benefits of the corresponding changes echoes, even remotely, some Lamarckian themes.

The dynamic RBV integrates two components from the three traditions. The intrinsic inheritability of variations that provides an advantage at the level of the organization can be attributed to Darwinism. The adaptation and fit notions, dear to Spencer, abound in this approach of organizational evolution, and raise the classical shortcomings of ex post justification of success, tautology, and teleological inferences (Porter, 1991; Williamson, 1999; Durand, 2000; Priem and Butler, 2001). Imported from Lamarckism, the habit argument leading to changes in functions and, via replication, to fostered advantages is typical of that stream of literature.

Current approaches of organizational evolution exhibit composite descent vis-à-vis evolutionary traditions developed in biology. Let us turn now to the Campbellian model and study its genealogical connections with the three nineteenth-century evolutionary traditions.

VSR MODEL – NEITHER LAMARCKIAN, DARWINIAN NOR SPENCERIAN

The VSR model integrates the cumulativeness and ratchet effects of socio-cultural learning processes, reminiscent of Lamarckian habitual and hereditary notions. However, the VSR model is populational, for it devotes itself to the study of the emergence, diffusion, and historical aggregation of selected ideas, independent of the individuals who propound them. This trait is clearly anti-Lamarckian and rather pro-Darwinian. Also, variations in this model are Darwinian in inspiration. Campbell's insistence on 'blind' variations is characteristic of this lineage. However, it seems that Campbell does not completely support an open-ended socio-cultural world as in biological evolution, where the sexual and natural selective forces incessantly model populations' fitness functions. In socio-cultural and organizational evolution, path-dependency and vicarious learning involve viscous knowledge and immaterial supports of replication that interfere with more classical biological determinants of human action. This contention of a socio-culturo-organizational evolution that is open-ended but neither non-random nor regressive in trend is colored with Spencerian teleological representations, while distant from Spencer's naïve overtones. The following two quotes show how Campbell differentiates himself from Spencer's close analogies between biological and sociological entities as well as the rough teleological content of his views:

> By intent at least, this paper aspires to more specific and cautious generaliza-
> tions than those offered by Emerson, Gerard, and Spencer. By intent, it stays
> closer to specifiable selection criteria. More specifically, the course of social evo-
> lution is not committed to such global goals as increased social homeostasis
> and integration. (Campbell, 1969: 81)

> We must avoid Herbert Spencer's passive panglossian evolutionism: Let things
> alone and everything will optimise. (Campbell, 1994: 23)

However, when citing sociobiologists or contradicting his own well-advised
contentions and methodological precautions, Campbell, like Spencer, sometimes
employs questionable blanket analogical reasoning:

> Socially organized human beings achieve much greater ultrasociality than do
> the naked mole rats – much greater division of labor, collective action, self-
> sacrificial bravery in warfare, fully comparable to those of the most caste-ridden
> of the ants. And we do this *without sterility among the cooperators*. (Campbell,
> 1994: 26; emphasis in original)

These odd animal-human contrasts obscure Campbell's eventual position vis-à-
vis Spencer's legacy. Overall though, the VSR model is neither Lamarckian, nor
Darwinian, nor Spencerian. Borrowing from the different traditions, it attaches
itself to an encompassing framework that might describe any cultural, social,
organizational, or human evolution process.

IMPLICATIONS

Four major implications derive from the comparison between organizational evolution approaches and evolutionary traditions. First, as Campbell underlined, what
matters are not the entities, but the evolutionary (namely, cumulative socio-cultural
and organizational) processes. With that thought in mind, and in line with the many
imports from biological traditions in each of the organizational evolution approaches,
we suggest that the analogical or metaphorical uses of biological entities to characterize organizational entities should be avoided as much as possible in our academic
works. They are misleading and specific to the biological traditions. A gene, a cell,
an organism mean many things according to 'who' speaks – Darwin or Mayr,
Mendel or Fisher, Gould or Dawkins. They drive people interested in organizational
evolution and strategic management to facile connections that, under the guise of
verisimilitude, conceal the peculiarities of organizational reality. That does not imply
that biological analogies are superfluous in other situations. (For instance, in peda-
gogical contexts, they can be used efficiently to transmit knowledge.) Nor does it
imply that the study of biology's history is useless. But, as far as the advancement of
organizational evolution thinking is concerned, it seems good practice to avoid inappropriate, ambiguous, and deceptive analogical notions.

Secondly, the common association of authors or research streams in the field
of organizational evolution with Darwinian, Lamarckian, or Spencerian biological
traditions should also be abandoned. These associations, often incisive or radical,

cannot characterize adequately the subtlety of these three nineteenth-century thinkers. Nor do they do justice to current works developed by organizational scholars. They are a form of 'name-dropping', and they perpetuate inappropriate association with what Lamarck, Darwin, or Spencer said and meant. As such, they are misleading too, artificially and knowingly labeling current developments with old – and often delusory – labels.

Thirdly, from the vantage point of what are now advanced biological ideas, our three nineteenth-century authors' thoughts are dated. They had some good insights, some bad. They pertain to their century. Referring again and again to their ideas, without a scrupulous look at current research advancements, entails another reference bias. It comes down to attributing truth to old ideas that have been refined or rejected by further theorizing and testing. We should not carry over outdated theorizing to present situations and problems, unless it is to show how research stumbles on similar obstacles when embracing ideas that are transversal to fields of inquiry.

Finally, in Chapter 3 we considered some false postulates that Lamarck posited, and we underscored at length some of Spencer's most blatant errors. The incorporation of the three nineteenth-century biological traditions within each of the three organizational evolution approaches contains the seeds for propagating not only errors endogenous to a very tradition but also the combinatory effect of crossing mistakes altogether. For instance, the combination of a priori heritable variations (from Darwin) with a posteriori heritable variations (from Lamarck) may raise concerns about logic. The acceptance of the 'survival of the fittest' argument (from Spencer) does not help elucidate selection criteria; instead, it casts doubt on the determination of selection criteria from observation of surviving entities (Campbell, 1969).

Knowledge of the genealogy of biological evolution theories is important for scholars committed to the comprehension of organizational evolution phenomena. However, when we engage in first, direct importations and analogues of biological entities, secondly, attribution of Lamarckian, Darwinian or Spencerian labels to contemporary research streams, thirdly direct references to these biological traditions as arguments for our current investigations, and fourthly incautious integration of the various traditions in a general model, we confuse a cursory framework for organizational phenomena based on biological resemblance with a thoroughgoing theorizing about organizational evolution.

Can the VSR model solve these issues? Based on a composite of past traditions, it focuses on a particular object of analysis and unfolds its own logic. A scrupulous inquiry on how population ecology, evolutionary economics, and the dynamic RBV correspond to its principles is in order, as well as a critique of its capacity to establish itself as the dominant explanatory framework devoted to cultural and organizational evolution.

4.4   A VSR MODEL APPRAISAL

The previous section compared organizational evolution approaches and the Lamarckian, Darwinian, and Spencerian traditions. It showed that organizational evolution must be treated independently of – but not ignorant of – references to nineteenth-century biological traditions, in order to avoid analogical, onto-logical, and logical traps. In this section, a second comparison positions each evolutionary approach vis-à-vis the Campbellian VSR model, and underlines convergences and nuances in the application of the dominant model in socio-cultural evolution. This comparison shows that the three approaches of organi-zational evolution used widely in strategic management literature avail themselves of the VSR model, but with particular angles and focuses. Thus, the VSR model needs to be re-examined carefully so as to find a way out of the clutches of the paradox: the VSR model as a plausible encompassing paradigm or as an intellec-tual system predicated upon ill-defined concepts. The analysis is conducted from two viewpoints: the VSR model's internal consistency, and its commensurability with strategic management.

VSR MODEL: AN OPEN HOUSE FOR EVOLUTIONARY APPROACHES

In his account of the evolutionary approach, Aldrich (1999: 21) indicates that evo-lution results from the operation of the VSR processes coupled with the struggle over scarce resources. In the traditional (B)VSR presentation of organizational evolution, organizations are shuffled as units of selection. Variation generates the raw material from which selection is made, and retention processes preserve the selected variation. These processes are deemed necessary and sufficient to account for evolution of social and organizational systems.

As Aldrich (1999) positions six perspectives on organizational evolution under the VSR banner, we position population ecology, evolutionary economics, and dynamic RBV vis-à-vis the VSR framework. Table 4.1 summarizes the convergent assumptions between the three theories with respect to the VSR framework and acknowledges some nuances. The identification of fundamental commonalities between these approaches demonstrates the overarching role of the VSR frame-work, despite some apparently irreconcilable features intrinsic to each perspec-tive. For instance, one can argue that population ecology and the dynamic RBV of the firm are irreconcilable, being representative of two poles of a continuum – environmental determinism and strategic choice. This has already been critiqued, and both research streams have eased their respective rigidities (Hrebiniak and Joyce, 1985; Child, 1997). Still, the three approaches present some nuances (too often watered down) in the application of the VSR model. They deserve mention. Looking at Table 4.1, from items related to Variation to those tied to Retention, we begin with the first obvious difference, the level of analysis.

Variation
First, and obviously, the approaches differ mainly in the level of analysis. Each approach places the varying, selected, and retained entities at different but connected

Table 4.1   A comparison of evolutionary perspectives from a VSR perspective

	Central elements	Population ecology	Evolutionary economics	Dynamic RBV	Driving organizational evolution
V A R I A T I O N	Level of analysis	Population of organizations	Firms and routines	Resources, competencies, and trajectories	Organizational evolution is a multi-level phenomenon
	Variation as a first step for selection	Various organizational forms and strategies	Firm idiosyncrasy	Resource heterogeneity	Different sources of variation can trigger the VSR process
	Status of blind variation	Blind perception for individuals	Actors are satisfiers (not optimizers)	Knowledge intangibility	Individual and firm rationality are bound together
	Importance of strategic management	Minimal	Variable	Important for orienting a firm's future	Strategic management as a blind spot?
S E L E C T I O N	Avoiding selection pressure	Difficult strategic reorientation; niche strategy	Path dependency; innovation	Path dependency; unique resources, processes, and trajectories	Firms have a low short-run capacity for action but can reduce selection pressure through some sort of uniqueness
	Selection criteria	Fitness and alignment	Cost and economic profit	Rent potential	Objective functions vary according to approaches
	Mode of selection	External selection	External and internal selection	Internal selection	Diverse selection modes operate concurrently
	Retention mechanisms	Reliability and accountability (structural inertia and institutionalization)	Routines	Learning	Firms have access to different but compatible retention mechanisms

levels of analysis. Population ecology deals with populations of organizations and organizational forms. Evolutionary economics considers firms and routines as the units of analysis. The dynamic RBV focuses on resources, capabilities, and trajectories. Therefore, the challenge in representing organizational evolution is to compensate for this multi-level characterization. However, there is a deep relationship between the different levels, for these are nested levels of variation. Besides, each level constitutes a layer of selection at which organizational units are either retained or eliminated (Baum and Singh, 1994b; Campbell, 1974, 1994).

According to the three approaches, heterogeneity and variation are the premises for selection. Population ecologists adopt this position: 'The ecological perspective focuses on the ways in which *various strategies* fit in with an environment that selects for or against these strategies by encouraging findings and discouraging failures' (Freeman, 1995: 222). Evolutionary economics and the capability view 'place major emphasis on the *heterogeneity* of the population of business firms and on the sources of that heterogeneity in the idiosyncratic internal features of individual firms' (Winter, 1995: 147). Variations, being at the form, firm, or resource level are therefore the first step in the evolutionary process.

Further, for all three perspectives, the rationality of actors is bounded. Individuals alone are unable to perceive the real sources of success, according to population ecologists (Hannan and Freeman, 1977). In recent studies, organizational identity appears as a constraining factor on rationality, favoring inertia and conformity. Accordingly, individuals are imperfect maximizers for evolutionary economists (Nelson and Winter, 1982). Individuals cannot render their capabilities explicit and transmit them to others (Teece et al., 1997: 525). In the dynamic capability approach, there is a cognitive resilience that maintains actors in their beliefs (Tripsas and Gavetti, 2000: Raff, 2000). This assumption is compatible with the (B)VSR model. Deliberate changes can be introduced by organizations, but due to the rational limitations and the organizational constitutive traits (identity, routines, ethos, or beliefs), the likelihood of pre-selecting an optimal variation is low, or at least not superior to the pure haphazard variation at the population level. As we mention below, there exist nuances about the strength of that assumption, and as we get closer to the internal constituents of an organization, the greater is our impression that latitude and discretion swell and are effective – namely, beat the odds of randomness.

As a consequence, another difference concerns the place of strategic management in the conduct of organizations, and whether or not strategic management has an active role relative to the VSR process. For population ecology, strategy has, at best, a reactive role. 'At any given moment, both adaptive and maladaptive firms inhabit local environments – the enigma is that we cannot tell which is adaptive until the environment selects out maladaptive firms' (Aldrich and Kenworthy, 1999: 28). According to this conception, strategic management cannot in fact influence an organization's likelihood of survival. Some evolutionary economists would share this view. Others would value strategy as a means to avoid companies being selected out. (See the replication strategy in Winter and Szulanski, 2001.) For its part, the dynamic RBV clearly offers strategic management an active role in defining processes, building positions, and controlling paths and trajectories (Teece et al., 1997; Volberda and Lewin, 2003).

In this context, all three approaches emphasize a low short-term capacity for strategic reorientation. Population ecology has been slow to recognize the possibility of strategic reorientation. When selection applies, its effects are not immediate. A firm does not suddenly cease all its activities, but it often does this only after a period of poor results, offering cues for a possible but costly reorientation.

Evolutionary economists use the notion of path dependency to account for time continuity and constraining effect on strategic action (Dosi and Nelson, 1994). As for the dynamic RBV, '… the capability approach sees value augmenting strategy as being difficult and costly. Moreover, it can generally only occur incrementally' (Teece et al., 1997: 529). Helfat and Peteraf (2003) develop a capability life cycle model wherein some inflection events enable the company to adopt one of six different types of 'branching', allowing some of them to avoid in the short-term the fate of disappearance.

The low short-term capacity of organizations to react induces them to commit to long-term paths. For the three approaches, this commitment is associated with a certain idea of uniqueness (Levinthal, 1995: 36). Population ecology considers niche strategy as a particular mode of fitting to environmental conditions. This niche strategy protects a firm against selection pressures from its environment but not from the density effect of the population occupying the niche (Carroll, 1985). Evolutionary economics emphasizes the enhancing power of innovation versus imitation – innovation being a means to create uniqueness and escape the grim reaper of mortality. The dynamic capability approach demonstrates how uniqueness and idiosyncrasy lead a firm to appropriate rents that are inaccessible to competitors due to the effects of isolating mechanisms. These mechanisms can be static (proprietary access to a technology or a material) or dynamic (a plastic organizational identity).

Selection

The selection criteria differ between approaches. Population ecology insists on fitness or alignment of an organizational form with its environment. While organizational identity summarizes uniqueness and commonalities, organizational form summarizes only inter-organization commonalities. Forms differ with respect to their environmental alignment, namely, their capacity to mobilize resources and to attract and retain members in that environment. Alignment may result from adaptive actions undertaken by actors, via structural network effects, and by a selective replacement of entities. The latter solution is preferred by ecologists. Evolutionary economists use criteria in their models and simulations to retain and eliminate firms (Metcalfe, 1994; Saviotti and Mani, 1994). They define thresholds that can be absolute, relative to industry average, or intrinsically time-varying. The great majority of these thresholds is tied to cost functions and profit realization. For this approach, therefore, the selection criteria are clearly economic (cost advantage and performance), and firms can undertake corrective and adaptive actions. The dynamic RBV uses a third series of selection criteria. Its proponents emphasize the rent potential associated with a bundle of resources or a time-combination of capabilities (Peteraf, 2003; Peteraf and Barney, 2003). Organizations capable of securing resources with high differential rent potential dominate in an industry, and they are more apt to preserve and build new advantages repeatedly. While they may be commensurable, these selection criteria echo different research traditions. Population ecologists evoke equilibrium models (Carroll and Hannan, 2000: 383), evolutionary economists path-dependent efficiency criteria, and capability defenders non-equilibrium and process effects that spawn idiosyncratic advantages.

Important considerations bear on the compatibility of these criteria, their cumulativeness or their mutual exclusion.

A way to conciliate selection criteria, as concisely presented by Aldrich (1999) and developed by Henderson and Stern (2004), consists in distinguishing selection forms depending on the location of the selecting forces. 'External selection' concerns forces external to an organization that affect its routines and competencies (Aldrich, 1999: 22). 'Internal selection' characterizes the selective mechanisms that affect the internal dynamics of an evolving system (Campbell, 1974). Some variation and selection principles involve historicity of various kinds, and some do not. Some derive from constraints – intrinsic, functional, and so on – that impose structure on the range of possibilities (Bickhard and Campbell, 2003: 272), and others do not. While population ecology studies factors that belong to external selection, evolutionary economics and, above all, the capability approach focus on factors that belong to internal selection. Therefore, integrating the various perspectives requires a cautious identification not only of the level of analysis but also of the dominant selection form, whether external or internal.

Retention

Finally, all three approaches share the view that the retention process guarantees the transition between past and future, protects actors against causal ambiguity and forgetfulness, and supplies material for the next round of variations. Thus, whereas each approach interprets the retention process as proceeding from a different mechanism, it is noteworthy that there is no incompatibility between these alternatives. Population ecology defends institutionalization through accountability and reliability as a process that helps newcomers to find the appropriate organizational form that has the greatest survival probabilities (Hannan and Freeman, 1984). The legitimation process ensures that an organizational form can expand. Evolutionary economics presents 'routinization' as a way to prevent a firm's satisfactory operations from being reconsidered at each use. Advantageous introductions are maintained and preserved, as part of the firm's capital. Dynamic RBV focuses on learning and knowledge protections (for instance, patents) as its favorite retention mechanisms (Grant, 1996).

A very last comparison (not reported in Table 4.1) could contrast the methods used to track the determinants of organizational evolution. Population ecologists use panel data, population analyses, and survival analyses. They explain the differences in founding rates and survival odds, the probability of the emergence of organizational forms, and other demographic outcomes. Evolutionary economists focus on innovation rates, profit profiles, and industry dimensions such as concentration and the nature of competition. They use mathematical models, computer simulations and, sometimes, empirical tests. Scholars from the dynamic RBV rarely propose large dataset studies to account for differential rent potential and organizational or capability trajectories. Instead, they utilize case studies and move slowly towards the study of influential event lineages as suggested, for instance, by Garud and Rappa (1994) and Van de Ven and Grazman (1999). These authors propose the identification and accounting of novel change events in the lineage of an organizational entity as a proxy for new routine generation. Rather than measuring the occurrence of routine appearance and disappearance via estimated rates of organizational births and dissolutions (which is typical in population studies), an event analysis within an organizational lineage helps capture how internal determinants of an organization impact its survival and performance (whether economic or not).

Overall, the three evolutionary approaches detailed in sections 4.2 and 4.3 appear highly compatible with the VSR model enunciated forty years ago by Campbell. However, they allow themselves certain adjustments that moderate their strict adherence to the original model. Hence, as observers, it seems that we are caught in a bind. Either we applaud the VSR model and erect it to the status of an aspiring evolutionary paradigm suitable for social, cultural, and organizational evolutions, or the malleability and plasticity of its concepts will tarnish its virtues and leave us with an encapsulating but loose and vulnerable intellectual system.

THE VSR MODEL'S INTERNAL CONSISTENCY

At first glance the VSR model seems seductive. It sheds unprecedented light on evolutionary processes, and it is elastic enough to garner the support of population ecologists and dynamic RBV advocates. But borrowing from past traditions in order to draw the contours of a novel representation of socio-cultural and organizational evolution bears some risks, first of these being an imperfect integration of the underlying concepts and principles proper to each tradition. In the following sections, we present four possible shortcomings of the VSR model that, if eluded, are likely to undermine its chances to become a vibrant and robust paradigm that couples organizational evolution and strategic management.

The immutability of criteria

Campbell himself pinpoints an inherent fragility in the VSR model: 'The primary sources of doubt lie in the selection process. This comes not only from the variety of intertwined selection processes but also with the difficulty of specifying the selective criteria independently of what they seem to have selected' (1969: 83). Selection criteria consist mostly of organization conservation, diffusion of variations between social groups, selective propagation of temporal variations, imitation between individual practices, selective promotion to leadership and educational roles, and 'rational selection' based on economic principles. A major difficulty resides in conceptualizing and theorizing how these criteria evolve on their own. If the evolutionary process seems immutable as it passes from V to S to R, does this imply that selection criteria remain stable over time? Probably not. Therefore another question crops up. How can a selection criterion be itself an object for change? Or, in more strategic terms: can an organization influence selection criteria and pressures – if not the evolutionary process itself – so as to increase their odds of success? And, if yes, how? (Durand, 2001). Additional questions arise from the list of selection criteria. Why this list? Is the list exhaustive? Can we rank the selection criteria and attribute gradual causal powers to them?

We must answer these questions if an evolutionary theory is to contribute efficiently to the advancement of research and practice. Today, the commonly shared definition of selection, which underlies our arguments about organizational evolution and strategic success, more often than not leaves these questions unanswered.

Inter-relationships

Baum (1999) asserts that entities at all levels strive to optimize their fitness; and, in the process, what is better for an entity at one level may be detrimental for the organizational hierarchy in general, or for one of its parts in particular. Differential selective mechanisms operate. They select positively (retain) variations at one level that higher level entities may select negatively (preventing that level from benefiting from the positive variation). Hypercompetition can be reinterpreted within that perspective. A 'successful' firm strategy consists in unfolding a succession of positive variations selected out over time and replaced by further variations, outpacing the capacity of the firm's rival to follow the rhythm of successive variations.

Indeed, in that representation, every entity competes at each level to attract resources that secure its odds for better persistence, development, and survival. Therefore, at the core of the organizational evolution (as, perhaps, in many contemporaneous debates in biology), lies a conception of a weak coordination between entities. Every entity pursues maximization of its survival, both immediate and future. In sum, these accounts of organizational evolution are based on a strict application of radical Darwinism, which, as mentioned in the previous chapter, was inspired by Darwin's followers more than by Darwin himself.

However, describing organizational evolution from such 'Russian doll' and 'beanbag' perspectives is eminently reductionist. An organizational entity (organization or organizational form) is not a bag of variables without significant interactions (Freeman, 1990). Inter-relationships between units of analysis at various levels happen and must play a role both in the V, S, and R sub-processes and in the content of Vs, Ss, and Rs. These interactions may offset and supersede all or part of each Russian doll's variable effects. To illustrate, the human genotype is nothing without the interactions developed by the individual owning that genotype. The inter-relationships of this individual with a plurality of characters (parents, teacher, policeman, rock star, …) activate potentialities that surely differ from individual to individual. Similarly, ignoring inter-relationships that occur within and between an organization's sub-units as well as marginalizing inter-organizational links bias the potential for valid evolutionary accounts. And then another danger lies in wait: an over-emphasis on the predominance of social ties and embeddedness to the detriment of intrinsic organizational characteristics.

Nested models

Evolutionary VSR models that include different levels of analyses (for example, resources, organization, and population) have been used primarily to describe organizational evolution. In general, however, a model applies at a given level of analysis (one of the Russian dolls) for which it gives a detailed evolutionary account, but the depiction of the evolution of other levels remains allusive. In general, also, scholars seek persistence and stasis of forms as a way to identify, first, what does not change. After that, for expert viewers, change pops out as a fish from calm waters. Finally, the evolutionary story is reset in a (chrono)logical order that fits into a VSR-like narration. The fish trajectory and waves in water can be situated in their context and explained ex post. However, research should not be content with these methods and should move toward a better multi-level analysis, depiction, and account of evolutionary phenomena for, in reality, selection acts simultaneously on emergent variations at various levels of analysis. To prolong the metaphor, not only should experts explain the fish trajectory, but they should also theorize simultaneously about what happened beneath the water level, whether the nature of the water changed or not, what outside conditions allowed the fish to leap, and whether the fish designed its jump purposefully. (After all, can a fish not be an artist jumper?)

However, the linearity (or circularity) of the VSR model does not hold up long when faced with an organizational nested hierarchy. How can we account for different variations taking place concomitantly? Which selection criteria matter more at each level of analysis? It appears that the structure of the nested hierarchy has seldom been used as an explanatory mechanism of organizational evolution. Campbell and his followers have certainly introduced the whole-part competition distinction to give emphasis to concurrent selection processes at various levels of analysis. Depending on the direction of causality (upward or downward, namely, from the smaller evolving units up to larger ones or from the upper levels down), the whole or the part increases its fitness independently of the impact of the selection on other units' fitness (Campbell, 1990). However, the application of both principles (whole-part competition and upward/downward causation) seems highly contingent, ad hoc, and hard to justify.

Furthermore, as evolution takes place in a nested hierarchy, frequency and amplitude of variations differ. Usually, a greater number of small variations are expected at lower levels due to a shorter time-scale for change and a lower complexity. However, it remains difficult to assert which are the drivers of eventual organizational evolution. In their exploratory study, Van de Ven and Grazman (1999) find clues that suggest differential patterns of lower- and higher-level variation influences, depending on periods. A first insight from their study discards the 'one-best-way' view. There exist equally viable paths of evolution for organizations facing the same environmental conditions (namely, health care organizations in Minnesota). In addition, top management events influence persistent organizational variations (branching) in scarce environmental periods, while in periods of abundance, prior organizational events explain current organizational events better.

However, one cannot determine easily the impact of a small variation at the lowest level of analysis relative to a huge reorientation decided at the highest level of analysis. In the absence of theoretical and empirical evidence on the determinants of the relative influences of simultaneous cross-level variations, organizational and strategic management scholars stay far away from the engine of change, and contemplate only the coachwork. In later works, Campbell (1990, 1994) lifts up the hood and explores several levels of selection, and proposes to determine multiple intermediate nodes of selection, such as face-to-face interactions (or 'primary groups'), getting closer to real mechanisms. But more work needs to be done to advance comprehension on mechanical and systemic effects.

VSR and strategic management

In Chapter 2 we distinguished strategy from strategic management in this way. Strategy is a theory about competitiveness that helps organizational members select among available resource utilizations and exchange modes. Strategic management is the set of concerted concrete actions that actualize (or not) the theorized competitive potentialities resulting from the combination of resources and modes of exchange. With this distinction in mind, we now consider several issues that arise when we seek to dovetail strategy and strategic management into the VSR model.

Strategy implies a willpower that allocates resources so as to achieve competitiveness. Strategic management entails a series of deliberate transformations aimed at aligning or positioning the organization within its environment and vis-à-vis rivals. However, for the VSR model, enunciated goals and purposive variations are not very significant. Fitness and correspondence to selection criteria matter more. Campbell maintains the supremacy of blind variations over deliberate variations. At the same time, he acknowledges what this assumption masks: 'For most applications of the selective retention model, the variation is taken as a descriptive given, as an unexplained part of the explanation' (1960: 394). However, this reductionism is unsatisfactory once the level of analysis is the organization and its strategic intents and operations. Strategists do not take variations (in technology, HR policy, portfolio, and so on) as a 'descriptive given'. They develop theories about intentional variations and competitive outcomes (Calori, 2000) and purposely orient their actions in certain preferred directions in order to beat the odds.

This Campbellian position would be less problematic were the VSR model entirely Darwinian. However, as shown before, it is not. It follows that the distinction between variations and selection might not be as radical as hypothesized, and that neither variation nor selection criteria are impervious to each other. Let us recall that behind the blindness argument resides a political conception of human action in history that befits Campbell. For him, the products of biological, organization-based, and cultural evolution on the one hand, and individuals on the other do not intersect. He believes that the individual qua individual – i.e., a person with a name, gender, history, etc. – cannot shape history. As a matter of fact, managerial actions and deliberate orientations are mere intrusions in a population-level conception of (s)elected variety. He notes the proclivity of professional managers to introduce change as a legitimation of their individual strategy, which comes down to being inimical to preservation of past firm-level adaptations (Campbell, 1994). For Campbell 'selection' rhymes with 'election', and individuals cannot elect themselves. It is the competition and the effect of selection that produce the possibility for strategic management to exist, while it remains highly improbable that what is taught in business schools influences the VSR process itself in any way (Campbell, 1994: 32).

Unfortunately, despite Campbell's arguments and defenses, it is hard to deny that many variations are intentional, and that, as such, they have integrated selection criteria and that their results are not random (Barron, 2003). Further, strategy involves more than the introduction of variations; it flirts with the selection process itself. Neither is retention absent from the organizing and allocation of resources. Yet, strategic management as a preemptive comprehension is unthinkable for Campbell, as is fashioning (namely, making, working, crafting) of selection criteria, because for him there are no principles of better and worse industrial organization and management. In a nutshell, the VSR model rejects both the possibility of deliberate strategic variations with non-random outcomes and the possibility of organizations fashioning selection criteria. These rejections impede the smooth integration of strategy and strategic management in the VSR model. Essentially, the VSR model does not accept these possibilities because of its assumptions about first, human nature (namely, the individual qua individual is impotent if alone and dominated by larger entities), secondly, the absence of an organizational hold on VSR processes, and thirdly, moral and ethical issues (the VSR model is ethics-free). These questions must find a more satisfactory answer in future models that connect organizational evolution with strategic management. The coevolutionary approach has been a tentative encroachment into these themes.

4.5   THE COEVOLUTIONARY APPROACH

Coevolutionary literature developed in the 1990s, urged on by the insightful remarks of influential scholars including Burgelman (1991), March (1994), Nelson (1995), and Barnett and Hansen (1996). But what does coevolution mean? Two evolving factors having an effect on a third factor describes a simple form of coevolution. For McKelvey (1997), coevolution characterizes the interdependence between firms, competitors, and niche resources: each changes as the other changes. In this case, coevolution is parallel evolution or correlated evolution. More often coevolution characterizes a process whereby there is a bi-directional causal effect between two entities. For instance, entities A and B (namely, populations) coevolve when a factor that relates elements of these entities has an impact on some properties of each, of both A and B (Murmann, 2003). Stuart and Podolny (1996) and Barnett and Hansen (1996) describe coevolution as one organization's search behavior affecting and being affected by the search strategies undertaken by like organizations within the same industry. Self-reinforcing and reciprocal effects of competitive search result in learning at the firm and industry levels.

Henderson and Mitchell (1997) call for an enhanced understanding of the endogenous and reciprocal relationships between firm capabilities, strategy, and competition. They state that, 'Reciprocal interactions at multiple levels of analysis between the market environment and firm capabilities shape business strategy and performance, while interactions between strategy and performance, in turn, shape both organizational capabilities and competitive environments' (1997: 6). In a more eclectic manner, Lewin and Volberda (1999) pose the 'prolegomena on coevolution'. They draw on a large array of inspiring literature having adaptation/selection as its central theme, dealing with: organizational sociology (population ecology), institutional theory, industrial organization, transaction cost view, behavioral theory of the firm, evolutionary theories, dynamic RBV of the firm, contingency theory, strategic choice theory, organizational learning, life cycle and punctuated equilibrium theories. Their definition of coevolution is the result of a process of cross-fertilization: 'We define co-evolution as the joint outcome of managerial intentionality, environment, and institutional effects. Coevolution assumes that change may occur in all interacting populations of organizations. Change can be driven by direct interactions and feedback from the rest of the system' (1999: 521).

To conduct research on such a fluid subject, several properties must be taken into account according to Lewin and Volbeda (1999): multilevelness, multidirectional causality, nonlinearity, positive feedback, and path dependence. Lewin et al. (1999) present a coevolutionary model in which coevolution forces relate, as follows:

1 Institutional environments (education systems, employment relationships, governance structures, regulation, rule-making, and capital markets) relate to a block consisting of industry characteristics in interrelation with firm components.
2 This industry-firm block relates to the extra-institutional environment (technological advances, demographics, social movements, new entrants, global interdependence, and management logics).
3 The institutional environment relates to the extra-institutional environment.

Relying on this system of interactions, the authors develop a series of hypotheses that intend to account for the generation of organizational forms. Gradually, their hypotheses move up in the nested levels of evolution, from an organization's balance between exploitation and exploration, to mediating effects of capitalism styles, and finally to extra-institutional forces of change.

The aim of this theorization of coevolution, found also in Volberda and Lewin (2003), is to avoid the dilemma of Darwinian selection vs. intentionality. According to these authors, pure selectionist models that do not admit a role for intentional behavior are incomplete and 'naïve', for two major reasons. First, naïve selection models attribute 'blindness' to variations, whereas intentional variations also exist. Secondly, naïve selection models recognize only a competitive selection view, whereas other types of selection may also be influential. For instance,

... top management may develop forms of anticipatory control systems in which prior knowledge functions as a selector, vicariously anticipating selection by the competitive environment. These deliberate variation-vicarious Selection-Retention engines in the multiunit firm create a more differentiated internal selection environment that bypasses purely blind variation by blocking perceived dangerous or inadequate actions before they are executed. Managed selection engines produce more complex micro co-evolutionary processes than naïve selection. (2003: 2118)

In order to explore the uncharted coevolutionary waters, empirical works have focused on particular links relating capabilities, strategy (intention), competition, and performance, with the objective of disentangling the causal relationships among all the involved entities and factors.

EMPIRICAL ISSUES

Many articles study cases of firms that have mustered ad hoc resources and developed capabilities in order to have their ideas, products, and organization selected and retained by the larger environment. Hargadon and Douglas (2001) studied Edison's robust design strategy that consisted of 'cloaking' his innovation, the light bulb, 'in the mantle of' well-established institutions, the gas companies, in order to impose it more easily on the market. Edison was able to gather adapted sets of resources to mimic the features of gas lighting. As a result of this strategy, generation and distribution of electricity were in part determined by the General Electric Company.

More advanced case comparison studies distinguish technical and institutional strategy and how they interact in prompting the diffusion of a new standard. For example, Das and Van de Ven (2000) show that the nature of the technology (novel or evolved) and of the market (concentrated or dispersed) influences whether firms use technical or institutional strategies to have their new product technology accepted by the market. They studied the video recorder and medical diagnostic imaging industries. They posit that a strategy is a pattern in the sequence of actions, usually deliberate, undertaken by firms for the attainment of a corporate goal. A technical strategy rests on three assumptions: first, the market selects among technological alternatives; secondly, selection is based on technical factors alone; and thirdly, the criteria for evaluating alternate technologies exist independently of the actions of the firm. By contrast, an institutional strategy relies on the following factors: first, firms, consumers, distributors, and regulators influence selection among alternatives; secondly, selection is based on how technologies perform on technical and non-technical factors; and thirdly, the criteria for evaluating alternative technologies do not already exist but are constructed through the interaction of firms, consumers, distributors, and regulators. Depending on the nature of the technology and the state of the market, more technically or institutionally oriented strategies increase the odds of success of the sponsored technology. Accordingly, such strategies introduce a pattern of coevolving relations between a firm's actions, the environmental selection criteria, and the degree of acceptability of their offerings in the marketplace.

Huygens et al. (2001) illustrate another example of a multi-case study, dealing with co-evolution in the music industry. Based on secondary sources, they studied the history of the music industry and identified the evolving capabilities of record companies. They relate how technological regimes changed over time at the industry level, from the invention of the phonograph and the gramophone to the advent of the CD. During the course of the twentieth century, the software shift (starting with recording companies) followed the technological lock-in on disks rather than cylinders, and was followed by the star system, the ascension of alternative music, the federal system (competition for labels), and the right shift (competition for catalogues). Huygens et al. give examples of how some companies introduced ruptures in the business model, based on new associations of resources and capabilities, and they highlight the role of what they call the search behavior as a pivotal influence in coevolutionary processes; the search behavior plays the interface role that accounts for both organizational changes (firm level) and new competitive regimes (industry level). However, they fail to describe the precise relationships between what could be considered as necessary and contingent factors. Neither do they clarify the respective role of firm and industry selection.

Peter Murmann's (2003) socio-historical work on the evolution of the dye industry from its inception to the beginning of World War One (1856–1914) shows how scientific, institutional, and organizational factors interweave to explain the loss of leadership of British and French synthetic dye companies and the emergence and long-standing domination of German chemical companies in this industry. He addresses, among other issues, collective actions by concrete firms to change their environment by modifying the selection criteria; explorative research mechanisms deployed by firms (for example, Hoescht) to select the best market-suited variations (color molecules); their cooperation with scientific institutions in order to foster the research process, protocols, and evaluation of these variants; and the locking-in effect of patent traditions in national contexts on the firms' appropriation of accruing revenues. Dye molecules were selected by firms, rather than by the market, as it was impossible for the market to attest to the value of each and every type of molecule. With this example, Murmann (2003) illustrates a typical internal selection mechanism of variants that do not even reach the marketplace, which is a complement to the internal selection mechanisms based on the voluntary cessation of product sales studied by Henderson and Stern (2004). Population influences also explain the dominance of German firms. Murmann's study emphasizes that Germany spawned more companies than other countries did, but also that more German companies failed, presumably fostering the selection-based learning from which survivors benefited.

But the touchstone of Murmann's entire survey is what he calls a 'theory of coevolution'. For him, '[T]wo evolving populations coevolve if and only if they both have a significant causal impact on each other's ability to persist' (2003: 210). Coevolution can take two forms: first, altering the selection criteria for the individual entities, and secondly, changing the replicative capacity of these individuals. In particular, Murmann is interested in decrypting how national populations of firms coevolved with both the population of existing dyes and the population of national universities. He shows that in-house R&D interacted favorably with the generation of new dye molecules. The cross-fertilization between the dye industry and the chemical research and teaching at German universities channeled the research focus into organic chemistry. More precisely, the exchange of personnel and the development of commercial ties (royalties, equipment, student training) between the university system and the industry reinforced German industrial dominance. Further, both spheres of influence worked hand-in-hand for national resources and lobbied governments to derive subsidies, educational spending, and legal advantages (patent regime) beneficial to academics and industry leaders.

Some studies measure empirically the nature and value of capabilities (namely, the potential for competitive advantage, superior performance, and survival). Business age is a typical proxy for capabilities, as shown by Silverman et al. (1997) in their study of survival rates of US trucking companies. Thompson, in a working paper (2003), addresses the important question of the traditional negative relationship between age and survival. He uses pre-entry backgrounds of firms as a proxy for firm capability in the shipbuilding industry. Empirically, this past experience had a significant and persistent effect on survival, emptying age of most of its explanatory power. Capabilities, more than age, were found to shape conditions of performance. Ingram and Baum (1997) argue that entries and exits in an industry should advise a focal firm on how to do business. They measure competitive experience in the hotel industry with a coarse indicator, business exits, but offer no concrete evidence that surviving hotels had a specific knowledge of the reasons why other hotels disappeared.

Another series of studies tackles both the theoretical and methodological issues raised by the multi-level reciprocal causal effects intrinsic to coevolution. Barnett et al. (1994) compare positional and capability advantages amongst retail banks in Illinois from 1987 to 1993. After the deregulation of the 1980s, retail bank units had the choice of taking over rival units and creating branches or remaining single-unit entities. According to an unmediated assumption about learning efficiency, the more competition an organization has faced over its history, the better it will perform today. In addition, selection pressures will also foster the propensity of an organization to perform by eliminating unprofitable variants. Barnett et al. (1994) hypothesize a trade-off between the evolution of distinctive competencies located in single-unit structures and the search for positional advantages by organizations using the multi-unit structure. The latter strategy buffers the organization from selective pressures but reduces its odds of beneficial learning processes that accrue to single-unit structures pursuing the former strategy. They conclude their study of differential effects of learning and selection by contending that, 'Rather than strategy and structure driving competitiveness, it is competition that drives evolution, which is then shaped by the strategies and structures of organizations' (1994: 24). Single-unit banks benefited from exposure to competition while multi-unit banks did not, but the latter gained very strong positional advantage via mutual forbearance at the expense of learning benefits.

Barnett and Hansen (1996) state that learning results from competition and that adaptive learners become stronger competitors, triggering further search and learning by their competitors. The focal organization then bears increased levels of competition, engaging it in a new round of learning and innovation. This reciprocal cause-and-effect relation constitutes what has been called the 'Red Queen' effect (a reference to Lewis Carroll's *Alice in Wonderland*, where the Red Queen tells Alice that one must run in order to stay still in a fast world). Barnett and Hansen separate an organization's own experience from an organizational rival's competitive experience. As in the Barnett et al. (1994) study, but with a different focus, competitiveness becomes an organizational property instead of a market characteristic. An organization's competitiveness is, therefore, measured by its effects on other companies' survival. Interestingly, Barnett and Hansen (1996) model the distribution of acquired experience facing different cohorts of rivals, assuming that a high variance among competitive relationships reduces an organization's viability.

Barnett (1997) further differentiates two aspects of an organization's competitiveness: the strength of an organization can be measured by its survival prospects. Alternately, it can be measured by its impact on the birth and survival of other organizations. 'I argue that when organizations are small, their evolution conforms to a baseline model where selection processes favor the survival of strong competitors. When organizations are large, however, selection instead leaves us with competitively weak survivors' (1997: 129). His data cover long periods: 1879–1935 for telephone companies in Pennsylvania, and 1633–1988 for American breweries. Results of the empirical studies on these two populations (breweries and telephone companies) indicate that 'for large organizations viability does not require competitive success because they can buffer their weak units from selection pressures and they can enhance their viability through institutional mechanisms not directly linked to market competition' (1997: 152). Therefore, selection can favor large organizations that are viable without being strong competitors.

Finally, we will mention a recent study that distinguishes three types of selection events and reconciles, both theoretically and empirically, external and internal views of firm selection. Henderson and Stern (2004) give the 'external selectionist' label to the population ecology tradition and to those branches of evolutionary economics where the economic environment culls out inappropriate variations and incrementally designs technological trajectories. Internal selection mechanisms are the bottom-up variations introduced by front-line employees or supervisors to broaden or shrink the portfolio of alternatives available to the firm. These generations of internal variation might be adaptive or not, depending upon their degree of 'stickiness' and inertia.

Environment selection need not equate with organizational failure. Selection events (jettisoned products, for instance) are sources of organizational learning, namely, selection-based learning. A clear distinction separates external and internal selectionist perspectives. External selectionists view the firm as having a single, monolithic core, whereas internal selectionists view the firm as having a multipart and modular center. Henderson and Stern (2004), who take internal selection into great account, define firms as loosely coupled collections of products, each embodying variants of a firm's core technologies. An internal selection event happens when a product is eliminated despite relatively strong sales, and the firm survives. A partial external selection event results from the elimination of a product due to poor sales, without dooming the firm to fail. A full external selection event occurs when the product is eliminated because its host organization dies. While in internal and partial external selection events the firm survives, the rationales for the survival are quite distinct, being intentional and internal in the former case but not in the latter.

Henderson and Stern (2004) find that internal and partial external selection events coevolve as each affects the other's future rate of occurence and the odds of a firm failure. They studied the population of personal computer manufacturers across a twenty-year period, and found:

Coevolution occurred because internal selection events had a negative and cumulative effect on future rates of full external selection, which occurs when the environment kills an entire organization and each of the products in its portfolio. Conversely, partial external selection, which occurs when the environment kills some of a firm's products, had a positive and cumulative effect on future rates of internal selection. One process that linked the internal and external realms was new product development. Internal and partial external selection each catalysed the creation of new products and firms that introduced more technological variations decreased their future odds of full external selection and organizational failure. (2004: 68–9)

Interestingly, the impact of partial external selection events is greater than that of internal selection events when it comes to pruning the product portfolio. Internal selection is more affected by internal politics: the winners of earlier resource battles gradually skew selection criteria away from market-driven realities toward their own personal or organizational interests.

COMMENTARY

To evaluate the contributions of the coevolutionary perspective, six comments seem in order. First, one can be concerned by the vastness of the coevolutionary program, in particular the search to integrate institutional and intentional and competitive factors (Lewin and Volberda, 1999; Volberda and Lewin, 2003; Oliver, 1997). What does coevolution seek to explain? Industrial dynamics? The emergence of organizational forms or strategic renewal behavior? A shift from a capitalist era to a post-industrial capitalist epoch? Population ecology has a clear agenda: to account for emergence and competition amongst organizational forms from a demographic perspective. Strategic management searches for explanations of firm performance, and breaks down competitive advantage according to internal learning returns and external positioning benefits (Barnett, 1997; Henderson and Stern, 2004). But what are the core dependent variables of coevolution studies?

The second problem faced by coevolution involves eclecticism. How do the different theoretical perspectives dialogue in the coevolutionary space? Are they really compatible? We strongly advocate exchanges between fields and theories, but not at the expense of a close examination of their deep assumptions. Is institutional theory compatible with strategic choice theory? What commonalities do population ecology and life-cycle theories share (see Chapter 2)? Put candidly, are population ecology, institutional approach, and managerial intentionality amenable to common definitions (of an organization, renewal, variation) and assumptions (organizational behavior, agent's rationality)? The need to clarify the commensurability and amenability of the different theoretical perspectives and traditions is overdue.

Thirdly, Huygens et al. (2001) argue, along with others (Iwai, 1984; Barnett and Hansen, 1996), that the race for imitation and innovation cancels out competitive advantage, competition being an equilibrating force that brings rivals back to an equivalent level of capabilities. That might not be entirely accurate. It may signify not a cancellation of effects, but successive retentions of new resources and capabilities. Along the same line, Henderson and Stern (2004) focus on the products as the selected-out entities and the vector of learning. As a consequence, they consider the fact that products and firms survive the selection processes (internal and external) to be a non-event. In our model, we will propose that the lower-level entity to be selected is not a product but a competitive advantage. Therefore, a pertinent event would be less the abandonment of a product by general managers (internal selection) or the firm's death (external selection) than the supportive set of resources acquired, built, and combined, leading to performance advantages. Furthermore, focusing on selecting-out events conceals the learning advantages gained from successes, and Henderson and Stern include no sufficient control for learning effects based on such positive selecting-in events (Lubatkin et al., 2001).

Fourthly, in some coevolutionary studies, mistaken Spencerian ideas resurface: fruitful causality, all-integrative models echoing principles of evolution, and encompassing analogies. People who are interested in coevolution (as most evolutionists are) and advocate for knowledge acccumulation and path-dependent effects should not forget lessons from the past. In this respect, clear methodological guidance is needed in order to avoid overinterpretation of facts that are reported ex post by actors or second-hand narrators. In addition, tests of alternative interpretations of cause-effect relationships should be more systematically undertaken, as in Kraatz and Zajac (2001), who formulate four not-entirely-compatible relationships between the nature of resources (level and quality) and propensity to change. They consider resources as barriers to learning, as environmental buffers, as commitments, and as facilitators. Looking at the US college education system, they find empirical evidence in support of a disincentive effect of superior resource endowments on strategic change decisions. Resource-driven disinclination toward change (due to better reputation, longer history, more supportive external relationships, greater financial resources, and more talented students) reduces the incentive to change and even moderates the positive impact of curricular change and enrollment growth for such endowed colleges. This finding seems to support a view in which resources appear as commitments. They use several empirical methods (OLS, fixed-effects, random models, and discrete-time event history analyses) to control for possible multiple result interpretations. Such methodological precautions must be commended and replicated in future coevolutionary works to avoid old Spencerian wrong tracks.

Fifthly, variegated efforts do not converge empirically into a common body of methods or, at least, of variables. Flier et al. (2003) investigate the connection between the speed of implementing regulatory changes and the pace of implementing technological changes in bank and insurance industries in three European countries. In their study, they modify their level of analysis from country-level down to particular companies' actions. They offer some metrics. Across countries, they calculate the average time lag of regulatory implementations and adoption of new technologies. At the country level, they compare the ratio of external vs. internal renewal actions and of exploitation vs. exploration by the firms operating in the industry. Internal actions originate within the firm (start-up, reorganization, job cuts) and external actions relate the firm to other entities (joint ventures, alliances, mergers and acquisitions). Exploitation refers to cost savings – dissolution of a range of products, sales of activities, or increase in the scale of activities. Exploration adds new activities or increases the geographic scope of the firm. At the firm level, Flier et al., detail the same ratios, and look at the volatility of strategic renewal using the standard deviations of these ratios over time. However, they do not evaluate the relative magnitude of the impacts nor the possible alternative effects. In addition, they lack exhaustive data required to conduct several tests, as performed in Kraatz and Zajac (2001) and in studies by Barnett et al. (1994; Barnett and Hansen 1996; Barnett 1997) which bring an interesting modelling of reciprocal effects at both firm-level and industry-level analyses.

Sixth, in order to advance co-evolutionary research McKelvey (1997) pleads for the use of idealized models and the switch to rate analyses. Idealized models help searchers to distance themselves from microstate details (the trees) and focus, instead, on the background law ensemble (the forest). Instead of concentrating their efforts on mean-variance observations, organizational scientists should study rates of occurrences of good and bad events. In such a conception, managerial actions could be evaluated 'on whether they are raising or lowering rates appropriately'.[3] In a defence of deductive-statistical explanations, McKelvey (1997) offers a rejoinder to the supervenience selection property presented in the next chapter: While the prediction of individual events in an organization is difficult, predicting distributions of events or event rates at the superior level, namely population or market, is more feasible.

4.6   CONCLUSION

This chapter has presented the VSR model as an overarching framework that integrates such different streams of research as population ecology, evolutionary economics, and dynamic RBV. It has also traced the descent of each perspective back to the three nineteenth-century evolutionary traditions: Lamarckism, Darwinism, and Spencerism. Each approach of organizational evolution, including the VSR model, consists of a conglomeration of Lamarckian, Darwinian and Spencerian notions and principles. Hence, this chapter advocates that we distance ourselves somewhat from these traditions when dealing with organizational evolution, without ignoring them completely. This chapter also shows that these different approaches of organizational evolution, while offering contrasting perspectives, are all compatible with a VSR model. Whether or not they are commensurable will determine the nature of the VSR model, as either a paradigm for organizational evolution or, more simply, a loosely encompassing envelope for evolving organizational patterns and forms in search of determination.

In particular, four significant doubts cast their shadows on the VSR model. First, without succumbing to the lethal charms of a regression ad infinitum, the immutability of selection criteria must be answered, leading to a fascinating but embarrassing question. Are selection criteria selected? Secondly, the rejection of the 'beanbag' conception of organizations, based on both realistic and theoretical grounds, requires us to take into account inter-relationships between units and entities. Thirdly, the Russian doll nested models of evolution, wherein units embed themselves into broader sets, obfuscate the logic of selection taking place at several places at the same instant. Four, blind variation negates the possibility of ex ante inflections of organizational evolution and eliminates managerial and organizational discretion as candidates for influencing the why and the wherefore of selection criteria.

Finally, coevolution studies provide interesting insights despite their own limitations. On the up side, we found that selection does not necessarily select strong competitors; firm competitiveness relates to a firm's impact on the performance and survival of other firms; comprehension of organizational selection requires an understanding of institutional and political factors. On the down side, lack of explanatory power, eclectics, over-generalization, finalism, and methodological hodgepodge risk to plague the co-evolutionary field.

In an effort to overcome these objections, another examination of biological thought is in order. Just as the careful study of the Lamarckian, Darwinian, and Spencerian traditions sheds some light on current theories of organizational evolution, recent works in biological evolution also deserve our attention. With their input, the Checklist Appraisal Grid for evolutionary models will be finalized, and new avenues will open to improve our understanding of organizational evolution and strategic management.

4.7 SUMMARY

	Key contributions
	Population ecology, evolutionary economics, or dynamic capabilities' views are composite descents from the original evolutionary traditions (Lamarckism, Darwinism, and Spencerism).
	All three approaches seem to adequately express their theory of organizational evolution under the guise of the VSR-encompassing model – despite certain issues in terms of commensurability and compatibility among their underlying assumptions.
On organizational evolution approaches	The coevolutionary approach brings to the fore interesting results:
	1 Institutional and cultural factors impact on industry selection processes and on firm selection events, both internal and external.
	2 Selection does not necessarily select strong competitors.
	3 Organizational competitiveness relates to a firm's effect on its rivals' survival; therefore, competition determines evolution, depending on the degree of every organization's competitiveness.
	4 Methodological issues concern the dependent variables and how the mobilized models account for reciprocal effects.
	5 A genuine coevolutionary theory should formulate its propositions using distribution functions and rate terms.

VSR harbors oft-ignored assumptions on:

- human nature
- a quasi-teleological view of evolution as progressive
- the political underpinnings of the model

On the VSR model

The VSR model is neither Lamarckian, Darwinian, nor Spencerian. It is a tentative encompassing framework for the study of organizational evolution, but it stumbles over:

- immutability of selection criteria
- theorizing inter-relationships between entities
- accounting for selection efficiency in nested models
- integration of strategy and strategic management

Implications

In our efforts to think seriously about organizational evolution and strategic management, we should try to:

- avoid biological analogies as proofs
- avoid misleading characterization of current reflections based on Lamarckian, Darwinian, and Spencerian labels
- avoid incautious mixtures of nineteenth-century traditions

But, this does not suggest that we should ignore the history of the biological theory of evolution – on the contrary.

NOTES

1 In Baum (2002), interorganizational evolution insists on the structuration of the relationships between organizations. Structuration may follow a market logic, a governance logic, or spatial arrangements (Greve, 2002). Organizational evolution concerns the selective pressure borne by organizations depending on their constitutive traits, the speciation of organizational forms leading to the creation of established populations, and the transfer and imitation among organizations belonging to peer or rival populations (Amburgey and Singh, 2002). Intraorganizational evolution, an under-studied but promising avenue for research, concerns numerous entities (Warglien, 2002): problems, rules, routines, initiatives, and other artifacts.

2 The following quote is representative of the conjunction of Darwinian and Lamarckian ideas: 'Relatedly, our theory is unabashedly Lamarckian: it contemplates both the "inheritance" of acquired characteristics and the timely appearance of variation under the stimulus of adversity' (Nelson and Winter, 1982: 11). However, Nelson and Winter's interpretation of Lamarckism is vague and misleading (see for example, Barron, 2003: 81).

3 An example of a rephrased hypothesis accounting for rates is: given conditions C and covering laws L in a population P, flow rates of occurrence of X will emerge with distribution D causing rates r of Y distributed across firms following an F distribution. C, L, and P are to be specified, and distribution D and F to be discovered.

5 INTRODUCING RECENT DEBATES IN BIOLOGY INTO THE CHECKLIST APPRAISAL GRID FOR EVOLUTIONARY MODELS

If blushing turns out to be an adaptation affected by sexual selection in humans, it will not help us to understand why blood is red. The immediate utility of an organic structure often says nothing at all about the reasons for its being ... All 12 combinations [of Cerion's shell whiteness] can be identified in Bahamian population, but would it be fruitful to ask why – in the sense of optimal design rather than historical contingency – Cerion from eastern Long Island evolved one solution, and Cerion from Acklins Island another? (Gould and Lewontin, 1979: 593)

Chapter 3 emphasized that our comprehension of the roots of evolutionary traditions is subject to improvements. We, as organizational scholars, tend to confuse Lamarckian concepts with Spencer's synthetic, but erroneous, evolutionism, and attribute to Darwin theses alien to his own theories. Chapter 3 constituted an effort to counteract both our laziness in not going back to original works, and our forgetfulness of past accomplishments, even if only 150 years ago.

Chapter 4 conducted a genealogical inquiry into current organizational evolution theories. From that inquiry, we learn that population ecology, evolutionary economics, and dynamic RBV appear to have a composite descent from Lamarckism, Darwinism, and Spencerism. These research streams all formulate their propositions using the Variation-Selection-Retention (VSR) language, albeit not stressing the same words. Hence, troublesome challenges loom before we can pose the VSR model as a paradigmatic panacea to the complicated relationships between organizational evolution and strategic management. Coevolutionary approach has responded imperfectly to these challenges while supplying interesting results and insights.

The raison d'être of this fifth chapter must be found in what we can learn from the most recent, intense debates that have flourished in the field of biology over the last three decades. Just as a close look at nineteenth-century biological and evolutionary thought helps to disentangle intertwined ancestry, a reading of contemporary debates in biology might help us to meet the still unanswered challenges related to organizational evolution and strategic management. These debates will help us complete the Checklist Appraisal Grid for evolutionary models.

In this chapter, we discuss four recent debates in biology that disrupted the apparent consensus on evolutionary synthesis of the 1950s to 1970s. Let us refer to them as 'the four cases': first, the case against micro-macro continuity reduces our chances of connecting micro-evolutionary processes to macro-evolutionary processes without additional ad hoc conjectures. Secondly, the case against selection points to the circularity of selecting the fittest. Thirdly, the case against adaptation revolves around both the teleological explanations of organisms' adaptations and the uselessness of fit as an explanatory factor in evolutionary theories. Fourthly, the case against organisms denies that individual organisms play a role in selection processes.

We examine each case in turn, and make every effort to be concise but precise. At the same time, we attempt to avoid our inclination toward insensitivity to take into consideration developments in adjacent fields, developments that concern critical aspects of our concepts and theories. Finally, as a general conclusion to this part of the book, we derive the Checklist Appraisal Grid for evolutionary models.

5.1 THE CASE AGAINST MICRO-MACRO CONTINUITY

Ernst Mayr tirelessly advocates for a synthesis that simultaneously reconciles opposing factors, such as chance and necessity, and constitutes a coherent narrative of the passage from micro-evolutionary processes to macro-observations.

> Evolution is neither merely a series of accidents nor a deterministic movement toward ever more perfect adaptation. To be sure, evolution is in part an adaptive process, because natural selection operates in every generation. The principle of adaptationism has been adopted so widely by Darwinians because it is such a heuristic methodology. To question what the adaptive properties might be for every attribute of an organism leads almost inevitably to a deeper understanding. However, every attribute is ultimately the product of variation, and this variation is largely a product of chance. Many authors seem to have a problem in comprehending the virtually simultaneous actions of two seemingly opposing causations, chance and necessity. But this is precisely the power of Darwinian process. (2001: 229)

Unfortunately, the widespread problem of comprehension mentioned in the above quote by Mayr affords us no way of concluding that two seemingly opposing causations act virtually simultaneously in evolutionary processes. There are still important gaps and theoretical alternatives if we are to connect micro-evolutionary processes and macro-evolutionary processes. Micro-evolution refers to changes within and among populations, including natural and sexual selection, micromutation, genetic drift, and gene flow. Studies of micro-evolution 'now represent the flagship for the presence and power of evolution' (Hendry and Kinnison, 2001: 2). Macro processes deal with the patterns of changes borne by higher entities and their populations. In a nutshell, micro-evolutionary processes concern internal, rapid, and frequent changes that occur in lower observable categories, while macro-evolutionary processes require longer periods of time and occur at the higher categories (species and above). Two key points are raised by the possibility of a micro-macro continuity: the question of difference in quality or quantity between the two patterns, and the possibility of asymmetrical influences (a micro factor having dramatic consequences at the macro level). Let us discuss each point in turn.

QUANTITY OR QUALITY DIFFERENCE?

What is the difference between micro- and macro-evolutionary processes? Is the difference in quantity or in quality? In the former case, the accumulation of micro-processes would account for macro-processes, while in the latter case, other assumptions must be introduced to fully account for the observable phenomena. Promoters of evolutionary synthesis, such as Dobzhansky (1937), Mayr (1942), and Simpson (1944), assert the continuity of nature between both processes. 'Experience seems to show, however, that there is no way toward an understanding of the mechanisms of macro-evolutionary changes, which require time on a geological scale, other than through a full comprehension of the micro-evolutionary process observable within the span of a human lifetime' (Dobzhansky, 1937: 12). The remarkable convergence of diverse species into comparable niches from different areas (islands, continents) constitutes a traditional argument for a deterministic path of evolutionary processes (Simpson, 1944).

Eldredge and Gould (1972) and Gould and Eldredge (1977) were among the first to shatter the complacent evolutionary synthesis. In their 1977 study, they contend that fossil and paleontological observations show long periods of minimal changes (called 'periods of stasis') interrupted by sudden manifestations of new species. In many instances, fossils do not exhibit gradual changes in phylogenic characteristics. A sudden replacement of long-standing species is the rule in observations from one geological layer to the next. The stability of species for such long periods of time (millions of years), followed by the observable extreme replacements are both at odds with synthetic Darwinism. Advocates for gradualism (namely, partisans of evolutionary synthesis) charge paleontological records, such as fossils, with being imperfect in tracing progressive changes. Indeed, some argue that long and gradual changes may appear instantaneous when brought down to geological time scales.

Gould and Eldredge (1977) focus on these 'glitches'. Punctuations can be explained as the result of partial isolation of a branch in a species. During these periods of isolation, the evolutionary rhythm of the isolated group outpaces the dominant species' own gradual evolution. Fossil records, due to the time aggregation they represent, do not exhibit the concurrent evolution race; rather, they reveal how quasi-static species were displaced and radically replaced by novel ones. Gould and Eldredge formulate the hypothesis that there must exist inertial forces that constrain individuals and species to remain stable. Internal forces in the developmental pathways of organisms impose restrictions on the acceptability of random and gradual variations. Furthermore, Gould (2002) argues that during the Cambrian explosion (namely, the brutal appearance of many sorts of living forms during the Cambrian era) chance played the most important part in retaining some and discarding other species. This interpretation leads to a great indeterminacy of evolutionary paths, far from the comfort of gradual synthetic evolution.

SMALL FACTORS, BIG EFFECTS

In contrast, at a micro-level of analysis, biologists seem to favor a rather deterministic explanation of evolution. 'Similar selective pressures acting on replicate populations tend to result in remarkably convergent (from different starting conditions) or parallel (from similar starting conditions) adaptations' (Hendry and Kinnison, 2001: 4). In elaborated models, biologists have hypothesized that evolution might occur along 'genetic lines of least resistance' or 'selective lines of least resistance' (Schluter, 1996, 2000). They say, for instance, that traits will vary progressively towards a peak of fitness. Sober (1984) has questioned the probabilistic nature of genetic evolution, and its implied determinism. He points to an interesting property of applied probabilities in the field of biology, noting that probabilistic reasonings suppose stretching of calculations *ad infinitum*. Therefore, what type of constraints does a limited number of individuals constituting a real-world finite population impose on these calculations? Microbiologists have since shown that contingent factors may or may not set conditions for evolutionary paths and also influence the manner by which adaptation takes place. When the starting populations are more divergent or smaller, the importance of contingent effects increases (what has been called the 'phylogenic effect' and 'founder effect').

The field of micro-evolutionary biology is fragmented into different approaches and sub-disciplines. Population genetics studies how the evolutionary forces (natural selection, random genetic drift, mutation, and gene flow) influence the allele frequencies within and among populations across time and space (Futuyuma, 1998). Developmental geneticists focus on the passage from genotype to phenotype. Since Fisher (1930), most of quantitative genetic theory (both populational and developmental) presupposes that infinitesimal changes at many loci cause evolutionary change. However, another hypothesis has surfaced, based on some evidence of the existence and determinant influence of Genes of Major Effect (GOME) on the evolutionary process (MacKay, 1996). According to this hypothesis, a few changes related to GOME could induce major changes in the phenotype. Developmental geneticists argue further that the impact on the phenotype varies depending on the timing of the mutation. In a nutshell, the earlier the effect of the mutation in the adaptation process, the stronger the impact on phenotypic characteristics.

Johnson and Porter (2001) argue for a synthesis of population genetics and developmental biology, distinct from the current synthesis of evolution and development with its emphasis on phylogenetic history. One of their conclusions indicates a way to integrate the micro-evolutionary streams: 'Often pathways are branched, allowing one gene product to interact with the regulatory sites of more than one other gene. Do the properties that make linear, regulated genetic pathways conducive for the evolution of reproductive isolation also apply to the more complicated branched pathways? We predict that they do' (2001: 54). Complex genetic branching could be reduced to simpler forms of pathways, giving a general and parsimonious explanation of the links between genetics and phenotypic development, namely, between probabilistic unobservable factors and embodied individuals.

The task of proposing a general and continuous theory of micro-to-macro evolutionary processes faces two hurdles: first, we cannot be certain that a closer examination of micro-processes will give the key to macro-processes, were the difference between the two to be a difference in quality. Secondly, measures, tests, and methods must yet be developed that would pry apart the many available alternative theories of developmental genetics – from intrinsic genetic developmental constraints to asymmetrical efficacies in gene variations (such as GOME).

For our purpose in this book, evolutionary biology is far from being the stabilized field of research from which we can blithely borrow concepts, theories, and models. If the punctuated equilibrium model were to be applied to organizational evolution, it should refer to major economic and organizational rearrangements at the century or, better, the millennium scale, i.e. since the inception of capitalism. This may be why the punctuated equilibrium model can only be an attractive but not entirely convincing analogy when applied at other time scales (see section 2.2.). However, whereas the 'small factor, big effect' phenomenon might likely impact organizational evolution, the differences in quality vs. quantity may be less problematic for organizational evolution than for biological evolution since the levers of organizational and economic growth are coarser, supposedly less numerous, and more observable than their biological counterparts.

5.2   THE CASE AGAINST SELECTION

A second criticism targets another pillar of Darwinism. After gradualism, natural selection is undermined as an omnipotent principle. A controversy has festered between biologists and philosophers regarding the thorny question of whether natural selection is a tautological principle or not. Sober's milestone book, *The Nature of Selection* (1984), offers an interesting tool to disentangle the problem.

OBVIATING THE TAUTOLOGY

Mayr (1991: 86) explains that 'there is no particular selective force in nature, nor a definite selective agent'. Many causes can account for differences in the survival of a few individuals. 'It is not the environment that selects, but the organism that copes with the environment more or less successfully. There is no external selection force' (1991: 87). The concept of selection characterizes relations between an organism and its environment; it does not determine the attributes of the organism. Envisaged at the individual level, selection is not a deterministic process, but an a posteriori phenomenon.

A major criticism looms as a challenge for the first and second Darwinian revolutions, bearing on selection efficiency. Natural selection, as an a posteriori phenomenon, is for many a tautology. By definition, it is always justified in its efficiency and effects. The ones who survive are fit to their environment, either in general or in some of their vital parts that contribute to their relatively greater survival odds or fertility. Natural selection is therefore a principle that states that survivors survive. Some phenotypic characteristics (horns, colored tail, and so on) hint to biologists that they offer, in sexual reproduction and sexual selection, a higher probability for males to mate. Biologists attribute the same function to the many less observable traits (that greatly outnumber the obvious ones) in a population's genetic pool – to benefit the fit of individuals who carry them.

Is the expression, 'survival of the fittest', a tautology? Sober (1984) demonstrates that this proposition is empirically-based and testable in its effect. He argues that fitness, as a dispositional property, can be assimilated as a cause of selection, and therefore under certain conditions is not a tautology.

> The fact that an organism has a certain level of fitness is not an *event*. An organism's fitness is more like a sugar lump's solubility than its sudden immersion in water. However, the fact that fitness is a dispositional property does not show that it lacks causal efficacy. Nor is the definitional connection of the fitness concept with (probable) survival and reproductive success a reason for holding that it is causally inert. (Sober, 1984: 84; emphasis in original)

Even if fitness includes a prioriness and tautology, it can remain explanatory and useful when disconnected from an individual attribute but included at higher levels of analyses such as populations. Therefore, personalizing fitness (namely, attributing to a particular individual or a particular organization a fitness greater than that of its rivals) leads to errors of judgment, as there is no causal power attributable to a particular individual fitness. The nature of fitness is probabilistic, not deterministic. Although the fitter individuals of a population should theoretically outlive the less fit members, they need not do so in reality. Finally, the 'survival of the fittest' contains a portion of explanatory power when applied at population levels of analysis, but no causal power at the individual level of analysis.

SELECTION OF, SELECTION FOR: SOBER'S NICE NIECE'S TOY

A core contribution of Sober (1984) revolves around a distinction applied to selection that helps to further avoid the tautology. Sober describes humorously one of his niece's toys. It consists of a multi-layered sieve. At the top level, holes are big, and each successive level contains holes of decreasing size, until the lowest level, with the smallest holes. The toy is filled up with balls of varying sizes and colors, with the noticeable property that the smallest balls are all green (and that no other balls are of the same color). Playing with this 'selection machine' involves shaking it. After a while, at the bottom of the toy, the smallest balls 'win'. As Sober remarks, this nice toy selects for smallness. But incidentally, it also selects green balls. Therefore, he writes:

> There are *two* concepts of selection we must pry apart. There is *selection of objects* and there is *selection for properties*. The smallest balls are the objects that are selected; it is equally true that the green balls are the objects that are selected. However, the concept of selecting for properties is less liberal. There is selection for smallness, but there is no selection for being green. (1984: 100; emphasis in original)

Individual traits such as greenness are not the business of natural selection. Phenotypic and genotypic properties of individuals cannot be explained by natural selection's theoretical domain when contemplated at an individual level. However, at the population level, natural selection can account for the probability of a trait's manifestation, because population-level explanations are not simple aggregations of individual trait characteristics. Evolutionary explanations range over statistical attributes of a population, not dynamic properties of individuals (Ariew, 1998). Therefore, 'the theory of natural selection is deterministic with respect to trait frequencies but not with respect to the survival and reproduction of individual organisms' (Sober, 1984: 118).

Two ideas proceed from this case against selection. First, the survival of the fittest can result from selective properties when fitness and selection rule at a higher level analysis (population for individuals, or individuals for genes). At this n+1 level of analysis, fitness represents a causal power that is not exhausted by the non-tautological proposition, 'survival of the fittest'. Defining an organization's fitness independently of its peers, however, is nonsensical. Moreover, fixing a priori the strategic value of fitness for an organizational population's properties does not mean anything specific for a given organization of this population. So, while the difficulty recedes it does not disappear, since the determinations of fitness (form, efficiency, conveyor, and so on) await definition and explanation. Secondly, selection selects for properties at upper levels of analysis, and does not select for individual properties.

Therefore, selection operates from the top down. Hence, the selection of entities engaged in a hierarchy of nested levels of selection – for which different properties entail different survival effects (like organizations) – goes downwards. Furthermore, we can demonstrate that the 'survival of the fittest' is not tautological. Defining an organization's fitness independent of its peers, however, is nonsensical. Moreover, fixing a priori the strategic value of fitness for an organizational population's properties does not mean anything specific for a given organization of this population.

5.3   THE CASE AGAINST ADAPTATION

The post-synthesis era is marked by the willingness of some biologists and naturalists to wade into the question of adaptation, a question that is often evoked by defenders of synthesis to justify every observable environment-organism association. Gould and Lewontin (1979), in particular, attack the Panglossian view of adaptation, which legitimizes every fact of nature. This view echoes the teleological adaptationist principle once supported by Spencer and subsequently revived in the mid-twentieth century. While selection is accused of selecting the fittest, adaptation also faces a tautological trap. Those who survive are the aptest to survive. Sober's niece's toy enables us to further defuse the intricate notion of fitness, entangled in both the Panglossian and the tautological adaptation arguments.

ARCHITECTURE IS CONSTRAINING

In a vibrant article, Gould and Lewontin (1979) denounce the optimizing power of natural selection as a form of a perfect adaptation. In the famous introduction to their article, they demonstrate that architectural constraints – such as the spandrels of San Marco's cathedral or the intermediate spaces in the mid-line of the King's College (Cambridge) chapel's fan-ornamented vault – have been so ingeniously decorated that these decorations seem to justify their own existence, and the existence of the building altogether. Anyone who tries to argue that the decoration precedes the structure succumbs to a Panglossian vision wherein things cannot be other than they are and everything is made for the best purpose (Hodgson, 1993). 'Yet, evolutionary biologists, in their tendency to focus exclusively on immediate adaptation to local conditions, do tend to ignore architectural constraints and perform just such an inversion of explanation' (Gould and Lewontin, 1979: 583).

Gould and Lewontin (1979) criticize the adaptationist agenda that breaks individuals into traits and parts and searches for explanations of their characteristics, shaped by adaptation and retained by natural selection. They argue that organisms are 'integrated entities, not collections of discrete objects' (1979: 585) for which any part must have – independently of the others – an optimal reason to be as it is. They object to the common practice of excluding potential explanations other than adaptation and natural selection, or limiting their relevance to minuscule and insignificant cases. Clearly, the human mind is fertile enough to provide new adaptationist 'stories' every time they are required. Since the criteria for story acceptability are loose, evolutionists can come up with a plausible replacement as soon as a previous one has been invalidated.

Gould and Lewontin (1979) offer five alternative explanations for the evolution of form, function, and behavior. First, in the case of no adaptation and no selection at all, a pure genetic drift will operate; namely, stochastic variations, or alleles, will be fixed in spite of natural selection because the vast majority of individuals will not retain a favorable mutation. Secondly, in the case of no adaptation and no selection on a specific part, the seemingly observable fit of the part at issue is a by-product of selection applied elsewhere. Thirdly, a decoupling of selection and adaptation gives two possibilities: selection without adaptation, and adaptation without selection. Fourthly, adaptation and selection operate, but without a selective basis for differences among variations. Finally, both adaptation and selection operate, but apparent utility is an epiphenomenon of non-adaptive structures, as in the architectural examples of San Marco and the King's College vault.

Interestingly, Gould and Lewontin (1979) connect embryology and developmental biology with evolutionary theory. Along with others, they conjecture that development occurs in 'integrated packages, and cannot be pulled apart piece by piece'. Therefore, an intrinsic restriction operates as an internal selective mechanism and impedes the effectiveness of certain variations at the phylogenic level. These architectural constraints have not been the result of adaptation, but rather the necessary consequences of the materials used in organic life.

In a conciliating turn, Sober (1984) distinguishes adaptedness from adaptation, and underlines their complementarity. Adaptation reflects the history of a trait in a given context, at the time of its appearance and currently. Adaptedness (namely, fitness) is a proxy for the future chances of reproduction and survival. A past adaptation may reveal a hindrance in a new environmental context. Chance may cause an adapted trait to arise. The terms are independent, a past adaptation not being a token of adaptedness. Sober defuses the quarrel: adaptation can be disconnected from a Panglossian view of perfection. However, the postulates about genetic or genomic architectural constraints on potential adaptedness advanced by Gould and Lewontin are still under scrutiny. Accordingly, Mayr (2001: 273) ends his Appendix on 'what criticisms have been made of evolutionary theory' with the following remark: 'There are many indications that separate domains exist within a genotype and that certain gene complexes have an internal cohesion that resists breakage by recombination. Up to now, however, these are only ideas; their genetic analysis still lies in the future'.

FITNESS, SUPERVENIENCE, AND SELECTION FOR PROPERTIES

Once we have said that fitness (adaptedness) is a future-oriented property of a population of organisms, we may have circumscribed the Panglossian problem but not the tautological one. More apt organisms have better survival odds or fertility than less apt organisms, by definition. Avoiding the circularity of the definition and the overgeneralization of its results requires us to highlight the following long-established characteristic of fitness: 'Fitness, although measured by a uniform method, is qualitatively different for every different organism, whereas entropy, like temperature, is taken to have the same meaning for all physical systems' (Fisher, 1930: 39, as cited in Sober, 1984: 49). There is an ontological difference between individual fitness and trait fitness, as they do not qualify the same levels of analysis. Individual fitness corresponds to the survival or reproductive chances attributable to the individual, given the ensemble of traits it possesses. Trait fitness is the average fitness of individuals in a population who possess a particular trait. As an aggregate, trait fitness is a population-level concept that does not require a specific individual to possess the particular trait. Natural selection and its causal effect on a population's trait fitness provides explanations for what several events that occur in a population have in common. Using a parallel reasoning, the fact that you have a longer life expectancy than I do is no guarantee that you will live longer than I will. Longer life expectancy is not a cause for life (or death).

Fitness is a supervenient property. A property is said to supervene when it fulfills two conditions: first, the property can apply to two different physical entities (namely, the property is not physically bounded). Secondly, two physically identical entities must both possess or both lack the property. Supervenience explains why evolutionary theory is opposed to vitalism: fitness is not an individually ascribable property. And, more importantly for the purpose of our argument, this explains our difficulty in locating, identifying, and formulating general causes for (individual) evolution; for there is no physical ascription of fitness at a given place as a given physical property. However, this does not imply the impossibility of a fitness theory and an evolutionary theory: 'Evolutionary theory provides general theories about fitness by connecting fitness with other *supervenient* properties' (Sober, 1984: 51; emphasis in original).

Sober's treatment of supervenience enables him to comprehend the development of populational genetics, and to regard any 'horizontal theorizing' as acceptable. Vertical embeddedness of concepts and properties, in a hierarchy of 'Russian-doll units' (species, individual, gene) hosts reductionist explanations. But demonstrating connections between supervenient concepts at a given level of analysis is, according to Sober, legitimate. It follows that population thinking 'is not best understood as an ontological thesis about the reality – existence or causal role – of much of anything' (Sober, 1984: 168). Selection selects the fitter. More precisely, selection selects objects that convey specific properties. But again, as for adaptation and adaptedness, there is neither equivalence nor bijective relationships between fitness and natural selection, which enables fitness to avoid the dual trap of teleology and tautology:

> When selection for and against various properties of organisms produces evolution, it must be true that the organisms differ in overall fitness. However, there can be selection for and against properties without this being reflected in differences in overall fitness. Conversely, the mere fact that there is variation in overall fitness does not yet establish why it exists. Fitness differences among organisms or traits do not by themselves reveal which properties are selected for and which are selected against. (Sober, 1984: 102)

The concept of fitness does not untangle the many factors that may determine an individual organism's destiny. Instead, it helps develop models that apply equally well at micro- and macro-levels of analysis, based on statistical distributions and relations. However, as one may object, explaining consequences without theorizing the sources is rather problematic. Indeed, 'it does not matter to the equations in population genetics why a given population is characterized by a set of selection coefficients, mutation and migration rates, and so on' (Sober 1984: 59). But not knowing what a trait distribution means for individuals involved in the population – about 'who is who' and 'what is what' – may appear as a severe limitation of supervenient evolutionary theories that mesh natural selection with fitness, as if one is disregarding individual cases. Individual organisms, which were the spearhead of Darwinian synthesis, are completely bypassed. Population thinking maintains a benevolent, although patronizing, attitude vis-à-vis evolutionary theories that propel individuals to the forefront of selection. Granted, individuals live and die. But the grim reaper of selection has higher views than mundane bodies and corpses. It selects for properties, not reified and corporeal individuals.

The challenge for organizational thought is, therefore, to abandon its cherished theme of organizational adaptation, as it is past-oriented and does not convey a causal determination of future odds of success. Yet adaptedness (namely, fitness) is a function that unifies current organizational properties with future outcomes, but at the population level only since fitness is a supervenient property. These reflections provide some explanatory elements about the controversy targeted at dynamic RBV and its tautological definition of a strategic resource as a priori adapted to competition. Dynamic RBV cannot rise to a stand-alone theory of competitiveness at the firm level as it takes 'objects' for 'properties'. A response to this attack must be found in the identification of selection criteria at the organizational and environmental levels of analysis, criteria that ensure certain resource properties a greater likelihood of competitiveness.

5.4 THE CASE AGAINST THE ORGANISM

Richard Dawkins is a British biologist who has been described by Bowler (2003: 361) as 'one of the most vociferous public advocates of the ultra-Darwinian position'. In a series of articles and books (1982, 1986, 1989), Dawkins proposes and vehemently defends a reversal or even a transfiguration of Darwinian selection theory (which brings Dawkins closer to the Weismann selectionist reinterpretation than to Darwin's original ideas). Using a hint borrowed from Hamilton and Williams in the 1960s, Dawkins strives to build and popularize a gene-based selection model. Williams (1966) stated that, since the selection process can be represented in terms of gene-level values of fitness, it is accurate to assess the single gene as the unit of selection. Dawkins goes on to develop a replicator view of evolution. In conjunction with this view, other thinkers, such as Hull (2001), argue that 'interactors' matter more than 'replicators' in the unfolding flow of evolution.

REPLICATORS AND VEHICLES

Dawkins emphasizes the role of replicators as crucial in the evolutionary process. A replicator identically reproduces its adapted forms over and over. Natural selection favors high-copying fidelity. Yet, copying errors are an essential prerequisite for evolution to occur. We have to assume that 'nothing wants to evolve. Evolution is something that happens, willy-nilly, in spite of all the efforts of the replicators (and nowadays of the genes) to prevent it happening' (Dawkins, 1989: 18). The important differences in genes emerge only in their *effects* (1989: 235). For many biologists inspired by evolutionary synthesis, selection sorts out individuals according to genetic variations and adaptedness. Bodies are intermediaries between genes and populations. For Dawkins, organisms are denied the possibility of replicating themselves. Dawkins turns classical biology upside down, considering genes as the major replicators, that use extended phenotypes (such as individual organisms) to survive and replicate themselves at the lowest cost. Replicators must drive the vehicles, as a racer drives a sports car. The success that this radical theorizing encountered in the public is undoubtedly linked to the vision that we, as individuals, are merely sports cars, rushing along at full speed, guided by compulsive genes seeking their replications. Individual and even social behaviors are reinterpreted as consequences of the 'long reach of the gene' (Dawkins, 1982). In some instances, like parasitism, genes can reach outside their own vehicle to influence phenotypes in other bodies (the host, in the case of parasitism).

There are two fundamental objections to ultra-Darwinian genic selectionism: the causal (in)transitivity and the many-to-many gene-phenotype correspondence.

First, for Dawkins, genes cause phenotypic effects, and phenotypes cause survival and reproduction success. But, as cleverly noted by Sober, it is far from clear that causality is transitive. For instance, let us assume that:

A has P that fulfills C and that C enhances S.
Can we then say that A causes S?

Certain conditions must be met for 'A causes S' to be true. First, having P does not imply a real, efficacious, and appropriate fulfilment of C in each and every situation. Impeding conditions can hamper P's fulfilment, for instance. Secondly, some ceteris paribus conditions have to be included: if Q is a fitter property than P, then there is a need to study the associations between P and Q in A subjects and non-A subjects before ruling on the truth content of the proposition 'A causes S'. Thirdly (and not last, even though we stop here), individual-level analyses are not tantamount to supervenient population analyses. The 'fact' that 'C enhances S' must be scrutinized because, while truly acceptable at a population level, that proposition might be misleading for an embodied individual A. (See the discussion above on fitness and supervenience.) Whether causality is transitive or not makes a huge difference. In the former case (transitivity), Dawkins' explanation is acceptable and very likely may be deeper than phenotypic explanations. In the latter (conditional transitivity or intransitivity), genic selection becomes less worthy as a theory. Sober (1984) provides intuitive reasons for rejecting the hypothesis of causal transitivity at a population level and for discarding the causal chaining sponsored by 'ultra-Darwinists'.

However, it is the second argument, namely the many-to-many gene-phenotype correspondence, that dents ultra-Darwinian underpinnings. Biological research has firmly established that a gene does not influence one function or phenotypic trait. There is not a one-to-one correspondence between genes and traits, but rather a many-to-many relationship. A gene or a gene complex can provide different phenotypic effects (a phenomenon called pleiotropy), and a phenotype may result from the interaction of several sets of genes (a phenomenon called polygenic effect). Remarkably, using the example of Sober's niece's toy, it is fairly clear that selection of a gene is not tantamount to selection for properties accomplished by a gene or a gene complex. Using the small example above, 'A has P that fulfills C', does not mean that P is based on a single gene G, with G leading to a single property P. But, if selection selects for P (instead of G), then the causality invoked by ultra-Darwinians does not hold.

In spite of the doubtful postulates on which it is rooted, Dawkins' theorizing has the merit of tackling a rather difficult question: why there is something like organisms on Earth rather than something else? Dawkins' (1986) 'blind watchmaker' goes back to deterministic processes at the genetic level without deterministic effects at both the individual and population levels. The last sentence of the second edition of Dawkins' book, *The Selfish Gene* (1989), gives the clue to 'what it is all about' for him: 'The individual body, so familiar to us on our planet, did not have to exist. The only kind of entity that has to exist in order for life to arise, is the immortal replicator' (1989: 266).

REPLICATORS AND INTERACTORS

In the 1970s, Hull (1976) and Ghiselin (1974) defended a view different from population thinking and supervenient forces that explains evolutionary phenomena. More than a simple contention against Dawkins' genetic selection theorizing, Hull offers an alternative to population thinking by regarding a species as if it were, itself, an organism. Species are not fixed in their characteristics and attributes, as Aristotelian physics and biology assumed and as some social-Darwinists and eugenicists asserted. Species are portions of a genealogical nexus. Relationships among organisms and the history of their relationships determine, to a greater degree than their genetic or phenotypic characteristics, the extent to which organisms are conspecific. That idea of interaction has come to play a central role in Hull's further theoretical developments, applied to biology but also to the evolution of science and scientific theories (Hull, 2001).

Hull joins the interaction process, which intersects with replication, to the incessant 'Dawkinian' replication process. Altogether, replication and interaction constitute the two inseparable facets of selection. Genes are certainly the primary (possibly sole) units of replication, whereas interaction can occur at a variety of levels, from genes and cells through organisms to colonies, demes, and possibly entire species. 'The unit-of-selection controversy concerns levels of interaction, not levels of replication' (Hull, 2001: 48). Interactors are similar to Dawkins' vehicles, with the difference being that their interactions with the environment causally impinge on the replication process. 'Interactors are those entities that interact as cohesive wholes with their environments in such a way as to make replication differential. Thus selection can be characterized generally as any process in which differential extinction and proliferation of interactions causes the differential perpetuation of the replicators that produced them' (2001: 22).

Replicators and interactors are the entities that function in selection processes. The term coined by Hull to refer to the evolving entities as outcomes of the replication process is 'lineage'. 'Lineage is an entity that persists indefinitely through time either in the same or altered state as a result of replication' (Hull, 2001: 110). Lineage is therefore a genealogical concept. Overall, the new terminology seems to give a novel angle to the evolutionary concept. Genes, organisms, and species have been replaced by replicators, interactors, and lineages. Hull offers to switch from a traditional hierarchy of units (from genes to populations) to a different logic that separates the units of replication from the units of interaction.

Hull (2001) redefines selection as a process in which the differential extinction and proliferation of interactors *cause* the differential perpetuation of the replicators. For Hull et al. (2001), selection entails 'repeated cycles of replication, variation, and environmental interaction so structured that environmental interaction causes replication to be differential' (2001: 53). Replication is a necessary condition for selection as it occurs in biological contexts, but it is not a sufficient condition. Hull defends a dual-process view of selection: first, replication that may, but does not necessarily, involve genetic variations, and secondly, interaction with the environment that causes variations in replication. Environmental interactions bias how and what information is passed on by replication. For these authors, 'We suspect that selection processes are able to produce genuine novelty and organization only *because* they are so incredibly wasteful. The efficient production of novelty and order may not sound like an oxymoron, but we suspect that it is' (2001: 93).

From these distinctions, the question of the level of selection must be separated into two sub-questions. At what levels does replication take place? At what levels does environmental interaction take place? Moreover, for Hull, there are no units of selection because selection consists of two subprocesses – replication and interaction. Therefore, what matters are the interactors that define an entity in its relationships with its surroundings and not the units of selection.

5.5 SUMMARY

In this short chapter, we presented four major debates on contemporaneous evolutionary thought (see Table 5.1). Assumptions and hypotheses, responses and prolongations, illustrate the vitality of this field of research, and may in turn nurture the necessary reflections about the VSR model, organizational evolution, and strategic management.

The case against micro-macro continuity poses the question of a difference of quantity or quality between analyses at the long-term population level and the short-term genetic level. Gould and Eldredge's (1977) punctuated model defends a difference in quality, namely, that different theories have to be developed according to the level of analysis. Tushman and Romanelli (1985) and Gersick (1991) transfer the punctuated equilibrium model into the organizational field, but their efforts remain unconvincing since the different levels of analysis and time

Table 5.1 'The four cases' summarized

Case	Argument against evolutionary synthesis	Mnemonic trick	Status
Micro-macro continuity	Difference in quantity or quality across levels	Punctuated equilibria (Cambrian era)	Argument not rejected; to be integrated in further research.
		Asymmetrical gene properties (GOME)	
Selection	Tautology: survival of the fittest	N + 1 level property (Sugar solubility)	Under certain conditions, arguments rejected.
		Selection for, selection of (Sober's niece's toy)	
Adaptation	Panglossian view	Embarked constraints on variations (San Marco cathedral)	Argument accepted. Adaptation is not a cause of better odds of survival and fertility.
	Tautology: survival of the aptest	Supervenience; adaptation vs. adaptedness (life expectancy)	Adaptedness can be integrated into an explanatory model of population-wide evolution.
Organism	The organism has little weight as a unit of evolution		
	Replicator and vehicle	Causal intransitivity and many-to-many gene-phenotype correspondence	Argument rejected for replicator-vehicle interpretation.
	Replicator and interactor: no unit of selection, level of interaction	Variation replication due to interaction Replicator, interactor, and lineage	Argument to be further analyzed and integrated for replicator-interactor interpretation.

frames are much closer in organization studies than they are in the genetic and paleontological realms. Efforts to reconcile micro- and macro-evolutionary processes exist nonetheless, and integrate the possibility of 'many genes-to-one phenotypic effect' or of asymmetrical gene influences (gene of major effect, for instance).

The case against selection examines the tautological property of selection, selecting the survivors. First, to eliminate the tautology, one must consider how fitness is statistically distributed among entities at the level just above that of the given entities, namely, fitness as an $n + 1$ property. Secondly, selection has to be assumed as selection for properties, not objects. Therefore, evolutionary theory can exist and can associate functions at an $n + 1$ level without falling into the tautology trap, but at the cost of ignoring material peculiarities of n-level entities.

The case against adaptation attacks the Panglossian view of fit and emphasizes constraints proper to the varying entity. Randomness in variation is contestable, for it depends on the materials that constitute the entity and the architecture of the entity itself. Evolution might occur notwithstanding the presence of adaptation and selection forces. However, a high degree of unpredictability results from this thesis. Further, the reflection about the supervenience property of fitness (adaptedness) helps avoid the tautological postulate that more adapted entities survive better. Evolutionary theory happens, then, to be a horizontal theorizing and modelling of $n + 1$ level properties distributed along statistical lines at the n level of entities. Meso-entities, squashed between micro- and macro-levels, are anecdotal conveyors of varying traits extolling adaptedness values expressible at an upper level of analysis.

Finally, the case against the organism reflects upon the organism itself as a topical meso-entity. A strict replicator view of evolution demotes the organism to a mere vehicle driven by powerful replicators in a quest for its replication and survival. This radical materialism is an extreme case of reductionism that can be invalidated; for it erroneously assumes both a causal transitivity (not demonstrated) and a one-to-one gene-phenotype correspondence (invalidated by empirical evidence). Another criticism of meso-level entities such as the organism concerns the 'interactor interpretation' of evolution, wherein interactors are manifold and not reducible to a coarse entity such as an organism. Interactions with likes and with environment affect the replication process. According to this interpretation, the search for an appropriate unit of selection becomes fruitless, since what matters are the levels of interactions.

CONCLUSION: THE CHECKLIST APPRAISAL GRID

In concluding the second part of this book, we synthesize the major accomplishments of our review under the Checklist Appraisal Grid. This grid evaluates evolutionary models used in organization and strategy science so as to first eliminate as many as possible stumbling blocks and pitfalls on the road toward an integrated model, secondly, to generate evolutionary models that leave space for intentionality and enable us to connect sound theory with good praxis, and thirdly, contain as many prior findings as possible and help accumulate new knowledge. The Checklist Appraisal Grid highlights the series of crucial points we came across during the preceding chapters of the book. Table 5.2 shows where we stand at the end of the second part of this book.

Table 5.2 Where we stand – synthesizing Chapters 2 to 5

Chapter 2	Organizational evolution	Strategy/strategic management
Time efficacy	Is there a time efficacy (final cause) in organizational evolution?	What is S/SM time efficacy? Does it drive real events (decoupling between discourse and action)?
Level of analysis	At which level of analysis does evolution operate?	Does S/SM have a real influence on organizational becoming?
Selection	Are selection criteria specified in their form, effects, and durability?	Does S/SM have an influence on the selection criteria?
Cause and consequence	Can evolution be, concurrently, a cause and a consequence?	Is S/SM a cause of organizational evolution or a later consequence?
End of evolution	Is there an ending/finality to organizational evolution?	Paradox of S/SM role and efficiency. Influence of intentionality?

Chapter 3	Key contributions
From Lamarck	Posing the question of inheritability Reflecting on the force of habit (at the individual level) Theorization of transformism
From Darwin	Decomposing levels of analysis (population and organism) Introducing population reasoning Developing selectionist model Freeing the analysis from teleological conceptions
From Spencer	Separating law and cause of evolution Avoiding finalism as scientific demonstration Avoiding biological analogies as evidence Providing a consistent evolutionary framework Defining causality

Chapter 4	Key contributions
	Population ecology, evolutionary economics, and dynamic resource-based view are composite descents from the original evolutionary traditions (Lamarckism, Darwinism, and Spencerism). VSR framework is neither Lamarckian, Darwinian nor Spencerian
	Coevolutionary approach stresses that selection does not necessarily select strong competitors and that organizational competitiveness is ontologically relative.

	VSR model is a tentative, encompassing framework for the study of organizational evolution. It stumbles over:
	
	    immutability of selection criteria
	    theorizing inter-relationships between entities
	    accounting for selection efficiency in nested models
	    positioning of strategic management

(Continued)

Table 5.2   (Continued)

Chapter 5	Key contributions
Remaining problem	An integrated multi-level evolutionary theory faces the micro-macro continuity problem (not solved in biology)
Solutions exist for	Selection tautology (survival of the fittest): $n + 1$ level property and distinction between selection of/selection for (Sober's niece's toy).
	Adaptation tautology (survival of the aptest): supervenience. Level of analysis problem: beyond the replicator-vehicle proposition, the replicator-interactor solution?

Chapter 2 presented the five major theoretical problems of organizational evolution and strategic management: first, complicated relationships between time, organizational evolution, and strategic management efficiency; secondly, determination of significant levels of analysis for the study of organizational evolution and for the definition of an efficient strategy; thirdly, specification of selection criteria involved in the process of organizational evolution and the real influence of strategy on selection; fourthly, intricate issues of organizational evolution and of strategic management, considered either as a cause or a consequence; and fifthly, the paradox of strategic intentionality and efficiency in association with the possibility of an end for organizational evolution. Chapter 3 fleshed out, in both conceptual and methodological terms, the contributions of three of the most influential evolutionary traditions, namely, Lamarckian, Darwinian, and Spencerian. Chapter 4 showed that current theorizing of organizational evolution does not belong to one or another of these traditions, but appears to be a patchwork of composite blocks. In addition, Chapter 4 posed the question of whether the Variation-Selection-Retention (VSR) model is a potential paradigm or an all-encompassing and loose framework. Finally, Chapter 5 presented four powerful debates that have emerged in recent decades in the field of biology, which may provide ways to address some of the problematic links between organizational evolution and strategic management.

A sound evaluation of an organizational evolution model commensurate with strategic management should integrate these many constraints. So we consider the conceptual puzzles discussed in Chapter 2, the cautions raised in Chapter 3 on Darwin's and Spencer's works (which also addresses Lamarck's contributions), the four challenges posed to VSR models (from Chapter 4), and 'the four cases' present in contemporary biological studies (examined in this chapter). Based on these elements, we present our Checklist Appraisal Grid (Table 5.3), the checklist of properties that should establish an evolutionary framework which applies to organizations and takes strategy into account.

Table 5.3   A checklist appraisal grid of an evolutionary model

	1	2	3
Conceptual puzzles about organizational evolution (Chapter 2)			
Is there a time efficacy (final cause)?			
At which level of analysis does evolution operate?			
Are selection criteria specified in their form, effects, and durability?			
Can organizational evolution be concurrently a cause and a consequence?			
Is there an ending/finality of organizational evolution?			
Cautions (Chapter 3)			
Decomposing levels of analysis			
Introducing population reasoning			
Developing selectionist modeling			
Freeing the analysis from teleological conceptions			
Separating law and cause of evolution			
Avoiding finalism as scientific demonstration			
Avoiding biological analogies as evidence			
Providing a consistent evolutionary framework			
Defining causality			
VSR limitations (Chapter 4)			
Immutability of selection criteria			
Conceptualization and integration of inter-relationships between entities			
Accounting for selection efficiency in nested models			
Positioning of strategic management			
Challenges (Chapter 5)			
Micro-macro continuity challenge			
Selection tautology (survival of the fittest)			
Adaptation tautology (survival of the aptest)			
Level of analysis challenge: replicator-vehicle vs. replicator-interactor			

1   The model responds very well to the issue.
2   The model takes the issue into account.
3   The model does not account for the issue.

PART 3   OFFERING POTENTIAL ANSWERS

In the first two parts of this book, we presented questions that are raised by an advanced reflection on organizational evolution and strategic management, and we suggested possible answers coming from biological and organizational studies. In this last part of the book, we offer some additional answers that bypass the difficulties encountered so far. There are two chapters in this part of the book.

In Chapter 6, a theorization effort is conducted that builds on the findings from earlier chapters and avoids the acknowledged pitfalls. Based on a revised conception of the components of the VSR model, the Organizational Evolution and Strategy (OES) model is drawn. The gist of the model lies in the idea that selection does not immutably reproduce itself as a constant, that selection criteria differ both from one level of analysis to another and from time to time, and that the crux of strategic management is to induce favorable selection criteria changes.

Chapter 7, the last chapter of this book, probes several implications of an approach to organizational evolution and strategic management literature that are akin to the OES model. The four implications we examine are epistemological, theoretical, empirical, and practical. First, epistemological implications involve i) the necessity, when reflecting upon selection, to deal with real and concrete actions, hereby entailing a posture oscillating between a moderated positivism and realism, ii) the difficulty for the VSR model to become an uncontested organizational evolution paradigm; iii) the recognition of influential individualities' freedom in open-ended organizational and economic evolution; and iv) the challenges that this freedom poses for every actor. Secondly, theoretical implications for strategy research, population ecology, evolutionary economics, the dynamic RBV, and the coevolutionary approach are mentioned. We distinguish between choices that preserve and reinforce current selection forces and those that transform selection criteria in a changing industrial context with conflicting institutional logics. Future studies in strategic management should include additional sociological indicators in order to control for alternative conceptions of selection and avoid sweeping and problematic generalizations (Denrell, 2003; Ferraro et al., 2005). Thirdly, empirical implications advocate for the convergent use of multiple methods (theoretical models, simulations, statistical studies, and qualitative studies) in order to find the causal mechanisms that relate strategy and strategic management to organizational evolution. Fourthly, and practically, the sketch of an original strategic diagnosis is proposed.

6 THE ORGANIZATIONAL EVOLUTION AND STRATEGY MODEL

Evolutionary theory now deploys a striking hierarchy of possible selection mechanisms. Indeed, it is a double hierarchy – of both objects and properties – that contemporary theory has to consider. Objects at different levels may be selected; and there may be selection for and against properties at different levels as well. (Sober, 1984: 368)

In this chapter, we propose to build the 'Organizational Evolution and Strategy' (OES) model. Section 6.1 develops the model's components. This model rests on prior conceptions – from Campbell, but also from Baum and Rao (2000), Durand (2000), and Volberda and Lewin (2003). Earlier, we showed that population ecology, evolutionary economics, and the dynamic resource-based view can be interpreted through the VSR model lens (see Table 4.1). All three perspectives contain their conceptions of variations, their selective mechanisms, and retention principles – although at different levels, applied to different entities, and based on various economic principles. Therefore, a model based on a VSR philosophy can serve as a starting point for developing tentative responses to the intriguing relationships between organizational evolution and strategic management. From this basis, we use the Checklist Appraisal Grid to answer the questions raised by evolutionary models and those that plague any VSR approach. Section 6.2 then offers a comprehensive discussion of whether and how the OES model satisfies the successive requirements of the Checklist Appraisal Grid. Finally, the last section completes the model by giving further details on the fourteen relationships that causally relate entities and levels in the OES model.

6.1 REPRESENTING A BASIC VSR ORGANIZATIONAL EVOLUTION MODEL

Baum and Rao (2000), Durand (2000), and Volberda and Lewin (2003) offered earlier models and representations of organizational evolution based on the VSR philosophy. We draw on these works to elaborate a first basic model of organizational evolution. To do so, we distinguish three levels and two 'hierarchies' (Figure 6.1 and Appendix 1).

ENTITIES AND HIERARCHIES

Organization is the central unit of analysis. It consists of resources and capabilities (at the intra-organization level), and belongs to markets (at the supra-organizational level). Inspired by a breakdown of multi-level analyses into two distinct hierarchies (as proposed by Baum and Singh (1994b) and Baum and Rao (2000)), these three levels serve as our starting point and constitute one of the two hierarchies of the model, called the 'genealogical hierarchy'. The genealogical hierarchy corresponds to an institutionalized memory of a given economic activity. For Baum and Rao (2000), the genealogical hierarchy consists of institutional lineages that continue over time, such as professional guilds, craftsmanship transmission, or internationalization of firms. In our setting, which does not include social entities such as guilds or unions, genealogical hierarchy refers to the three main entities of economic activity formerly captured in the literature: market, organization, and resources and capabilities. Thus, by 'genealogical', we mean the historical articulation of the entities and their relationships that we can retrieve through a genealogical inquiry – as the one conducted, for instance, in this book on the evolutionary traditions.

In the genealogical hierarchy, market is the overarching coordinating mechanism of economic activity. By 'market', we mean the legal and institutional definition of economic activity that makes possible the organizational activity. (Recent examples of institutional redefinition of markets include, for instance, the Telecommunication Act of 1995, the Sarbanes-Oxley Law, and the European deregulation of car dealerships.) Therefore, market definition is not restricted to profit-exchange places but contains, as well, a legal and institutional component that allows existing or emerging organization types to develop (Kondra and Hinings, 1998; Oliver, 1997).

Nested within markets, collective entities, called 'organizations', operate different economic activities. They may take the form of corporations, franchises, or holdings, among many other possibilities. An organization utilizes resources and capabilities to perform a set of tasks in a specific order. Resources and capabilities comprise the lowest-level entity of that hierarchy that we consider here. Resources are means of action endowed with certain properties and are able to perform various services (Penrose, 1959). These means of action can be direct (for example, a physical retail network, a computerized reservation system, a plant) and indirect (for example, reputation, brand, financial capacity). The properties that make resources strategic for an organization are characterized by three qualities – they cannot be easily imitated, transferred, or substituted (Barney, 2002; Grant, 1991). These properties enable rents to accrue to the controller of the resources (Winter, 1995). Each resource can render a plurality of services, most of them being mutually exclusive (Penrose, 1959; Sandberg, 2000). For instance, a computer can be used to store a database, do spreadsheet calculations, write texts, and browse information, but different people may not be able to perform all tasks concurrently on the same computer. A brand can be stretched, but should remain within certain limits to preserve its coherence.

A capability is measured by the ability of individuals in an organized collective to make use of the services of available resources in order to adequately perform a task. Being able to satisfy 95 percent of any client's requests in twenty-four hours, rejuvenate 60 percent of a product portfolio in a three year cycle, or broaden the sales of a brand while keeping marketing expenditures constant are examples of capabilities. Capabilities, therefore, express the rent potential contained in the resources. Resources are inert; capabilities are active. Resources are nouns; capabilities verbs (Durand, 2000). Resources involve value calculations, reflection on potential utilizations, and logical articulation of actions. Capabilities involve the psychological and social content of concrete actions. Some resources and capabilities are necessary for an organization to exist and be concretely expressed as a viable firm. They are all gathered in the single-individual company, and they are dispersed in larger companies. Over time, the ensemble of necessary resources and capabilities, retained in a sort of sedimentation process, may be supplemented by new resources and capabilities.

If one wanted to project *downward* in the genealogical hierarchy, one would likely encounter technological and scientific knowledge and identity traits as elements embedded within resources and capabilities (Cohen and Levinthal, 1990). Technological and scientific knowledge as part of public and private spaces modify the potential services rendered by existing resources (Shane, 2000). Identity traits, rooted in the psychological and social determinants of action, alter the individual perceptions and volitions present in an organization, and thus enhance or degrade a capability. Projecting *upward* in the genealogical hierarchy, different anthropological models of exchange (capitalist, socialist, and barter economies, among others) encapsulate market forms. Therefore, the model proposed in this chapter is part of a more general model of economic evolution.

Generally speaking, one may find a similar genealogical hierarchy in most regions of the world where economic philosophy coincides with the capitalist anthropological model of exchange. Despite this similarity, however, there are differing nuances in legal, institutional, and cultural definitions of markets and organizations, which may reflect, for example, the general mechanisms of incorporation and bankruptcy (Hall and Soskice, 2001) or the particular application of institutional or technological innovations in the European banking industry (Volberda and Lewin, 2003).

As mentioned earlier (see section 1.1 and section 3.2), the use of biological analogies and references to connect the representation of genealogical units and their actual expression creates a serious dilemma. The dual-hierarchy model presented in Figure 6.1. is one of the responses that addresses this difficulty. The ecological hierarchy consists of the actual manifestation of different types of organized activity located in particular time and space settings. Overall, a level of analysis is therefore constituted by a genealogical-ecological entity pair, such as market-industry, organization-firm, and resource and capability-competitive advantage. The ecological hierarchy represents historical materializations of genealogical entities. 'Ecological' refers to the principles of organization of concrete and living milieus in which industries and firms compete and evolve. As an illustration, Nike, Reebok, and Adidas belong to one ecological hierarchy since they are exemplars of a particular type of firm that barely existed before World War Two namely, global footwear and sportswear companies.

While the corresponding manifestation of organizations is a concrete firm, the concrete expressions of (genealogical) markets are specific industries which emerge or disappear over time. At the finest level of analysis considered here, resources and capabilities take the actual form of what can be called 'competitive advantage'. Competitive advantage, therefore, exists as the concrete manifestation of the rent potential resulting from the conjunction of resources (with isolating properties) and capabilities (actualizing resources' potential services) that are capacitated by an organization (Durand, 2002) and selected by real firms in industrial contexts (Wiggins and Ruefli, 2002). These conjunctions of resources and capabilities provide the garnering firm with a rent advantage over its rivals, intentionally or not. But we must remember that selection selects properties and not objects or resources per se. Therefore, competitive advantage is a conjunction of rent-accruing properties possessed at given times by resources and capabilities, and the dynamic RBV has mistaken objects for properties (for example, the brand for its inimitability or employees' benevolence for their non-transferability). The strategic interest is not which resource or capability matters for competitiveness (to have a brand or to favor employees' benevolence); rather, the strategic interest is the conditions under which the selection forces induce changes in the properties that resources and capabilities possess – changes that increase or decrease the likelihood for an organization to be competitive. In certain situations, temporary monopoly can annihilate the inimitability advantage brought by a brand and very low labor cost can compensate for all the benevolence of dedicated employees.

At a level of analysis below competitive advantage are products (as far as manufacturing industries are concerned) or deployed services (since services comprise more than two-thirds of the national GDPs of developed capitalist economies). These products and services epitomize the technological knowledge and identity traits belonging to the lowest-level corresponding entities of the genealogical hierarchy. Therefore, in this ecological hierarchy, one is able to collect fine specimens of a concrete history of products over time. This always incomplete collection materializes the fascinating story of the never-ending efforts made by firms to satisfy or orientate their demanding patrons (Lubatkin et al., 2001). Successful products (Braun's electric razor of the 1950s, PCs, iPods) convey the discernable (or not) marks of a competitive advantage once possessed by a given firm. As such, industrial museums or design exhibitions where old cathode tube TV sets cohabit with contemporary flat screens evidence the production of an economic history on the march, a history *fashioned* by organizations. Moving one step above industry in the ecological hierarchy, we find entire economic systems and governing institutions – such as the late GATT, extant IMF, or transnational regulative bodies – which correspond to the anthropological model of exchange present in the genealogical hierarchy (Djelic and Quack, 2003).

RELATING LEVELS AND HIERARCHIES

Obeying the VSR logic, the two hierarchies structure themselves over time in relation to the three distinct VSR processes.

Variations at any of the three genealogical levels (market-industry, organization-firm, and resource and capability-competitive advantage) condition the selection possibility that occurs effectively in the ecological arena. In this representation,

Figure 6.1   Basic elements for a VSR model of organizational evolution

Market is the overarching coordinating mechanism of economic activity; it is not restricted to profit-exchange places; it contains a legal and institutional basis that allows (**or not**) existing and emerging organization types to develop.

Organizations are purposive social collections of controlled resources, building exchange relations and interacting with other entities, and developing strategies for reaching objectives.

Resources are means of action endowed with certain isolating properties and able to perform various services.

A *capability* is the capacity of individuals in an organized collective to make use of the services of the available resources in order to perform a task adequately and to express the rent potential contained in resources.

Industry is the concrete manifestation of a market.

Firm is a concrete manifestation of an organization applied to a specific type of offering.

Competitive advantage is the concrete actualization of the rent potential resulting from the conjunction of resources (with isolating properties) and capabilities (actualizing resources'potential rent-accruing services) capacitated by firms in industrial contexts.

variations are due to the retention of selected former variations at and below that level of analysis. Cumulative learning and retention of practices derived and retained from the competitive advantage selected over time fuels the variation process at the resource and capability level (Zollo and Winter, 2002). Resources and capabilities can vary for other reasons, as well. Science increases the services certain resources can render, while education develops individual and collective human capabilities to explore and exploit these available services. Organizations vary under at least a twofold pressure. First, retained resources and capabilities accumulate over time to modify the genealogical definition of an organization (Nickerson and Silverman, 2003). Secondly, the selection of existing firm types is also retained at the organizational level, and this retention in turn nurtures organizational variations. For instance, the different structures of organizations (U-form, M-form, J-form, and so on) are examples of organizational variations that are selected by concrete firms and later retained in the genealogical hierarchy as a basis for other variations (Kraatz and Zajac, 1996; Jacobides and Winter, 2005). The necessary reporting and symbolic management capability of large public companies,

Figure 6.2   A simple VSR model of organizational evolution

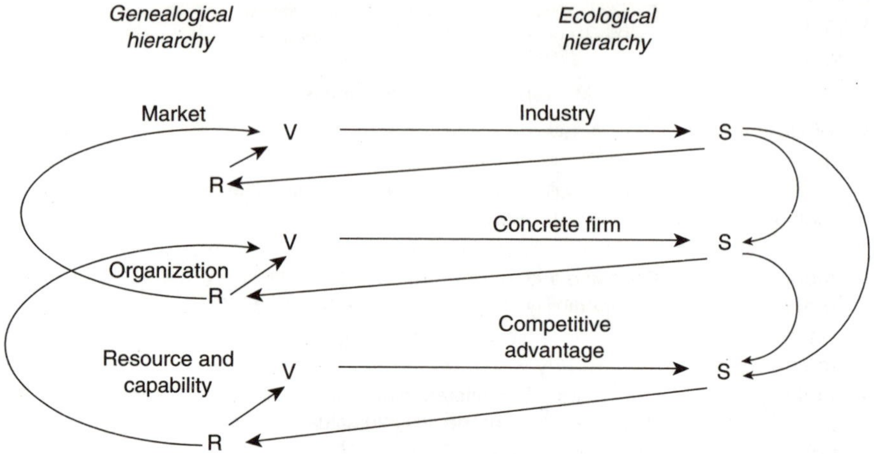

retained at the resource and capability level, impacts the definition of such an organization and fuels further variations which may be selected by concrete firms (Zuckerman, 1999). Finally, the organizational variations, selected in the ecological hierarchy and retained in the genealogical hierarchy, induce variations in the very conception of markets. Markets need adjustments and delimitations, as the retention of concrete selected market variations by concrete industries imposes some recall of the laws and rules of markets (Fligstein, 1996). This is where the law, regulation, and deregulation play their part.

Therefore, an upward process integrates the modifications of the resource-capability coupling into the definition of organizations, which, in turn, may affect the definition and working principles of a market. For instance, the gathering within the same organization of generation and distribution resources may or may not affect the functioning of energy markets; namely, vertical integration of energy operators may or may not violate market principles in one place at a given time. It follows that the genealogical definition of a market may be altered as well as the definition of an energy operator, distributor, and so forth, due to the resources and capabilities owned and utilized by operative organizations. To use the VSR terminology, this upward process is the retention process that nurtures variations at a given genealogical level (resource and capability, organization, and market) and also at the next higher level (resource and capability retention affects organizational variation, and organization retention affects market variation).

The concrete actualization of market variations is to be transferred into real industries – where newcomers can intrude, concrete firms vie with each other for clientele, and buyers value expressed capabilities in offerings mastered by concrete firms (competitive advantage). A downward process relates selection amongst ecological entities to each other. Industry characteristics influence how and which firms are selected as well as the nature of competitive advantage. Firms select organizational arrangements and available resources and capabilities in order to establish a positive differentiation in their offerings, namely, to muster a competitive advantage (independently of assuming whether a deliberate choice guarantees a higher likelihood of selection or not, as potential random combinations could lead to a competitive advantage). Figure 6.2. illustrates a first representation of a VSR-based model of organizational evolution and strategic management.

Some significant remarks about the proposed evolutionary model follow:

- While the selective downward process in this representation is similar to the findings of Baum and Singh (1994b), Baum and Rao (2000), and Volberda and Lewin (2003), this model, in contrast to theirs, does not integrate multi-level influences of retention on other entities' variations in the genealogical hierarchy. For the sake of simplicity and parsimony, the OES model focuses on the likely dominant influence of retention at level n (namely, variation at level $n + 1$). While n to $n + 2$ and n to $n - 1$ retention-variations relationships may exist, we did not find enough evidence to support theories that they would dominate over n to $n + 1$ effects.
- In the model, resource and capability variations are mainly influenced by one process. That does not imply that other retention processes beyond the sphere of organization theory cannot influence these variations. We briefly mentioned that scientific accumulation and knowledge diffusion impact how resource and capability vary. Other factors may also enlarge a concrete firm's potential opportunities to use resources and capabilities (Moran and Ghoshal, 1999). One can think of socio-cultural movements, individuals' identification processes, and so on (Rao et al., 2003).
- We do not use the 'blind' label to qualify variation, nor do we employ the 'competitive' selection or the 'deliberate' selection as in Volberda and Lewin (2003). At this stage, it is unclear what these adjectives bring to the picture. 'Blind' means that the probability to be selected is unknown, and that is by definition included in the model. Knowing that others failed or extrapolating as to why they succeeded cannot be logically transformed into guarantees about how and why one will fail or succeed (Romanelli, 1999). Therefore, in the absence of 100 percent certain outcome, any action is blind, which supports our abandonment of this adjective. 'Competitive' distinguishes a selection process for which an agent cannot control the outcome, while 'deliberate' qualifies the effective purposefulness of the agent enacting the intentional changes. However, in the organizational context, selection is by nature competitive; and even though a selection may be intentional (for instance, the selection process conducted by a firm to obtain a competitive advantage), there is no guarantee that what will eventually be selected and retained is precisely the intentional choice of that agent. Being deliberative does not cancel out the competitive nature of selection. Therefore, we judge these attributive adjectives to be superfluous and perhaps even misleading.
- The nature of competitive advantage determines which properties of the resources and capabilities are required for a given theoretical organization to compete, allowing the inclusion of concrete activities (customer segmentation, HR motivation techniques, etc.) into the definition of the genealogical entities. In a sense, it is possible to describe a history of competitive advantage from the marketing basics of the 1950s, the HR tools of the 1960s, the internationalization process of the 1970s, the finance mastery of the 1980s, the IT craze of the 1990s, the process outsourcing of the years 2000–10, and so forth.
- This dual-hierarchy model supplies a representation of diverse disciplines interested in economic activity and organizations (Figure 6.3). The field of micro-economics looks at the relationships between two genealogical entities:

Figure 6.3 Positioning research fields

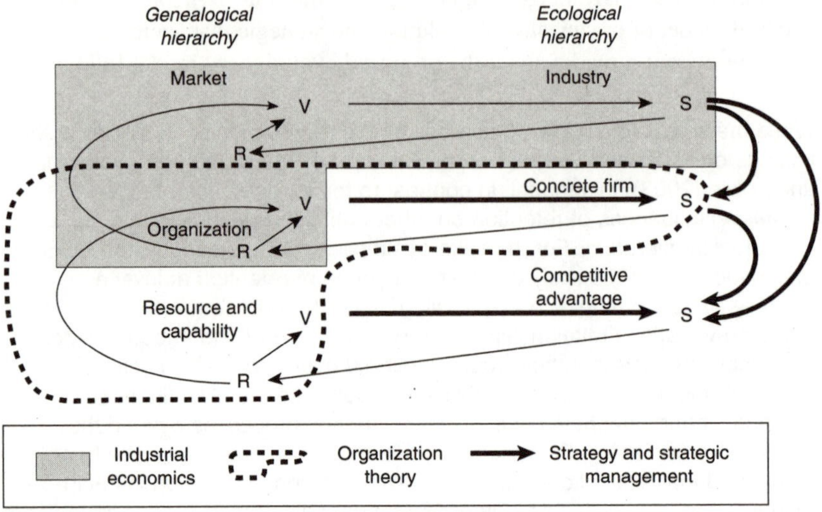

market and organizations. Industrial economics studies and tests the empirical manifestations of economic organizing principles on concrete ecological observations. Of utmost relevance for this book is the fact that organizational evolution and strategic management involve entities from both hierarchies. Organizational evolution (organization theory) concerns not only the upward movement from resources and capabilities that may transform organizational definition, but also the lateral correspondence between genealogical and ecological characterizations (namely, organization and concrete firms). Strategy and strategic management imply the pragmatic activity of maneuvering existing firms in order to select appropriate resources and capabilities that suit buyers' demands and might serve as a competitive advantage, depending upon the industry's requirements.

6.2 APPRAISING THE OES MODEL

Based on the Checklist Appraisal Grid (Table 5.3), we can assess the OES model.

PUZZLES AND CAUTIONS

Prior discussion about coevolution affords us some responses to most of the conceptual puzzles. The question of time efficacy in the model is resolved. In the OES model, final causes do not impinge on current events. Future times do not cause present events. There is an ontological decoupling between intentional behavior that meshes experience and foresight, and concrete causal mechanisms that imply that a cause precedes its consequence. Therefore, if a time efficacy

Table 6.1.   An appraisal of the OES model

	1	2	3
Conceptual puzzles			
Is there a time efficacy (final cause)?	✔		
At which level of analysis does evolution operate?	✔		
Are selection criteria specified in their form, effects, and durability?		✔	
Can organizational evolution be concurrently a cause and a consequence?	✔		
Is there an ending/finality of organizational evolution?	✔		
Cautions			
Decomposing levels of analysis	✔		
Introducing population reasoning	✔		
Developing selectionist modeling	✔		
Freeing the analysis from teleological conceptions	✔		
Separating law and cause of evolution		✔	
Avoiding finalism as scientific demonstration	✔		
Avoiding biological analogies as evidence	✔		
Providing a consistent evolutionary framework	✔		
Defining causality		✔	
VSR limitations			
Immutability of selection criteria	✔		
Conceptualization and integration of inter-relationships between entities	✔		
Accounting for selection efficiency in nested models	✔		
Positioning of strategic management	✔		
Challenges			
Micro-macro continuity challenge	✔		
Selection tautology (survival of the fittest)	✔		
Adaptation tautology (survival of the aptest)	✔		
Level of analysis challenge: replicator-vehicle vs. replicator-interactor	✔		

1   Basic model responds very well to the issue.
2   Basic model takes the issue into account.
3   Basic model does not account for the issue.

were to exist, it is the 'efficacy' of past times through learning, experience, and habit, and not the efficiency of future times.

The model meets, at least partially, the requirement of placing the loci of organizational evolution – and of showing why, under certain circumstances, evolution can be conceptualized as a cause and a consequence of change (depending on the part of the diagram one focuses on). Evolution operates at various levels of analysis: industry, firms, and competitive advantage. However, it is possible to adjoin higher and lower levels. At higher levels of analysis, institutional factors, for example, impact the very conception of markets (the distinction between private and public, the distribution of control, monitoring, and sanction powers to ad hoc agencies (Dobbin et al., 1994; Hoskisson et al., 2004)). At lower levels, product lines and service ranges embody the declination of competitive advantage into real artefacts (Lubatkin et al., 2001). Researchers can position themselves at various levels and study particular relationships and effects. Using the OES model, we can postulate what selection criteria are likely to matter at which level, responding to the concern of specifying the form, effects, and durability of selection criteria.

Ultimately, it is difficult to answer the last question about the finality of organizational evolution. There is no reason to make assumptions about a given ending of organizational evolution. However, as selection criteria are variable and proceed downward from macro levels to micro levels, a directionality of organizational evolution might be uncovered under the veil of social, political, and ideological movements that affect the very definition of markets. But, again, there is a great distance and even a likely decoupling between these movements, the terminology they use, the actual succession of events they bring about, and an assigned finality to organizational and economic evolutions.

The simple model of organizational evolution takes into account the diverse cautions noted in Chapter 3, the exceptions being the distinction between the law and the cause of evolution and, more importantly, the definition of causality. Several of the co-evolutionary studies strive to unravel the cause-effect relations of organizational evolution and succeed in their efforts (Barnett et al., 1994; Barnett, 1997). In the OES model, antecedents can be related to consequences at each level of analysis, and combinations of causal relationships exist at a multi-level analysis. Laws of organizational evolution, if they were to be defined, would likely follow the perspective suggested by McKelvey (1997); namely, they would express propositions in terms of distributions and frequency rates of events within and between populations. The OES model is not teleological and avoids finalism as a scientific demonstration. However, the model does not exclude intentionality as a potential vector of change and evolution. As for the definition of causality itself, it is a pending issue that we will evoke in section 7.1, 'Epistemological Implications'.

VSR LIMITATIONS

The OES model enables us to position the field of strategic management in a more satisfying manner than does the traditional Campbellian VSR model of socio-cultural evolution. First, the immutability of selection criteria finds a reply. In the OES model, selection criteria vary in a twofold manner. They differ from one level of application to another. For instance, selection criteria causing the elimination of market variants (from the genealogical hierarchy) depend on principles such as property rights (Murmann, 2003), customer protection, and economic surplus apportioning inscribed into economic law and enacted in existing industries (for example, bank deregulation as studied by Barnett et al. (1994; Barnett and Hansen,1996) in the ecological hierarchy). The selection criteria eliminating concrete firms from industries are not identical to the selection criteria that eliminate market variants and concern learning advantages or positional advantages, for instance (Barnett and Hansen, 1996; Murmann, 2003). Moreover, selection criteria vary over time; they are not immutable. There is a spiraling effect implying that a focal firm's rivals increase their learning and internal selection capability to match the focal firm's efficiency, spurring a dynamic of increasing competition (Henderson and Mitchell, 1997). Adding new selection criteria to the list of the necessary mastered dimensions so as to play in an industry is, therefore, a fundamental trait of strategy and strategic management (Kim and Mauborgne, 1997) which does not contradict the VSR logic as it is described in this chapter.

Secondly, the OES model may lack a clear integration of relationships between entities. In particular, a broad set of studies in strategy centered on alliances, partnerships, and networks appears to be at odds with the stand-alone entities of the model (Baum and Korn, 1999; Uzzi, 1999). Again, coevolutionary reflections instill a more plastic definition of firm boundaries. Relationships with public entities (such as research centers and universities), structural forms (single-unit or multi-unit firms), and even alliance formation and management can be represented in our model. Each of these relationships between and across firms and entities takes the form of capability variations and new rent-accruing properties that are selected because they add competitive advantage (ecological hierarchy), and they are retained and integrated at the organization layer (genealogical hierarchy), leading in turn to organizational variations. Pursuing the logic one step further, one may understand why and how industry boundaries dissipate when mergers and acquisitions combine various resources, capabilities, and organizations under the same structural arrangements. This theory of ecological entities is more coherent with an interactor view (Hull, 2001; Hodgson and Knudsen, 2004) than with a vehicle view of evolution (Dawkins, 1989; Weeks and Galunic, 2003).

For instance, the personal digital assistant (PDA) technological movement led Palm to create two entities, PalmOne and PalmSource, to cater to different customers' needs. The frontier between PDA and mobile phones has been evaporating, pushing PalmOne to develop relationships with phone companies, aimed at the convergence of terminals. At the same time, competition has raged among operating systems (although differently between Europe and the US, where PalmSource has been leading the competition with a more than 50 percent market share for years). In this case, the concrete firm Palm had to determine what type of competitive advantage to build by: first separating technical resources and capabilities of the hardware from the software, and secondly, developing cooperative capability on the hardware branch. These resources and capabilities led to a competitive advantage for Palm for several years, and they have been retained as necessary elements of organizations in order to compete in this market. In effect, this retained competitive advantage has modified the organization's constitutive genealogical traits and, thus, the nature of concrete firms potentially operating in the PDA industry (extending the market to computer, software, and telecommunication companies with comparable technical and cooperative capabilities). Further, this evolution has affected the delineation of telecommunication and computer markets concretely expressed at the industry level. Therefore, the OES model can cope with the vertical relationships in the two hierarchies as well as with the horizontal relationships amongst units and between hierarchies – relationships that complicate organizational evolution phenomena and strategic management field.

Thirdly, even the difficult question of selection efficiency in nested models may find a tentative answer, based on works such as Barnett (1997) and Henderson and Stern (2004). Earlier, we found that selection criteria vary in nature across levels and over time, and we assumed a downward causation process amongst selection levels, implying that selection criteria at an upper level must be met before selection criteria at lower levels can be met. We also know that survivors need not be the strongest competitors, and that the likelihood of full external selection is reduced by the intensity of innovativeness and prior internal selection events. Therefore, we can argue that the whole-part selection problem may be less definite in organizational evolution than in biological evolution, because in organizational evolution a downward causal selection process seems more acceptable. However, this does not prevent interactions and mediating effects from operating, as shown in Henderson and Stern (2004). Overall, we have arguments to contend that selection processes are likely to be directional (downward causation), changing in their content (selection criteria are amendable), and not purely efficient (weak competitors can be strong survivors).

Finally, the OES model integrates the positioning of strategy and strategic management as one of its key components. Designing an organizational arrangement that capacitates the exploitable services of firm and environment resources within a firm is at the core of strategy. Implementing techniques and processes that select competitive advantage and fuel the retention process is at the core of strategic management. That selection criteria are not immutable frees space for an organized intervention, materialized in facts and events which alter the selection properties at various levels of analysis.

CHALLENGES

The study of contemporaneous debates in biology revealed four challenges. Two of them are easily addressed. The micro-macro continuity challenge is found to be less problematic in organizational evolution phenomena than in biology because: first, there is less time discontinuity between macro-economic factors (public investment, interest or exchange rates) and micro-economic factors (industrial development, competitive success) than between geological or paleontological observations and genetic materials; secondly, the relative accessibility of observable elements in economic and organizational life enables researchers to test possible relations at various levels of connection; and thirdly, the combinatory complexity is lower in economic and organizational evolution than in biological evolution. In the latter, the genome contains exponential possibilities, the transformation principles from code to matter are eminently variegated and intricate, the layers of interactions are multifarious, and the external shocks are likely to impact survival in numerous ways. Consequently, the probability of finding a meta-theory connecting micro-processes (such as genomic development) to macro-processes (such as population dynamics) is less in biology than it is in evolutionary organization and economic theory.

The replicator-vehicle vs. replicator-interactor interpretation can also be accounted for. While genetic material happens to be the replicator in biological evolution, some biologists argue that organisms are mere vehicles that ensure the replication process on behalf of the replicator and, potentially, to the detriment of the organism and the organism's associated counterparts. In the extended phenotype model, parasites affect their host's genetic material on their own behalf, parasites being themselves vehicles of a genetic replicator in competition with other replicating materials. The interactor interpretation ascribes to the organism different properties and roles. In particular, interactors make replication differential. Indeed, Hull (2001) redefined selection as a process in which the differential extinction and proliferation of interactors cause the differential perpetuation of replicators. To use Hull's terminology, firms would be the interactors that, via the organizational retention process, will lead to organizational lineages in the genealogical hierarchy. Accordingly, in a footnote, Murmann (2003: 203) emphasizes that the interactor in his research setting would be the business firm, whereas the replicator would be the business model.

As demonstrated by the tentative OES model, concrete firms are clearly closer to being interactors than they are to being vehicles. Their interaction with available variants and varying resources and capabilities, as well as with industry-selective pressures, generates differences in replication processes (Maritan and Brush, 2003). By the same token, competitive advantage could depict an interactor gathering a plurality of properties (contained in resources (and their associated services) and capabilities (and their exploitative quality)) that, in their relationships with their environments (organizational and competitive), cause new variations in replication. But the difference between biological interactors and economic and organizational interactors lies in the purposive generation of differential replication processes. This is why the reductionist materialism of gene-vehicle metaphor is even more inappropriate for the study of organizational evolution. This also explains why the replicator-interactor biological image could be used to reflect on organizational evolution, contingent upon three major adjustments: first, firms purposely generate differential replication in search of competitive advantage. Secondly, firms select modes of replication that change the replicated content (while replicators usually reproduce unchanged). Thirdly, firms as interactors connect the organizational evolution phenomenon to the sociology of networks at various levels through their exchanges (Burt, 1997; Uzzi, 1999).

While we have addressed two of the challenges presented by the micro-macro continuity and the replicator-interactor interpretation, two additional challenges – the selection and adaptation tautologies – remain to be overcome. From the coevolutionary discussion, one may find ideas for conciliating selection and adaptation notions without falling into the tautological traps.

The survival tautology claims survival of the fittest, namely, those with the highest survival possibilities. Two elements contribute to casting doubt upon the selection tautology criticism. First, if we consider the notion of fitness as a population property (and not as an individual characteristic or an event), it is possible to attribute explanatory power to fitness and derive testable propositions. Secondly, in this context, selection forces bear more on properties than on objects. Coevolutionary studies have shown that selection criteria differ from one level of analysis to another, that firms – by their actions – augment the list of selection criteria, and that survivors are not the strongest competitors. There are several ways to survive; for example, via learning advantage, structural disposition, positional arrangement. Therefore, the culling action of firm selection does not rely on immutable, invariable, and absolute criteria. Survival does not concern the fittest individuals. It concerns a cohort of individuals wherein occurrences of distributed properties cohabit as both a stand-alone and compound state. Hence, it is the distribution of properties at the industry level that determines firm selection; and, at the firm level, it is the distribution of competitive efficiency present in resource and capability combinations, called 'competitive advantage'. At the n + 1 level, selection theory can be said to be deterministic in terms of the relationship between property distribution and survival. However, at the n level, selection theory has little to say with respect to a given entity's survival. Therefore, in the OES model, selection never selects a particular firm.

The adaptation tautology presents adaptation as an ineluctable outcome (a Panglossian view of adaptation). Two elements help to override the adaptation tautology. First, architectural and material constraints shape the adaptation path. Adaptation is not fine-tuned, but irregular and patchy. Secondly, 'adaptedness' differs from 'adaptation', the former being an n + 1 distributed forward-looking property, the latter a historical and actualized result of past selection. Adaptedness is a supervenient property, being equally applicable to a plurality of individuals (unboundedness) provided that they all possess or lack the property (exclusive association).

Architectural and material constraints impose uneven selective processes on firms in their attempts to reach competitive advantages. Further, structural inertia, prevailing logic, and social conformism reinforce the contra-Panglossian view of adaptation. In addition, the fact that firms strive to find the right combination of factors leading to a competitive advantage is independent of the actual adaptedness of the firm, because adaptedness is a supervenient property. A firm does not actually adapt; rather, it adopts characteristics in terms of resource combinations and exchange modes. A set of firms can exhibit more adaptedness relative to another set of firms. A firm can be more adapted to a given environment based on ex post analysis of the environmental conditions and the examination of the individual firm's traits. However, one can not relate this higher adaptation to an individual adaptedness (since adaptedness is a supervenient property); nor can one assume that the intended actions that were once formulated in a firm's strategy actually resulted in greater adaptation (because a theory of action does not coincide perfectly with real operations and outcomes). Therefore, a firm can be said to be better adapted than another only as an ex post observation – adaptation does not contain any predictive power at a firm level. It is possible to ascribe a greater degree of adaptedness to a firm only as a member of a cohort. In this case, the predictive power of adaptedness relates the cohort of firms to an explicit environmental property. Using a statistical distribution for adaptedness in the cohort, some firms receive more adaptedness than others. However, in practice this property ascription does not purport to identify which firm receives which adaptedness value, since the reasoning applies at the cohort (industry) level.

Therefore, the use of 'adaptation' should be banned from our scientific inquiries and analyses of organizational evolution when we seek to predict and experiment. We might prefer to use 'adaptedness' for a cohort of firms and use 'adopt' each time we refer to an individual firm, thus avoiding the adaptation tautology trap. Instead of saying, 'The firm adapts to its environment', consider, 'The firm adopts properties A and B'. This will help to eliminate the self-fulfilling, erroneous causal power ascription at both a level and a unit of analysis deprived of such capacity. Furthermore, we should not attribute any causal power to the fact that a firm's adoption of a practice (say, 360-degree evaluations) 'adapts' it to its local context. As interactors, firms bias replication processes, willingly or not. But the practice's attunement to a firm context does not explain competitive advantage, performance, and survival, for such an explanation falls into the tautology trap. What matters is the retained and replicable traits, properties, resources, capabilities, and so on that, from the firm's adopted actions, constitute selective differential events at the cohort level – a succession of events that we call economic history.

A positive facet of the OES model is that, overall, it is receptive to cautionary remarks, and it faces the various challenges posed by a serious approach to evolutionary phenomena. Further elements that amplify the potential value of the model follow.

6.3   OFFERING FURTHER PROPOSITIONS TO CONNECT ENTITIES AND RELATIONS

This section provides further details on the evolutionary stages and relationships involved in the OES model. It has two aims: first, to complement the OES model with additional information in terms of both the sources and nature of variations, retention, and selection processes, and secondly, to examine the fourteen intra- and inter-hierarchy relationships represented by arrows in Figure 6.2. Figure 6.4. synthesizes the propositions.

THE FOURTEEN ARROWS

Organizational variations take the form of new resource combinations, capability arrangements, and decision structures that are to be selected by concrete firms. We have defined strategy as a theory about competitiveness that helps organizational members to select among available resource utilization and exchange modes. At the organization-firm level, corporate strategy is, therefore, a selection of an organizational variant in line with the firm's theory of competitiveness (arrow 1).

Organizational variations are spurred by organizational integration, namely, the assimilation of influential resources and capabilities retained from the successively actualized competitive advantages (arrow 6). We call this retention process the resource sedimentation (arrow 4), whereby resources and capabilities participating toward a competitive advantage become vital for a firm to operate. The other major source of organizational variations concerns the structural rearrangements (arrow 8) proceeding from the retention of prior selected organizational

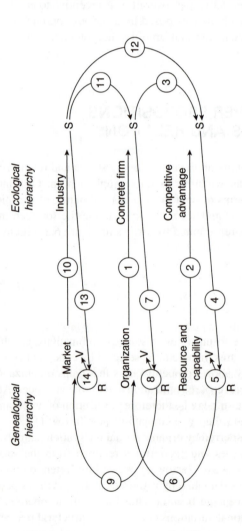

Figure 6.4 A representation of the Organizational Evolution and Strategy model

Relationships

1. Corporate strategy
2. Business strategy
3. Strategic management
4. Resource sedimentation
5. Opportunity generation
6. Organizational integration
7. Organizational incorporation
8. Structural rearrangements
9. Institutionalization
10. Industrial filtration
11. Full external selection
12. Partial external selection
13. Market assimilation
14. Market redefinition

Level	Sources of variation*	Retention processes**	Selection criteria**
Market – industry	*Institutional, ideological, and political movements* Market redefinition (14) Institutionalization (9)	Market assimilation (13) due to degrees of theorization and legitimization	Economic efficiency Social reproduction
Organization – firm	Structural rearrangements (8) Organizational integration (6)	Organizational incorporation (7) due to competitors' imitation	Governance efficiency Administrative coherence
R and C – competitive advantage	Opportunity generation (5) *Scientific research* *Socio-cognitive capabilities of individuals*	Resource sedimentation (4) due to imitation (managerial fads), learning, and professional institutionalization	Transactional efficiency Resource valuation

* Normal: in the scope of this book
Italic: out of the scope of this book

**Non-exhaustive lists

variants by concrete firms. We call this retention process at the organization-firm level the organizational incorporation (arrow 7).

But strategy is also about selecting resources and capabilities. Arrow 2 represents business-level strategy, namely, the selection of resources and capabilities which, combined, enable a firm to engender a competitive advantage according to the firm's theory of competitiveness. These resources and capabilities vary in their nature and properties, depending on what we term the opportunity generation (arrow 5). Opportunity generation refers to the many theoretical possibilities that exist in combining the sedimented resources and capabilities with existing or new ones. Opportunity generation leads to resource and capability variations (Denrell et al., 2003). Other series of variations correspond to the technological improvements, breakthroughs, and sense-making capability of individuals and firms that associate variants with existing elements in order to constitute a competitive advantage (Moran and Ghoshal, 1999; Rindova and Fombrun, 1999; Shane, 2000). As formerly defined, strategic management (arrow 3) is a set of concerted concrete actions that may (but do not necessarily) actualize the theorized competitive potentialities resulting from the combination of resources, organizational arrangements, and modes of exchange. This, in turn, may result in a competitive advantage.

The second major selective influence on competitive advantage comes from industry. As mentioned in the works of coevolutionists (Henderson and Stern, 2004), arrow 12 represents the partial external selection mechanism that selects parts of an organized firm but does not select the entire firm. Full external selection (arrow 11) refers to the selection of an entire concrete organizational arrangement controlling resources and exchanges, namely a firm (Barnett and McKendrick, 2004).

In turn, concrete industries are selected expressions of market variations. Incumbent companies and new entrants (de novo firms or diversifiers) tinker with the available market variants, enforce rules of acting, and use uncharted interpretations of those to undertake actions (Beckert, 1999; Fiss and Zajac, 2004; Garud et al., 2002). We call this selection process industrial filtration (arrow 10), which actualizes market variations into concrete industrial situations.

Market variations proceed from the upward accumulation of numerous organizational traits that trigger legal, regulative, and normative variations at the market-level definition (Dobbin, 1994, 1995). Broadly speaking, we refer to this inter-level retention process as institutionalization (arrow 9). We have already mentioned that institutional negotiations, ideological battles, and political movements can introduce further variations at the market level definition, which are then filtered by industries and their corresponding constituents, firms (Casile and Davis-Blake, 2002; MacKenzie and Millo, 2003; Rao et al., 2003).

Market variations are also triggered by the retention of selected industrial variants (arrow 13) that, in turn, trigger new variations (arrow 14). Thus, arrow 13 represents market assimilation of concrete industrial forms that legitimizes industrial structures (for example, oligopolies and vertical integration) and functioning such as technological standardization through joint consortium, retail agreements, and so forth (Kogut and Walker, 2001; Kogut et al., 2002). Market redefinition (arrow 14) spurs market variants based on former real market organizations and recently-actualized industrial forms.

THE VARIATION, SELECTION, AND RETENTION PROCESSES

Figure 6.4 depicts the relationships between the involved entities and the VSR processes. Sources of variations come from different relationships, some within the scope of this book and others beyond it. The retention processes could be further analyzed; for example, market assimilation (arrow 13) is a function of the degree of theorization and legitimization at the market-industry level. By theorization, we mean the degree of industrial logic articulation needed for an industrial organization to endure (Lounsbury, 2002, 2004). For instance, the French industry structure favors the retention of particular types of market variants. An industry leader, deeply connected with the state through personnel, finance, and purchase relationships, commands an ensemble of first-circle private suppliers, which guarantee business for a second-circle of small enterprises (Hancké, 2001). By legitimization, we refer to the generally accepted economic structure resulting from the selected market variants (Dobbin, 1995; Fligstein, 1996). For instance, Japanese keiretsu have seemed to be out of fashion, Korean conglomerates have streamlined their operations, and opaque connections between US accounting and consulting agencies needed clarification. All three examples illustrate fading legitimacies of once-praised industrial arrangements.

At the organization-firm level, organizational incorporation relies mainly on imitation. A selected organizational variant may be adopted by rivals and spur a diffusion process (Greve, 1998). As a consequence, the initial advantage of the selected organizational arrangement is likely to be reduced, but it is retained in the genealogical hierarchy and spawns a new variation.

At the finer level, resource sedimentation springs from several factors. Imitation among and between top executives leading to managerial fads can influence the retention of a set of resources and capabilities (Fiss and Zajac, 2004; Westphal and Zajac, 2001). Learning, both within a company and derived vicariously from others' experiences, undoubtedly enforces retention of certain proven resources and capabilities (Miner and Raghavan, 1999). Identity movements in professions (Rao et al., 2003), which are specifically related to capabilities, generate retention processes that impact opportunity generation (arrow 5) and organizational integration (arrow 6). While this list is not exhaustive, it shows how the applicability of the general framework is not restricted to fixed entities, levels, and relationships.

Concerning selection, we found that selection criteria differ both from one level of analysis to the next and between periods. At the market-industry level, the selection criteria deal with economic efficiency and social reproduction. Regarding economic efficiency, on the one hand, national and regional economic systems confront each other along diverse dimensions, such as financing of education systems, public vs. private appropriation of research findings, balance between direct and indirect taxes, and incentives to individual initiatives (Hall and Soskice, 2001; Kogut et al., 2002). These diverse dimensions demonstrate different degrees of economic efficiency in terms of both new industry generation and current and new firm competitiveness. On the other hand, social reproduction characterizes how social structures endure inside and across firms, conveying prejudice and privilege, entitlement and justification, and so on – phenomena that in theory and practice bias individual and collective agents' economic attributions of rewards and survival probabilities (Benjamin and Podolny, 1999; Hayward and Hambrick, 1997; Hayward et al., 2004; Rao et al., 2001).

At the organization-firm level, selection criteria include governance efficiency and administrative coherence. Governance efficiency concerns who presides over companies, on which sociological and political bases, and under what types of control and accountability conditions (for example, Davis and Greve, 1997; Jensen and Zajac, 2004). Administrative coherence concerns the degree of coherence between and amongst the various resources and capabilities mobilized for rent generation and appropriation, as well as the correspondence between this resource and capability portfolio and the selected organizational arrangement. For example, too much diversity in the resource and capability portfolio leads to underperformance, while franchise or alliance as specific types of organizational arrangement enable a firm to earn rents based on a limited set of well-mastered resources and capabilities (Palich et al., 2000; Winter and Szulanski, 2002).

At the finer level of analysis, transactional efficiency and resource valuation determine the selection of available resources and capabilities (Jacobides and Winter, 2005). Transactional efficiency covers the cost-and-benefit structure of the procedures that are in order to perform exchanges (Poppo and Zenger, 1998; Williamson, 1985, 1999). It depends on the frequency and nature of exchanges as well as the position and behavior of the involved parties (for example, Michael, 2000; Stabell and Fjelstad, 1998). Resource valuation refers to the ability of agents to estimate the rent potential of available resources and capabilities in an organized setting. It is dependent upon resource and capability properties, potential services and extant know-how, and opportunity recognition (Makadok and Barney, 2001; Moran and Ghoshal, 1999; Denrell et al., 2003).

Overall, the proposed relationships, sources of variations, retention processes, and selection criteria are not definitive but tentative conceptualizations that help to integrate the OES model with more concrete notions, observable factors, and previously-researched fields. Future refinements are needed in order to establish closer connections between the different ideas and disciplines and to present a more coherent and workable theory of the links between organizational evolution and strategic management.

ANTICIPATING THREE DIFFICULTIES

While the OES model does not presume to solve every difficulty innate to organizational evolution and strategic management, this sub-section hints at how to address three among these remaining difficulties. First, like any model inspired by a VSR approach, the OES model ignores discontinuous changes. One may ask how the OES model accounts for abrupt changes of economic regimes and whether it is compatible with the dialectical motor of evolution often discussed in political and organizational sciences. The OES model seems fairly gradual; however, this criticism is not as strong as it might appear. In fact, nothing prevents anyone from envisioning radical opportunity generations (arrow 5) and market redefinitions (arrow 14) that disrupt the standing theories of competitive advantages. Christensen (1997) presents convincing arguments explaining how and why disruptive strategies can supplant incumbents' taken-for-granted strategies. We do not see incompatibilities between disruptive models of strategic change and the OES model. We do not consider the succession of intense periods of trials (eras of ferment) and stabilizing phases (dominant designs) promoted by Utterback (1994) to be incompatible with the OES model. However, the OES model eliminates the adaptation magic from the explanation. Instead of invoking natural evolutionary patterns, it prefers to account for the ebbs and flows of technological races by utilizing the factual characteristics of competition for rent-bearing technologies. There is no necessity for life cycles. Remember, competition drives evolution, not vice versa.

A second criticism is that the OES model would leave the inner workings of the firm in the dark. The OES model would mobilize few mechanisms of organizational action. Organizational rationalities, behavior, and process would remain under-represented. However, research shows that the OES model can address these concerns, via two means at least. The resource valuation selection criteria and the role they play in the OES model (Figure 6.4) provide the first opportunity to enter the black box of firms in relation to their counterparts' and rivals' valuation abilities and to connect organizational behavior and cognition research with the OES model (Greve, 2003). The other possibility of integration concerns the moderating impact that these inner mechanisms have on, at least, both the downward selection processes (external selection and strategic management) and the strategy formulation (both corporate and business). Efforts are pending to dovetail the rich extant literature in organizational behavior with broader evolutionary models, such as the OES model.

Finally, what is intriguing about these evolutionary descriptions is the absence of certain simple questions: is strategic change always necessary and good? Is resistance to strategic change legitimate? Who benefits from the decisions? Top executives run companies and would guide evolution (Lovas and Ghoshal, 2000). Embedded in their organizational position is the power to formulate strategies and objectives, to address stakeholders' queries, and to magnify energy and logic in order to realize those strategies and objectives. However a large space separates formulation from implementation (Fiss and Zajac, 2004; Westphal and Zajac, 2001). Within it, stakeholders' interests diverge dramatically. So far, few evolutionary and ecology researchers have dealt with these issues although some business school scholars have considered the ethical values and social implications that strategy and strategic management promulgate (Clegg, 2002; Durand and Calori, 2006; Walsh and Margolis, 2003). Since the OES model insists not only on actions and events but also on values and theories that strategy applies and extends between and among organizations, an overlap exists between the OES model and deeper philosophical views of human desires, volition, and action.

6.4   SUMMARY

The OES model reconciles the respective imperatives raised by the coincident study of organizational evolution and strategic management. Most of the questions, cautions, and challenges raised in the earlier parts of this book seem to have been dispelled by the OES model (Table 6.1. and Figure 6.4.). Noteworthy points of the OES model include the following:

- Final causes neither drive nor cause organizational evolution.
- Several levels of organizational evolution are observable, depending on the process involved (variation, selection, and retention) and the type of relationship under scrutiny.
- Competition drives evolution.
- Selection criteria vary across levels and over time. Selection processes are directional (downward causation) and not purely efficient (weak competitors can be strong survivors).
- There is no ascribed ending to organizational evolution.
- There is not such a high discontinuity between micro- and macro- processes as in traditional biological research. Vertical and horizontal relationships between entities are more conceivable and observable than in biological research.
- Strategy and strategic management constitute an integral part of the OES conceptualization.
- The dual-hierarchy OES model is compatible with higher and lower levels of analysis and interpretations, in terms of political, sociological, and psychological influences. The latter are conducive to variations, they influence retention processes, and they affect the definition of selection criteria.

Moreover, the survival and adaptation tautologies have been eliminated. Selection does not select individual firms; rather, it selects distributed properties in liaison with environmental conditions. Adaptation as a problematical notion seems inapplicable to the scientific study of organizational evolution at the organization-firm level. We offered two tricks to avoid the adaptation trap: to replace the verb 'adapt' with 'adopt', as the former underscores the teleological and Panglossian nature of adaptation whereas the latter stresses the firm's influence on modifying the frequency of practices at the industry level; and to reserve adaptedness as a supervenient property applied at a collective level – such as a cohort or an industry.

Although our progress is encouraging, some issues deserve further clarification. Notably, the nature of causality in the proposed model is incomplete. Also, the epistemological nature of the VSR framework, questioned in Chapter 4, has not yet been solved. Epistemological and empirical considerations are now in order, to further appreciate the applicability and validity of the OES representation.

Baum and Singh (1994b)		Baum and Rao (2000)		Volberda and Lewin (2003)		Durand (2000) This book, Figure 6.1.	
Genealogical hierarchy	Ecological hierarchy	Genealogical hierarchy	Ecological hierarchy	Genealogical hierarchy	Ecological hierarchy	Genealogical hierarchy	Ecological hierarchy
Polyphetic group/species/ organization/ routine	Ecosystem/ community/ population/ organization/ work group/job	Organizational form/ organization/ routine	Community/ Population/ Organization/ Job	Competencies/ capabilities/ routines	Population/ multi-unit firm/ unit	Market/ Organization/ Resource and capability	Industry/ Concrete firm/ Competitive advantage

APPENDIX: ENTITIES IN THE ORGANIZATIONAL EVOLUTION MODEL

Figure 6.1 represents the two hierarchies and three levels of analysis. While both hierarchies are present in Baum and Singh (1994b) and Baum and Rao (2000), a comment is in order on the differences between the entities we use in the OES, tentative representation.

Why, in Figure 6.1, do we use: market/organization/resource and capability (genealogical hierarchy) and industry/firm/competitive advantage (ecological hierarchy), as in Durand (2000: 277)?

Baum and Singh's (1994b) work seems imbued with biological analogies and imperfectly relates to organizations, what they do (production and delivery), and what they use to act (resources and capabilities). In addition, genealogical hierarchy consists of four levels in their model, whereas the mirroring ecological hierarchy has six different levels, which raises the problem of correspondence between the two hierarchies.

Baum and Rao (2000) reduces the number of levels but contains some other problems. Organization is present in both hierarchies, for instance. The notion of 'job' is sociological in nature and matches imperfectly with a competitive view of organizational evolution. However, units used in our Figure 6.1 are very close in inspiration to Baum and Rao (2000). One major difference is our use of 'market' instead of 'organizational forms'; population ecology is Baum and Rao's principal theoretical basis while it is only one stream of research in this book. The second difference concerns 'competitive advantage' instead of 'job'. Competitive advantage is a concept that relates a firm's selective actions to its competitiveness and theoretically provides the firm with higher odds of success, be it profits, survival, or another outcome; job, on the other hand, is agnostic as far as performance or survival is concerned, which is problematic for selection and retention stages.

Finally, Volberda and Lewin's (2003) proposition, while interesting, bears a risk of misunderstanding. Their genealogical hierarchy lacks clarity on a certain point, as competencies, capabilities, and routines in the genealogical hierarchy belong to the same genre of factor. They do not display differences in the level of action. Finally, they do not match the corresponding three entities in the ecological hierarchy, as competencies, capabilities and routines might be attributed to any of the three ecological entities (population, multi-unit firm, and unit).

7 IMPLICATIONS

Given the abandonment of positivism by current philosophers, the misconception of positivist epistemology by social science postpositivists, and lack of a coherent replacement epistemology that conforms to the expectations of normal science and higher status sciences, the field of organization science is in great need of a new organizational epistemology. (Baum and McKelvey, 1999: 5)

Observers of business life (scholars and practitioners together) face contingent and sometimes contradictory cues that blur their understanding of the role and importance of strategy and strategic management in organizational evolution. The prevalence of one analysis level over the others (industry vs. firm vs. resource), the decoupling of human intention from organizational outcomes, and the complex intra- and inter- relationships within and between organizations make the elaboration and implementation of strategy an arduous task. The OES model fixes certain parameters that help reduce complexity and uncertainty. Strategy is a firm-level theory about competitiveness that helps organizational members to select among available resource utilizations and exchange modes. Strategic management is a set of concrete actions that strive to actualize the theorized competitive potentialities resulting from the combination of resources and modes of exchange. Henderson and Mitchell (1997: 12) define strategy and performance as 'an ongoing sequence of capabilities-conditioned adaptations by firms which, in turn, become exogenous events in the environments of the managers of other firms'. We prefer to modify their definition and represent the relationships between strategy and performance as an ongoing sequence of selection-criteria adoptions about capabilities and organizational arrangements by firms that, in turn, become exogenous events in the environments of the managers of other firms.

The OES model offers answers to the five original questions about strategy and strategic management raised in Chapter 2. They are as follows: first, strategy does not possess a particular time efficacy of its own. Secondly, however, it has a real influence on a firm's becoming, for it leads to reinforcement or attrition of selection criteria at various levels of analysis: competitive advantage, firm, and industry levels. Thirdly, the essence of strategy is its influence on selection criteria, either directly or indirectly. Fourthly, strategic management is a cause of organizational evolution, as it is a concrete series of actions that impose utilizations, constrain choices, and shape meanings. Fifthly, the influence of intentionality on organizational evolution is subsumed into the real and concrete actions undertaken by firms when implementing the envisioned strategy; intentions and theories do not directly fashion reality (McKelvey, 1997: 361).

Strategy, therefore, is about articulating a theory of competitiveness, electing selection criteria (wittingly or unwittingly), and making decisions to support or reverse them. Evidence shows that selection does not act as a rapid and smooth optimizing principle contrary to the hypothesis of historical efficiency; and, therefore, an evolutionary perspective must acknowledge how selection processes affect and are affected by the pace and path of strategic change (Barnett and Burgelman, 1996). The OES model explicitly recognizes the importance of the different types of selection determinants and renders it worthwhile to distinguish between different levels of selection criteria. It is also important to recognize that selection criteria can be firm specific, and that a good-strategizing firm can increase its rivals' selection pressure. For instance, strategically betting on search routines, creative capabilities, and knowledge absorption can help a firm ease its selection constraints or increase its competitors' selection constraints (Durand, 2001). From this, it follows that selection criteria must not be considered as immutable, blind, and exogenous dimensions; in fact, they are the core of strategic analysis, formulation, and implementation.

These ideas express the distinct facets of what could be called 'evolutionary strategic management'. Evolutionary strategy is not limited to the effects of actions on performance criteria. It also encompasses the influence of the decisions on future selection criteria and pressure at the market, organization, and resource levels. Selection criteria do not have a timeless value. Thus, managers should take advantage of the determinants that shape selection criteria in order to escape the pressure of selection or to enhance selection in other industries. Furthermore, a firm can concurrently undertake several changes whose selection contents differ, a situation that is often ignored in research but not in practice. (For instance, firms can, over the years, combine goals and actions that preserve and transform selection criteria in an effort to hedge risks.) Future studies in strategic management should conduct research in these promising directions.

In this last chapter we develop some of the epistemological, theoretical, empirical, and practical implications of the OES model. At the epistemological level, four questions attract our attention. What is the epistemological posture required to produce cumulative knowledge? Can the VSR model serve as a paradigm? What is the role of individuals in evolution? And what is their responsibility in choosing selection criteria? At the theoretical level, we suggest extensions for the various subfields of research presented in this book. At the empirical level, we plead for an integration of four methodological realms: mathematical models, simulations, statistical analyses, and qualitative studies. Finally, at the practical level, a four-step strategic analysis is outlined.

7.1   EPISTEMOLOGICAL IMPLICATIONS

Four important epistemological implications permeate this book.

First, an epistemological stance holds throughout. In this book, as in many others, reality is thought to be governed by causal relationships between entities, which a scientific examination will uncover (Ackroyd and Fleetwood, 2000; Bunge, 2001). Organizational evolution is caused, and organization science strives to reveal the why and the wherefore. This does not deny the possibility of and interest in deconstructing texts, scripts, and discourses. On the contrary, the capacity to identify and document ideological inflections and to produce interpretative knowledge is necessary in order to relate theories of action to concrete actions, namely, parts of strategic discourses to effective strategic management. However, when it comes to scientific (namely, testable, falsifiable, and replicable) knowledge, misgivings arise about epistemologies that are imbued with an insufficient ontology of objects and properties (incessantly redefined by actors and observers), an instrumental theory of what is true, a moderate exigency of coherence in propositions, and an omnipotent conception of beliefs (Ackroyd and Fleetwood, 2004; Durand and Vaara, 2005; Tsang and Kwan, 1999). From the OES perspective, as illustrated by the quote that opens this chapter, we should favor epistemologies that rely on definable objects and properties, demand a certain degree of correspondence between the concepts and the objects, command a high degree of coherence among propositions, provide a sound definition of causality, separate testable propositions from beliefs, and encourage replication (Donaldson, 2003; Durand, 2002; Fleetwood, 2004; Huber and Mirowski, 1997; Kwan and Tsang, 2001). Many epistemologies gather these characteristics within a range that includes what has been qualified as moderated positivism, various forms of realism, and even certain aspects of moderated constructivism.[1]

Secondly, we suspended our response to the question of whether the VSR model is a paradigm or a loose framework. Although further study is needed, the reproaches addressed to the traditional VSR model seem valid and, therefore, we should perhaps consider the VSR model too slim a reed on which to build a paradigm for organizational evolution. Specifically, it is weakened by its acceptance of relatively heterogeneous theories (population ecology, evolutionary economics, dynamic RBV, and sociocultural evolution) as well as its difficulty in articulating human intentionality with intangible selective mechanisms. Nonetheless, this book uses the legacy of prior VSR formulations and attempts to devise an integrative model, although, like its predecessors, this formulation is not exempt from limitations. But the OES model does successfully offset some of the VSR model's existing deficiencies and could perhaps be a step on the road toward a more complete representation of the intertwined relationships between strategic management and organizational evolution.

Third, as a substantially modified version of the original Campbellian model, the OES model must tackle the ontological question confronting the reality of individuals against the reality of organizations (Hayward et al., 2004). Campbell asks us to consider organizations as ontologically real, and he downplays the influence in sociocultural evolutions not of individuals in general but of any individual qua individual (see sections 4.1 and 4.4). Apart from Campbell's theses, the OES model integrates the ideas of influential individuals along with organized capacities to fashion selection criteria at various levels of analysis. Thus, individual expression and personal human freedom, in theory as well as in practice, affect the path of history, be it organizational, economic, social, or political. Firms are not vehicles for genetic replication but for the embodiment of individual aspirations (Lounsbury and Glynn, 2001). However, as interactors, firms adopt choices and are selected on grounds almost entirely independent of these individual aspirations (economic efficiency, social reproduction, governance efficiency, administrative coherence, transactional efficiency, and resource valuation). In other words, while individual aspirations may be causes for an individual's participation in a concrete firm, individual aspirations are not the cause of the firm's competitive advantage and survival odds.

Finally, while evolutionary frameworks do not conventionally deal with human nature, relationships between individuals, and ideology, the OES model provides the minimal elements for a more realistic theory of organizational evolution in place of the tame references to genuine favorable trends or super-human individual traits. Power, ethics, and philosophical dispositions of actors count among the long-neglected dimensions of strategic change and organizational evolution models (Stern and Barley, 1996; Hinings and Greenwood, 2002; Durand and Calori, 2006). The OES model proposes explicit connections between theories about competitiveness (and the supportive ideologies that come from historical, institutional, and political traditions) and the applied actions that implement techniques to exploit resources, value capabilities, and extract rents. The OES model does not excuse anyone from playing her role in the vibrating organizational evolution generator. Everybody tinkers with selection criteria. The OES model requires that CEOs, VPs, managers, and every organizational member – not to forget business schools' scholars – face their historical responsibility and accountability.

7.2   THEORETICAL IMPLICATIONS AND IDEAS FOR A RESEARCH AGENDA

This section assesses how the OES model could help to advance the fields of organizational evolution and strategy by drawing them closer to each other, avoiding high- and low-church infighting disputes, and having the field cohere around simple and falsifiable principles. In this section we provide some suggestions for advancing the various theoretical approaches that have been presented in this book.

CONTRIBUTIONS TO STRATEGY RESEARCH AND STRATEGIC CHOICES

The OES model assumes that every firm's action is a choice that influences the value of existing selection criteria. No resource selection or organizational arrangement choice can be neutral on competition. On the one hand, we have shown that adaptation theory arguments are misplaced due to the intrinsic conceptual limitations of fit and the epistemological trap of the very notion of adaptation. On the other hand, inertia arguments assume that respect and maintenance of current selection criteria is the best passport to performance and survival. The OES model prefers to associate any firm decision with its relevant selection criteria (Figure 6.4.) At the market-industry level, selection criteria concern economic efficiency and social reproduction. At the organization-firm level, they are governance efficiency and administrative coherence. The criteria at the resource-competitive advantage level are transactional efficiency and resource valuation. A firm must decide whether its selection-criteria choices should respect the prevalent industry structure, social reproduction principles, and competition logic or transform these conditions. Hence, we could distinguish two categories of strategic choices: selection-preserving choices (SPC), and selection-transforming choices (STC).

In the OES model, every firm's choice equals a selection-criterion choice that increases or relaxes the selective pressure on competitors. In other words, an SPC maintains established rules of action and puts pressure on competitors to conform to the current model of competition, whereas an STC requires the firm's competitors to react to new selective rules and criteria. Increase in the rivals' selection pressure may enable a firm to reduce rivals' profitability, in absolute and relative values. For example, an offering respectful of local and historical traditions preserves the extant selection process and price-fixing mechanisms whereas another offering combining imaginatively technologies, services, and cultural symbols compel competitors to elaborate a new theory of their competitiveness and act accordingly. As a consequence, SPC and STC are not *ex post* concepts (as fit), and the nature of the environment is not given *a priori* (turbulent or not, competitive or not) but results from the nature of the firm's choices (and not vice versa). The environment is no longer independent of the undertaken choices; rather, it derives from them.

SPC and STC have different consequences for a firm. External consequences pertain to the effects of a choice on the image and social categorization of the firm within its industry (Dutton and Dukerich, 1991; Gioia and Thomas, 1996), namely, vis-à-vis the social reproduction criteria. For instance, the distinction between the social determinants of status and its economic components is especially important in globalizing high-tech or cultural industries, where cost strategy does not entirely explain competitive advantage. In particular, in cultural and artistic industries, social reproduction selection criteria are of the utmost importance, as competitive advantage relies more on socially-constructed and accepted signals (like awards, grades, or rankings) than on economic indicators of quality such as energy consumption, power, and obsolescence (Phillips and Zuckerman, 2001; Washington and Zajac, 2005). External agencies and third parties participate in the social stratification, endowing or severing status to competing firms (Zuckerman, 1999). Accreditation agencies, watchdog associations, and rating agencies, to cite a few examples, do more than provide an accepted evaluation on product quality; they also confer a position in terms of firm social status (Rao, 1998; Durand and McGuire, 2005), and past studies have shown that positional rank is associated with advantages related or not to prior performance (Washington and Zajac, 2005).

SPCs exploit the current knowledge and firm identity to improve a firm's image as being an innovator within the same social order. Innovative but conforming actions reduce the selection pressure for the focal firm. By contrast, STCs exhibit the capacity of a firm to fashion its environment. STCs seek to draw on new knowledge and business logic and to favorably alter the image of the firm, appearing as a genial rule-breaker and/or an 'ambidextrous' organization mixing tradition and novelty, combining exploitation and exploration. These alterations are cues captured by participants in the social order who potentially value such a differentiation, as evidenced by their willingness to pay a premium price for STC. Thus, SPCs illustrate how an organization deploys its innovativeness and deftness in a category. Ability to maintain a higher rate of SPCs than its competition should favor a firm's competitive advantage. However, while riskier than SPCs, STCs are probably more likely to enable the firm to increase its expected profit differential from the industry average.

Other factors may moderate the direct influences of SPC and STC on competitive advantage. First, both choices have different impacts on a firm's organization. Internal consequences deal with the competencies of the firm (Teece et al., 1997), its learning capacity and the identity of organizational members (Elsbach and Kramer, 1996; Scott and Lane, 2000). Overall, STCs are more likely than SPCs to put at higher risk the firm's competence, learning capacity, and identity. Secondly, the relationships between SPCs, STCs and competitive advantage must be considered relatively to rivals' actions. Whether one changes more or less than a competitor is as consequential as how much one changes in absolute value (Barnett and Hansen, 1996; Deephouse, 1999). Thirdly, decision-makers select concepts and visions from available theories of actions and make them perform into concrete strategic managerial actions. How intensely and how many of these existing theories of actions populate the environment moderate how firms' individual SPCs and STCs impact competitive advantage. For instance, in an industry that features a quarrel of moderns against ancients, the question comes down to which of SPCs, STCs, or a mix of SPCs-STCs provides a greater performance. One may track over time the many actions of a firm extolling modernist philosophy and choices and scrutinize whether the firm mixes or not actions, products, and offerings that belong to both categories – with a strategy of hedging social and identity risks. One could compare such a hedging strategy vis-à-vis conforming firms that do not intertwine philosophies and actions. Interestingly, in contexts where a plurality of philosophies are present, a distinction between different types of STCs could shed further light on which of the underlying values and concepts that pervade groups of competitors end being retained into resources, capabilities, and organizational traits.

The OES model may help strategic and organizational literature avoid certain predicaments regarding STCs and SPCs. In particular, part of the literature touts the merits of STC on the grounds of adaptation to an organization's environment, while other works contend that STCs are disruptive and likely inefficacious. As a consequence, strategists and practitioners are left in a quandary as to whether STCs contribute to performance or not. In sum, they are asked to make transformative choices, but not too much nor too often. We believe that the inclusion of SPC and STC relative to peers within a framework such as the OES model may alleviate, at least in part, the contradictions that derive from inappropriate assumptions dear to organizational evolution works (individual reductionism on the part of adaptation advocates, and ultra-selectionism for the inertia proponents). SPC and STC are not incompatible; they can be conducted concurrently by a firm. They both contribute positively to a firm's advantage although differently depending on a firm's characteristics, and the other companies' choices. Therefore, the OES model can accommodate apparently irreconcilable arguments and recommendations.

Future studies in this area would extend research in five directions. First, viewing firm choices as preserving or modifying prevalent selection criteria offers a new lens through which to evaluate a firm's choices that goes beyond the notion of strategic balance (Deephouse, 1999), the models of strategic fit and adaptation (Siggelkow, 2001), and the approaches in terms of inertia (Hannan and Freeman, 1989), which suffer from severe drawbacks. Secondly, while numerous studies have explored whether change is beneficial or harmful, the OES model offers a framework in which to focus on both the content and process effects of choices on competitive advantage. One can study not only if, when, and how often decisive actions occur but also the nature of these actions (Barnett and Carroll, 1995) as preserving or transforming the prevalent selection criteria in many changing industrial contexts with conflicting institutional logics. Thirdly, such an approach defines the sets of actions undertaken by firms to deliver their competitive offering, assuming a preeminent role of firms in the process of industry evolution – rather than considering industry influences as a given to be integrated into a firm's adaptive reaction. Fourthly, this approach is amenable (as detailed below) to elaborated regression models that take into account many of the criticisms directed against conventional variance analyses (see section 2.2. earlier in this book). Finally, this approach contributes to a realistic understanding of how competitive advantage is being built and improved in the socially-bound contexts of industries. Therefore, we advocate for a social characterization of firm choices that would complement an economic valuation to better explain strategic outcomes, such as competitive, status, and pricing advantages.

CONTRIBUTIONS TO POPULATION ECOLOGY

A great difference between the OES model and population ecology resides not only in the distinction of two genealogies but also in the integration of three levels of selection, pointing to the infra-level as essential for the dynamics of retentions and variations. In a sense, population ecology models of the 1970s to 1990s are over-focused on exclusive identification of the sources of selection in the firm's environment. To an extent, this corresponds to nineteenth-century 'fixism', in which species, populations, and codes are displaced and replaced due to exogenous shocks. In particular, while insisting on legitimacy and competition, these models miss the sources and explanations of legitimacy and competition, which is a serious problem. At worst, they could be considered as mere empirical extensions of mathematical and statistical properties of groups, populations, and ecological environments.[2] At best, they comfort scholars by pointing out that, with certain restrictions on the definition of an organization and a population, organizational populations respect deduced patterns and phenomena observed in other contexts (species dominance and genetic diffusion, among others). But if one uses definitions of organization and population that respect the assumptions of the extant biological and ecological models, why would it be otherwise? There is a great risk of seeing organizations in terms of what is required for a model to perform its task: justifying the observers' perception and their *ex ante* methodological intuition. Empirical results would be method-laden. Besides, the novel agenda of population ecology cannot compensate for these inherent deficiencies (Polos et al., 2002; Hannan et al., 2003). Human agency is still ethereal, definitions of codes remain almost as exogenous and fixist as organizational forms were, and selection effects still require materiality and better connection with embodied actors (Durand et al., 2004). At the root of these deficiencies, this book argues, population ecology falls short on theorization despite its remarkable attempt.

Notwithstanding these shortcomings, population ecology research has provided building blocks to erect a sounder conception of organizational evolution. One way to fortify the results of population ecology is to integrate into its theories and models more indicators that account for governance characteristics (such as ownership types, sociopolitical assets embodied in owners, founders, and managers), transaction efficiency (wherein organizations are seen as interactors more than as vehicles), and resource valuation. Tying together these individual assets (that are representative of broader sociological, economic, and cognitive properties) would help to avoid the probably delusory quest for abstraction of population laws (Baum and Dobbin, 2000).

Another avenue for further reflection hinges on deepening the theoretical use of the supervenience property. Instead of focusing on forms, populations, and codes, population ecology might reorient its agenda towards a trans-form attribution of properties across individuals. Inspired by Sober's niece's toy, it could reconceptualize part of its theoretical roots, and move away from its oftentimes limiting selectionism. For instance, legitimacy would not derive *ex nihilo* from the demographic characteristics of populations, but from the social qualities of an organization's members (including affiliation, status, and capital). Organizational ecology would then reflect the selection of socialized attributes and properties, branching its analysis out to the history of political and ideological disputes.

Finally, as a matter of fact, population ecology needs more theorizing not on the relationships between its entities, but on the entities themselves. As philosophers remark (Sober, 1984: 168; Matthen and Ariew, 2002), population thinking is not an ontological thesis about existence or the causal impact of anything. It puts things in relation to one another. Yet, what organizational scholars need are deeper approaches to concepts – such as resources, organizations, agents, institutions, codes, and so forth – and to their associations with the properties and attributes that cross-cut organizations. Whereas we understand what a green sphere refers to, since the concepts of greenness and sphere are recognized cognitive categories, we have less understanding of what a specialist organization competing within a complex environment refers to. Interpretations of the latter notions of specialization and of environmental complexity are wide open, leading to theoretical and methodological holes that plague results with qualms and doubt. Maybe a different light can be shed on organizational selection, and in particular on how organizational actions influence the selection criteria, based on the OES model.

In sum, from this book's perspective a further integration of selection criteria (governance efficiency, transactional efficiency, and resource valuation), a reflection about trans-form properties, a better definition of the ontological nature of concepts, and a more plastic notion of selection will enable organizational ecology to unfold and thrive.

CONTRIBUTION TO FIT AND ADAPTATION DEBATES

Fit and adaptation have been presented as representative of 'magical holistic' concepts. *Magical* because the fit's dimensions of correspondence, coherence, and complementarity are unexplained blanket assumptions that relate an entity to its surroundings. *Holistic* because an entity's fit implies a larger property above and beyond the entity's individual properties – the properties that determine whether the entity matches its environment. There is a magic trick in attributing a property to an entity that surreptitiously concerns a broader and external unit. Adaptation is also problematic. The very idea of adaptation does not acknowledge the incredible wastefulness of trials, but concentrates on the 'successful' observable results of evolutionary processes which have not yet been theorized (Hull et al., 2001). Moreover, it concentrates most of our research efforts whereas non-adaptive alternatives of technological change and organizational evolution exist (see section 5.3; Dew et al., 2004). What was stated in Chapter 6 bears repeating. Adaptation intrinsically contains a teleological component that condemns it to be sidelined from a scientific approach to studying organizational evolution.

Magical holistic concepts such as adaptation and fit oversimplify the analysis: they save the researchers from the need to attribute fitness value to organizational entities. We as scholars tend to generalize fitness properties at different levels of analysis (a resource fits in an organizational setting, an organization fits in an environment) without detailing or justifying if fitness is or means identical things at each level. Studies that involve magical holistic concepts like fit and adaptation often employ techniques such as mathematical models or computer simulations independently of the nature of entities and levels. Therefore, saying that organizational evolution depends on organizational fitness adds little value to the analysis. The concept of overall fitness and the idea that there is selection of entire organizations fail to capture the causal structure that the concept of selection for properties is designed to characterize. 'The claim that we want to make is that while predictive fitness values are predictors of trends in populations, and may thus be considered probabilistic causes, they are not causes in the sense appropriate to fundamental processes' (Matthen and Ariew, 2002: 79).

This book therefore pleads for a thoughtful use of the fitness notion based on three simple rules: first, do not apply fitness at an individual firm level, but only at a collective level. Secondly, spell out the density function of fitness as applied to the collections of entities. Thirdly, signal which observable attributes correspond to the properties that fitness associates with replicative and/or competitive advantages. As for the fit and adaptation notions, we have recommended not using it in our scientific inquiries as causal mechanisms. Each time the adaptation idea emerges in researchers' minds, they need to switch 'adapt' to 'adopt' (such as, 'adopt an action that preserves or transforms selection criteria') in order to avoid falling into the Panglossian trap.

CONTRIBUTION TO EVOLUTIONARY ECONOMICS

Recent models in evolutionary economics cultivate mathematical sophistication and computer simulations. However, their fundamental bases remain unchanged. They explain technological diffusion, industrial structure, and performance, relying on simplistic path-dependent varying selective thresholds and behavioral assumptions of firms (Lomi and Larsen, 2001; Silverberg et al., 1988). A great effort is needed to encompass sociological stratification effects on firm selection and feedback effects of organizational incorporation on organizational variations (see Figure 6.4., arrows 7, 11, and 12). Selective thresholds must not limit themselves to a cost advantage; rather, they need to integrate sociological determinants (social reproduction selective criteria) as well as economic efficiency selection criteria. Technological innovations entail considerably more consequences than cost reductions do. They take the form of social acceptance of body control, social contrast, and personalized individuation. Furthermore, the definition of firms used in evolutionary economics needs to encapsulate findings from strategy literature in terms of governance efficiency and administrative coherence. Moreover, simulations should integrate more asynchrony in their models to account for idiosyncratic characteristics of firms. Indeed, evolutionary economics possesses the assets to conceptualize anew temporality in competitive models. Firms still experience time simultaneously and identically in evolutionary models despite the existing research that shows how organizational times differ within and between organizations (for example, Huy, 2001). In relation to a universal clock, computerized agents could act for and against selection-preserving and selection-transforming determinants at their own rhythm (based on perceptual, cognitive, and technological capacities.) The resulting evolution, based on an asynchronous competitive behavior that relaxes time uniformity across firms, should impact industry traits (price, differentiation, performance) and technological characteristics (diffusion, lock-in, inertia). Finally and more generally, dependent variables of interest in evolutionary economics research should consider other dimensions of performance, such as transactional efficiency and resource valuation capabilities.

CONTRIBUTION TO DYNAMIC RBV

Chapter 6 states that the culling action of firm selection does not rely on immutable, invariable, or absolute criteria. Survival concerns a cohort of individuals for whom occurrences of distributed properties cohabit in both stand-alone (in a controlled resource) and compound states (in a capability that activates the services of unused resources.) Hence, at the firm level, the distribution of rent-accruing properties present in resource-and-capability combinations leads to competitive advantage. The reference to an n + 1 level is necessary to deduce an effect of resources on performance (for instance, a 'capable' organization, as in Durand (2002)). It follows that the RBV is tautological if located only at the resource level, since it is logically impossible to assert the causality between a resource and the purported resulting advantage materialized at the firm level (Powell, 2001). Traditional RBV mistook objects for properties. What is being selected are the properties conveyed by some resources and capabilities (for example, a marketing team's ability to sense cultural trends before competitors do and to exploit existing brand portfolios) and not the resource and capability themselves (for example, higher marketing budgets or a well-known brand).

By the same token, the recent theorization of dynamic capabilities is flawed because its underlying theory of evolution is not fully expressed and is isolated from a thoughtful conception of fitness and supervenience. If 'dynamic' means the possibility of sequentially activating untapped services of controlled resources, there is no reason to reject the dynamic RBV. If 'dynamic' refers to potential ad hoc and (currently) unsuspected potentialities that match future environmental conditions, then magical holism again permeates our analysis as we blithely attribute *ex ante* adaptation properties to the capabilities. In addition, the dynamic RBV is still reluctant to integrate behavioral hypotheses into its reflections on resource valuation, which is an important selection criterion according to the OES model. These hypotheses include organizational rationalities, foresight, risk behavior, and intentionality. In a nutshell, there are many obstacles to be overcome before the dynamic RBV can offer first a sound theorizing of evolution that avoids the adaptation trap, secondly, a model that embeds dynamic capabilities within a coherent theory of organizations and markets, and thirdly, a valid test of its hypotheses. Perhaps the OES model can allow the dynamic RBV to set its contributions within a broader framework, one that integrates a theorization of dynamics and evolution and also connects dynamic RBV with other research fields.

CONTRIBUTIONS TO CO-EVOLUTIONARY STUDIES

The principal relevance of the OES model for co-evolutionary studies lies in the determination of clearer dependent variables that go beyond typical performance and survival indicators. Once specified and included in the different levels of analyses, future studies may concern selection-preserving and selection-transforming choices, types of organizational arrangements, and forms of competitive advantages based on transactional efficiency or resource valuation characteristics. The OES model may also provide useful definitions of processes and relationships worthy of deeper scrutiny. For instance, understanding how external selection and strategic management influence resource sedimentation processes might complement cognitive and psychological models about organizational memory. International comparisons could show how national institutions and regulative systems influence market redefinition and market assimilation, as well as the pace of selection events, the rhythm of competition, and regional modes of organizational evolution. We can therefore extrapolate that nations, regions, and industries possess their own preferred selection patterns within which discourses about strategic action embed and enact reality (Djelic and Durand, 2003).

7.3   EMPIRICAL IMPLICATIONS

A direct importation of methods used in biology and in cybernetics gives undoubtedly a scientific facade to organizational evolution studies. Yet one may wonder whether these methods bring any analytical power at all once their underlying assumptions are left behind. Certainly, similarities in demographic patterns have been found empirically across organizational populations. However, are organizations commensurate to each other? Under which conditions is it valid to employ the rule of aggregation that constitutes population from individualized organization? Because geneticists such as Yule, Fisher, and Wright developed mathematical models representing population genetics scenarios in the early 1900s, does it entitle current organizational scientists to reuse the same properties and equations? Where is the critical evaluation of these model equations in each discipline – both the source (most often biology) and the destination (organizational science)? What relation exists between a simulation and reality (between a simulacrum and an event)? How can we generate, replicate, and accumulate knowledge on organizational evolution knowing of these imperfections?

There are four major methodological realms that can enable us to accrue knowledge on organizational evolution and strategic management. First, theoretical models can be developed from applied mathematics, as those used in biology. Population genetics has an abundance of theoretical models accounting for mutations, which belong to two grand families (Hartl and Clark, 1997). In the first family, mutations are assumed to be present in population (models by Fisher, Haldane, and Wright). Selection effects caused by the mutation can be constant, frequency dependent, and density dependent, and may or may not vary over time. The second family of models assumes that mutations occur at random intervals in time. Mutations are said to be selectivity neutral or nearly neutral (Kimura, 1983). Elaborated versions of these classes of models have given rise to a plethora of refined specification that organizational theorists could learn and borrow from (Tomiuk et al., 1998). Intrinsic limitations of such methodological importations are: first, the underlying analogies assumed to connect biology with organization science – and mathematical modeling with biological reality, secondly, the method-laden results, thirdly, the problematic application of mathematical modeling to the concrete reality of the social maneuvering that is implied by strategy, fourthly, the 'so what' pending question about results derived from mimicry of applied mathematics, and fifthly, the ignored flaws of theoretical biological models that are imported into the organizational realm. For example, many biological models assume a constant, year-to-year selection intensity. In contrast, Grant and Grant (1995) explore an hypothesis of selection intensity that fluctuates from year to year; and other researchers show how selection can fluctuate over an individual lifespan. Granted these limitations, theoretical models could explicate archetypal forms of organizing that could serve as the idealized envelope of possible events, observable or not in industry and firm history.

The second category of methods involves computerized simulations. At least since Nelson and Winter (1982), simulations have been populating academic journals dealing with evolutionary problems. Lomi and Larsen (2001) provide a rich introduction to the different simulation protocols that can be utilized in organizational evolution research. The January 2005 issue of the *American Journal of Sociology* offers various examples of simulation protocols applied to the diffusion of norms, the emergence of network structures, and the micro-emergence of macro-social forms. The issues that remain to be addressed concern the epistemological nature of simulations (relationships between simulation and reality) and their degree of adhocracy (when they exhibit well-suited threshold values, apposite parameters, and insufficiently justified functions). Despite these shortcomings, it is indeniable that simulation protocols will eventually provide increasingly fruitful avenues for research.

Thirdly, the most widely accepted method concerns the statistical verification of deduced hypotheses. Variance approaches have been criticized due to reductionist assumptions, while process approaches have been touted for their greater grasp of longitudinal phenomena (see section 2.2). However, it appears that recent generations of statistical models and estimations can withstand cross-time effects, violation of observation-to-observation independence (autocorrelation), and correlations between error terms and regressors. In particular, fixed-effect and random models of pooled repeated observations cope with these limitations of classical variance approaches, and are inspired by process approaches. The Hausman test facilitates the choice between those two models relative to the question of whether or not unobserved individual effects correlate with included variables. When the Hausman test does not reject the hypothesis that the individual effects are uncorrelated with the other regressors in the model, a random effects regression must be used. Random effects models split the residual of each observation into a firm-specific residual and the 'usual' residual, and allow for firm-specific variation across years. Fixed effects models require exhaustive multi-year population information, while random effects models compensate for sampling restrictions. When there is within-cluster dependence of yearly observations in multi-year individual datasets, a Huber-White sandwich estimator is required to obtain robust standard errors. Again we should not idealize biology and its statistical prowess. Organizational scientists are, after all, better suited than biologists to follow organizations for decades and to track events throughout their lifespan.[3] In any case, these models imply archival efforts, historical analysis, and socio-logical perusal of facts in order to access both the socio-cognitive capabilities of influential individuals and the institutional, ideological, and political movements at stake when selection criteria come about.

Finally, qualitative studies take their place in this methodological concert. As strategy is ultimately a local epitomized theory about competitiveness, the study of strategic theorizing and discourses is crucial to understanding the ideo-logical foundations of the discipline. Although evidence for ideas' perfomance in the study of organizational evolution needs reinforcements, it is undeniable that – as sources of variations – economic concepts and political values inter-twine with strategic theories about competitiveness (Lounsbury and Glynn, 2001; MacKenzie and Millo, 2003). There exists a constant production of theses and practical ideas (particularly from consulting agencies and legitimating agen-cies) that pervade the ecological hierarchy of the OES model, influence strategy and strategic management, and eventually may alter the very definitions of resources, organizations, and markets (via the processes of resource sedimenta-tion, organizational incorporation, and market assimilation.) Thus, companies' missions, strategic fads, and management fashions not only belong to the strate-gic discourses but also transfer into concrete practices (Rao et al., 2001). As such, they are powerful selection regimes, created and diffused by organizations themselves. At each level of analysis, qualitative studies can therefore bring ele-ments of ideological inflections, relevant and useful for examining how theories impact (when mediated by action) variation sources, selection criteria, and reten-tion processes.

Our feeling is that the four methodological realms can converge, complement each other, and produce cumulative results around a coherent OES model. Table 7.1 diplays examples of indicators that could be used in studies belonging to any of the four methodological domains.

7.4   PRACTICAL IMPLICATIONS

Managers can use the OES model in their analyses and decisions. The essence of strategy resides in the managers' comprehension of and influence on the selection criteria prevailing in a given context. There is no one best strategic way to perfor-mance. In some regions and industries, diversification will be an efficient way to hedge risks over different activities because property rights and transactional efficiency cannot be guaranteed (Kogut et al., 2002). In others, due to the preva-lence of stock markets in the valuation of companies (pressure on governance inefficiency), diversification needs to be moderate, activities related to each other, and administrative coherence high (Zuckerman, 1999). We should therefore envis-age a certain variability in 'do's and don'ts' lists, best practices, and key lessons derived from experience across regions when analyzing the merits of alliances, acquisitions, mergers, FDIs, and so forth. What matters in a given economic and

Table 7.1 Operationalization of selection criteria

Selection criteria	Examples of variables	Details
Economic efficiency	Structure of industry	Fragmented, concentrated, national champion, …
	Characteristics of banking system and finance	Professional, risk-adverse, independent, role of VCs, …
	National or regional innovation support	National and regional funds and policies, …
	Education quality …	% of graduates and postgraduates …
Social reproduction	External evaluation and vertical structuration	Third parties in social stratification (guides, rankings, accreditations) …
	Award	Awards, prizes, honors, …
	Social capital	Inter-generational connectedness, …
	Network structure …	Embeddedness in social networks, form and stability of the networks, …
Governance efficiency	Nature of shareholders	Private, public, blocks, …
	Type of control	Monitoring, incentive structure, …
	Exposition to capital and labor markets …	Debt and equity structure, family-business, international exposure, …
Administrative coherence	Degree of diversification	Portfolio relatedness, organizational form
	Exploitation/exploration	Technological trajectories, patent lineages …
	Type and changes in structure	Magnitude and frequency of reorganizations
	Diversity …	Human resources, identity, …
Transactional efficiency	Complexity of transaction	Technical and legal specifications, …
	Specificity of underlying asset	Technical, cultural, symbolic values, degree of uncertainty, …
	Relative position of exchanging parties	Asymmetries in the exchange
	Modes of exchange …	Frequency of exchange, type of contract, cooperative strategies, …
Resource valuation	Opportunity recognition	Forecasting ability, entrepreneurial resources
	Prior exploitation of potential services	Variance of returns from past undertaken changes, economies of scope, …
	Content of choices …	SPC and STC relative to peers, cumulative number of SPCs and STCs, time since last SPC and last STC, …

socio-political space is the capacity to influence the nature and pace of shifts in selection criteria. The OES model may help uncover the structural mechanisms that explain why, in a given context, one determinant of organizational evolution supersedes others, whereas in different contexts the influence will be reversed.

Four steps for governing the elaboration of a strategy according to the OES model will be suggested. Before studying each step, remember that four major assumptions support the practical application of the OES model: First, organizational evolution is non-teleological. Secondly, firms adopt selection-preserving or selection-transforming choices. Thirdly, avoiding selection pressure or increasing selection pressure on competitors is the royal method of strategy. Fourthly, strategy is about generating and protecting rent sources (anchored in resources and capabilities' properties) more than about short-time profit. The four steps are partially described below:

Step 1 How durable are the selection criteria?

At the three levels, every entity (industry, firm, and competitive advantage) can be selected out. Managers should assess the durability of selection criteria in order to avoid pressure or to pass it on to competitors. Table 7.2 presents typical questions that may enable strategists to identify shifts in selection criteria and help them to formulate a diagnosis.

Step 2 What is my firm's ability to intervene on selection criteria?

Based on prior assessment of the selection criteria's durability at the various levels of analysis (step 1), managers have to evaluate their ability to impact on selection criteria and decide whether to fight against or accelerate the shift in selection criteria (so as to reduce selection pressure on their firm or to increase selection pressure on their competitors). A gradation of actions is, in fact, available: stop, slow down, anticipate, accompany, push forward the selection criteria shift. Social capital, political sense, legitimacy, status and privilege, symbolic power, uniqueness, and size are all elements that contribute to a firm's capacity to influence the pace of selection criteria shift.

Step 3 At which level will adopting actions have the greatest (desired) impact?

Because of the downward causation selection effects, the more managers have the possibility to intervene directly at the market-industry definition level, the more influence they get. Numerous examples exist of companies that were able to protect rights and rents (including monopoly rents in the energy and transport industries, for instance) due to their capacity to hamper market redefinition (often via slowing down deregulation). However, depending on the strategic problem and the intensity of competition, intervention at the organization-firm level or at the resource and capability-competitive advantage level can suffice. For instance, imposition of a new organizational format (consortium, club, association, grouping, network, etc.) can stabilize the pace of change and prevent diffusion of alternative efficient organizational arrangements (Dyer and Nobeoka, 2000). The rapid diffusion of new features based on idiosyncratic resources and capabilities can powerfully increase selective pressure on competitors, via the development of a novel competitive advantage that is later integrated at the organizational level. A corollary question focuses on whether to act alone or muster forces in a collective

Table 7.2 Selection made simple

For all the questions below, use a 10-point scale (with 1 as the weakest marker and 10 as the strongest). Then, sum up the points, and refer to the commentary. Please note that the questions are general and do not purport to be exhaustive. The goal is to introduce an original screening of available information, place it onto the OES model, and bring about a different estimate of a firm's competitive position and strategy.

Determine the selection pressure in your industry
Over the last five years, has the focus of your main activity changed?

What is the importance of market redefinition phenomena in this process?
i.e., the fact that

- certain industrial practices have been accepted (although traditionally rejected before)
- traditional foes have been playing at rapprochement
- entrants have been establishing within your industry

What is the importance of new organizations' institutionalization in this process?
i.e., the fact that

- new organizational arrangements (e.g., cooperation, franchise, long term contracts, etc.) become stronger than before
- legal and regulatory inflexions have modified competition

What is the importance of a changing societal perception (by your buyers) in this process?
i.e., the fact that

- new values are prompted by competitors and are becoming accepted and even demanded by buyers
- the mechanisms of attributing a social value to your offerings (e.g., good, beautiful, fair, safe, virtuous, true, etc.) are displaced due to cultural, demographic, or institutional reasons

The higher your score on these questions, the greater the likelihood that selection criteria at the market-industry level are changing (new selection criteria are emerging for both economic efficiency and social reproduction). You risk bearing partial or full external selection unless your economic position and social status in the industry enable you to influence these criteria.

Determine the selection pressure at the firm level
Over the last five years, did your company reorganize its activities often?
i.e., the fact that

- you changed from an offering- to a client-centred organization
- new professions emerged in your organization (e.g., key account managers, design and graphic, IT marketing professionals, etc.)
- new demands emerged recurrently from buyers, enticing your company to reorganize to satisfy them

Does the variety of organizational arrangements increase in your industry?
i.e., the fact that

- your old and new competitors modify their organizations in different ways and more often than you do
- full external selection (failure of an entire competitor) has occurred or is likely to happen soon
- the definition of your business is changing due to the increasing presence of differentiated, co-integrated, and technologically convergent offerings?

Table 7.2   (Continued)

The higher your score on these questions, the greater the likelihood that selection criteria at the organization-firm level are changing. You risk bearing full external selection unless you are able to increase your governance efficiency and your administrative coherence in order to influence these criteria.

Determine the selection pressure at the competitive advantage level
Does the variety of resources and capabilities *necessary* to elaborate your offerings increase?

Does the variety of resources and capabilities *available* to elaborate your offerings increase?

What proportion of your benefits proceeds from positional rents vis-à-vis resource-based rents?
i.e., the fact that

• your competitive advantage depends more on positions in markets due to historical, political, and socio-cultural reasons than on specific resources and capabilities (e.g., brand, loyalty, enforceable patent, marketing savviness, financial expertise, etc.), and their associated properties (values, rareness, non-imitability, etc.)

How fast is the process of resource sedimentation?
i.e., the fact that

• new combinations of resources and capabilities are copied, borrowed, or substituted by competitors, depleting the rent-potential benefit of your competitive advantage

What degree of opportunity does your business generate?
i.e., the fact that

• the definition of the activity changes rapidly due to valuable recombinations of resources and capabilities
• rent-generating combinations (participating to a firm's competitive advantage) of resources and capabilities spawn new possibilities of business (based on economies of scale and/or economies of scope)

The higher your score on these questions, the greater the likelihood that selection criteria for competitive advantage are changing. You must make choices that increase your transactional efficiency and foster your resource valuation capability. Were you absent from the resource sedimentation and opportunity-generation processes, you would have less chance of maintaining yourself in the business.

---

action in order to affect the selection criteria. Advantages of collective action are obvious but depend on the capacity of the firm to maintain loyalty, trust, and alignment among the joint allies (Stuart, 1998). Shared interests and benefits are a first source for ensuring cohesion, an alternative being threat and coercion. Good examples of collective actions include standardization processes in the music and video industry.

Step 4 Communicating and implementing strategy
Once a firm's strategists have produced a strategy (namely, a theory about competitiveness), what is the firm's capacity to communicate and implement – internally and externally – the mission, objectives, and decisions? Behavioral organization

science lessons apply at this stage, inspired by psychology, psycho-sociology, and cognitive science. Techniques to implement the selection-preserving and selection-transforming choices count in their ranks (among others) communication, negotiation, conviction, motivation, emotion management, creativity management, manipulation, enforcement, and coercion. Again, it is not the theories per se that are influential but the derived concrete actions that causally impact reality – hence the fundamental importance of managerial techniques in organizational evolution.

This four-step strategizing process, inspired by the OES model, avoids the unsolvable debate of what matters more: industry trends or firms' idiosyncratic traits. What matters is the capacity for a firm to act on the nature and pace of selection criteria changes, at the three key levels represented in the OES model, and perhaps beyond. Eventually, each individual actor, from her position decides whether or not to actualize the potential contained in available resources, guided by an underlying theory of competitiveness. Organization and strategy scholars attend and participate to the many variation, selection, and retention processes that constitute the firm and market evolutions. As such, our responsibility is engaged in the future we prepare for the next generations.

NOTES

1   In fine, the definition of causality separates these epistemologies. Positivists see causality as an empirical invariance relating phenomena and a correspondence between observed phenomena and a reality, beyond the scope of our mundane faculties, that scientific research and method can uncover piece by piece. Realists also believe in transcendental reality, but indicate that we must analytically distinguish between empirical (observable phenomena), actual (events that take place) and real (underlying structures, processes and mechanisms) domains. Realism argues that a constant conjunction of events is neither a sufficient nor a necessary condition for the manifestation of a causal law, as the effects of causal powers may not always be observable or can be counteracted by superior power. Moderated constructivists define causality as a meaningful and coherent association between concepts, and they subscribe not to a correspondence view but to a coherence view between phenomena and perceived reality.

2   Early on, Hannan and Freeman pushed aside the criticism of being simply metaphorical or analogical. 'Instead of applying biological laws to human social organization, we advocate the application of population ecology theories' (1977: 962). Fifteen years later, Hannan and Carroll said:

> Do special features of populations and their histories dominate, or do population histories work out minor variations on common patterns? We are far from knowing the answer to this question. Lacking a clear-cut answer, we take the view that *there is no hope of finding general processes unless we look for them, and we operate on the assumption of generality in the processes at work.* Testing its implications provides information about the utility of this assumption. If we are mistaken in thinking that the same general patterns apply to all kinds of organizational populations, then orderly patterns are unlikely to result when we use the same analytic structure to analyze diverse populations. (1992: 37–8; emphasis in original)

More recently, pursuing the abstraction effort, Hannan, Polos, and Carroll declare:

> Organizational ecology and demography have spawned a variety of thriving theory fragments and bodies of related empirical research... These strands can sensibly be regarded as fragments in a larger research program because they (1) build on a common conception of the organizational world shaped by the process of selection and (2) share methodological presumptions and practices. ... We intend that the theory be understood as applying to all populations of organizations, and we are not aware of any exceptions. (Hannan et al., 2003)

3   Sample size has been incriminated for not enabling biologists who search on wild populations to uncover the force of selection pressure and its directionality. The median sample size in the studies reviewed by Kingsolver et al. (2001) is N = 134, preventing statistical models from revealing even an average magnitude of selection.

REFERENCES

Abernathy, W. and Utterback, J. (1978) 'Patterns of innovation in technology', *Technology Review*, 80: 40–7.

Ackroyd, S. and Fleetwood, S. (2000) *Realist Perspectives on Management and Organisations*. London: Routledge.

Ackroyd, S. and Fleetwood, S. (2004) *Critical Realist Applications in Organisations and Management Studies*. London: Routledge.

Alchian, A. (1950) 'Uncertainty, evolution and economic theory', *Journal of Political Economy*, 58: 219–29.

Aldrich, H.E. (1979) *Organizations and Environments*. Englewood Cliffs, NJ: Prentice Hall.

Aldrich, H.E. (1999) *Organizations Evolving*. London: Sage.

Aldrich, H. and Kenworthy, A. (1999) 'The accidental entrepreneur: Campbellian antinomies and organizational foundings', in J.A.C. Baum and B. McKelvey (eds), *Variations in Organization Science: In Honor of Donald Campbell*. Newbury Park, CA: Sage, pp. 19–34.

Amburgey, T., Kelly D., and Barnett, W. (1993) 'Resetting the clock: the dynamics of organizational change and failure', *Administrative Science Quarterly*, 38: 51–73.

Amburgey, T. and Singh, J.V. (2002) 'Organizational evolution', in J.A.C. Baum (eds), *Companion to Organization*. Oxford, UK: Blackwell Publishers. pp. 327–43.

Amit R. and Shoemaker P. (1993) 'Strategic assets and organizational rent', *Strategic Management Journal*, 14: 33–46.

Anderson, P. and Tushman, M. (1990) 'Technological discontinuities and dominant designs: a cyclical model of technological change', *Administrative Science Quarterly*, 35: 604–33.

Ansoff, H.I. (1987) *Corporate Strategy*. Harmondsworth: Penguin.

Ariew, A. (1998) 'The probabilistic character of evolutionary explanations', *Biology and Philosophy*, 13: 245–53.

Arthur, W. (1989) Competing technologies and lock-in by historical small events, *Economic Journal*, 99: 116–31.

Baldridge, D.C., Floyd S., and Markoczy, L. (2004) 'Are managers from Mars and academicians from Venus? Toward an understanding of the relationship between academic quality and practical relevance', *Strategic Management Journal*, 25: 1063–74.

Barnett, W.P. (1997) 'The dynamics of competitive intensity', *Administrative Science Quarterly*, 42: 148–60.

Barnett, W.P. and Burgelman, R.A. (1996) 'Evolutionary perspectives on strategy', *Strategic Management Journal*, 17: 5–19.

Barnett, W.P. and Carroll, G.R. (1995) 'Modeling organizational change', *Annual Review of Sociology*, 21: 217–36.

Barnett, W.P., Greve, H., and Park, D.Y. (1994) 'An evolutionary model of organizational performance', *Strategic Management Journal*, 15: 11–28.

Barnett, W.P. and Hansen, M.T. (1996) 'The red queen in organizational evolution', *Strategic management Journal,* 17: 139–57.

Barnett, W.P. and McKendrick, D.G. (2004) 'Why are some organizations more competitive than others? Evidence from a changing global market', *Administrative Science Quarterly*, 49: 535–71.

Barney, J.B. (1991) 'Firm resources and sustained competitive advantage', *Journal of Management*, 17: 99–120.

Barney, J.B. (2001) 'Is the resource-based "view" a useful perspective for strategic management research? Yes', *Academy of Management Review*, 26(1): 41–56.

Barney, J.B. (2002) *'Gaining and Sustaining Competitive Advantage'*. Englewood Cliffs, NJ: Prentice Hall. (second edition).

Barron, D. (2003) 'Evolutionary theory', in D.O. Faulkner and A. Campbell (eds), *The Oxford Handbook of Strategy*, Vol. 1. Oxford: Oxford University Press, pp. 74–97.

Bartholomew, S. (1997) 'National systems of biotechnological innovation: complex interdependence in the global system', *Journal of International Business Studies*, 28: 241–66.

Baum, J.A.C. (1999) 'Whole-part coevolutionary competition in organizations', *in* J.A.C. Baum and B. McKelvey (eds), *Variations in Organization Science: In Honor of Donald Campbell*. Newbury Park, CA: Sage, pp. 113–35.

Baum, J.A.C. (eds) (2002) *Companion to Organizations*. Oxford, UK: Blackwell Publishers.

Baum, J.A.C. and Dobbin F. (2000) 'Economics meet sociology in strategic management', *Advances in Strategic Management*, Vol. 17, New York: JAI Press, Elsevier Science.

Baum, J.A.C. and Korn, H.J. (1999) 'Dynamics of dyadic competition', *Strategic Management Journal*, 20: 251–78.

Baum, J.A.C. and McKelvey, B. (1999) *Variations in Organization Science: In Honor of Donald Campbell*, London: Sage.

Baum, J.A.C. and Mezias, S.J. (1992) 'Localized competition and organizational failure in the Manhattan hotel industry', *Administrative Science Quarterly*, 37: 580–604.

Baum, J.A.C. and Oliver C. (1991) 'Institutional linkages and organizational mortality', *Administrative Science Quarterly*, 36: 187–99.

Baum, J.A.C. and Rao, H. (2000) 'Evolutionary dynamics of organizational populations and communities', in S. Poole and A. Van de Ven, (eds), *Handbook of Organizational Change and Development*. Oxford: Oxford University Press.

Baum, J.A.C. and Singh, J.V. (1994a) 'Organizational niche overlap and the dynamics of organizational mortality', *American Journal of Sociology*, 100: 346–80.

Baum, J.A.C. and Singh J.V. (1994b) 'Organizational hierarchies and evolutionary processes: some reflections on a theory of organizational evolution', in J.A.C Baum and J.V. Singh (eds), *Evolutionary Dynamics of Organizations*. Oxford: Oxford University Press, pp. 3–22.

Beckert, J. (1999), 'Agency, entrepreneurs, and institutional change: the role of strategic choice and institutionalized practices in organizations', *Organization Studies*, 20(5): 777–99.

Benjamin, B. and Podolny, J.M. (1999) 'Status, quality, social order in the California wine Industry', *Administrative Science Quarterly*, 44: 563–89.

Bennis, W.G. and O'Toole, J. (2005) 'How business schools lost their way?' *Harvard Business Review*, 83 May: 96–102.

Bergson, H. (1911) *Creative Evolution*. New York: Henry Holt and Company (2nd edition, 1983).

Bickhard, M. and Campbell, D.T. (2003) 'Variations in variation and selection: the ubiquity of the variation-and-selection-retention ratchet in emergent organizational complexity', *Foundations of Science,* 8: 215–82.

Bonardi, J-P. and Durand, R. (2003) Sustaining competitive advantage in high-tech markets: managing network effects, *Academy of Management Executive*, 17(4): 40–53.

Bourgeois, J.L. (1984) 'Strategic management and determinism', *Academy of Management Review*, 9: 586–96.

Bowler, P.J. (2003) *Evolution – The History of an Idea.* Berkeley and Los Angeles, California: University of California Press.

Brewer, M.B. and Collins, B.E. (eds) (1981) *Scientific Inquiry and the Social Sciences.* San Francisco: Jossey-Bass.

Brittain, J. (1994) 'Density-independent selection and community evolution', in J.A.C Baum and J.V. Singh (eds), *Evolutionary Dynamics of Organizations.* Oxford: Oxford University Press, pp. 355–78.

Brown, S.L. and Eisenhardt, K.M. (1998) 'Competing on the edge: strategy as structured chaos'. Boston, MA: Harvard Business School Press.

Bruderer, E. and Singh, J. (1996) 'Organizational evolution, learning and selection: a genetic algorithm based model', *Academy of Management Journal*, 39: 1322–49.

Bunge, M. (2001) *Scientific Realism-Selected essays of M. Bunge*, Amherst, New York: M. Mahner (eds), Prometheus Books.

Burgelman, R.A. (1991) 'Intraorganizational ecology of strategy making and organizational adaptation: theory and field research', *Organization Science*, 2: 239–62.

Burt R. (1997) 'The contingent value of social capital', *Administrative Science Quarterly*, 42: 339–65.

Calori, R. (2000) 'Ordinary theorists in mixed industries', *Organization Studies*, 21: 1031–57.

Campbell, D.T. (1960) 'Variation and selective retention in creative thought as in other knowledge process', *Psychological Review*, 67: 380–400.

Campbell, D.T. (1969) 'Variation and selective retention in sociocultural evolution', *General Systems*, 14: 69–85.

Campbell, D.T. (1974) '"Downward causation" in hierarchically organized biological systems', in F Ayala and T. Dobzhansky (eds), *Studies in the Philosophy of Biology.* London: Macmillan, pp. 179–86.

Campbell, D.T. (1990) 'Levels of organization, downward causation and the selection-theory approach to evolutionary epistemology', in G. Greenberg and Tobach (eds), *Theories of the Evolution of Knowing*, Hillsdale, NJ: Erlbaum.

Campbell, D.T. (1994) 'How individual and face-to-face group selection undermine firm selection in organizational evolution', in J.A.C. Baum and J.V. Singh (eds) *Evolutionary Dynamics of Organizations.* New York: Oxford University Press, pp. 23–38.

Canguilhem, G. (1998) *Du développement à l'évolution au XIXe siècle*, Quadrige: PUF

Carroll, G.R. (1985) 'Concentration and specialization: dynamics of niche width in populations of organization', *American Journal of Sociology,* 90: 1262–83.

Carroll, G.R. (1993) 'A sociological view on why firms differ', *Strategic Management Journal*, 14: 237–49.

Carroll, G.R. and Hannan, M.T. (1989) 'Density delays in the evolution of organizational populations: a model and five empirical tests', *Administrative Science Quarterly,* 34: 411–31.

Carroll, G.R. and Hannan, M.T. (2000) *The Demography of Corporations and Industries*, Princeton, New Jersey: Princeton University Press.

Casile, M. and Davis-Blake, A. (2002) 'When accreditations standards change: factors affecting differential responsiveness of public and private organizations', *Academy of Management Journal*, 45: 180–95.

Chandler, A. (1962) *Strategy and Structure*. Cambridge, MA: MIT Press.

Chandler, A. (1990), *Scale and Scope*. Cambridge, MA: Harvard University Press.

Child, J. (1997) 'Strategic choice in the analysis of action, structure, organization, and environment: retrospect and prospect', *Organization Studies*, 18: 43–76.

Christensen, C. (1997) *The Innovator's Dilemma: When New Technologies Cause Great Firms to Fail*. Cambridge: Harvard Business School Press.

Clausewitz, C. von (1976) *On War*. Harmondsworth: Penguin.

Clegg, S. (2002) 'Lives in the balance: a comment on Hinings and Greenwood's "Disconnects and consequences in organization theory?"', *Administrative Science Quarterly*, 47: 428–41.

Cohen, M. and Bacdayan, P. (1994) 'Organizational routines are stored as procedural memory', *Organization Science*, 5: 554–68.

Cohen, M., Burkhart, R., Dosi, G., Egidi, M., Marengo, L., Warglien, M. and Winter, S. (1996) 'Routines and other recurring action patterns of organizations: contemporary research issues', *Industrial Corporate and Change*, 5: 653–98.

Cohen, W. and Levinthal, D. (1990) 'Absorptive capacity: a new perspective on learning and innovation', *Administrative Science Quarterly*, 35(1): 128–52.

Crow, J.F. (2001) 'The beanbag lives on', *Nature*, 409: 771.

Dacin, T., Goodstein J., and Scott, W.R. (2002) 'Institutional theory and institutional change: introduction to the special research forum', *Academy of Management Journal*, 45(1): 45–57.

Darwin, C. (1859) *On the Origin of Species by Means of Natural Selection*. London: Murray.

Darwin, C. (1871) *The Descent of Man and Selection in Relation to Sex*, London: Murray.

Das, S. and Van de Ven, A. (2000) 'Competing with new product technologies: a process model of strategy', *Management Science*, 46: 1300–16.

Davis, G.F. and Greve, H.R. (1997) 'Corporate elite networks and governance changes in the 1980s', *American Journal of Sociology*, 103: 1–37.

Dawkins, R. (1982) *The Extended Phenotype: The Gene as the Unit of Selection*. Oxford: W.H. Freeman.

Dawkins, R. (1986) *The Blind Watchmaker*. Harlow: Longman.

Dawkins, R. (1989), *The Selfish Gene*. Oxford: Oxford University Press (first edition 1976).

Deephouse, D.L. (1999) 'To be different or to be the same: it's a question (and theory) of strategic balance', *Strategic Management Journal*, 20(2): 147–67.

Delacroix, J. and Carroll, G.R. (1983) 'Organizational foundings: an ecological study of the newspaper industries of Argentina and Ireland', *Administrative Science Quarterly*, 28: 274–91.

Denrell, J. (2003) 'Vicarious learning, under-sampling of failure, and the myths of management', *Organization Science*, 14(3): 227–43.

Denrell, J., Fang, C. and Winter, S. (2003) 'The economics of strategic opportunity', *Strategic Management Journal*, 24: 977–90.

Dew N., Sarasvathy S.D. and Venkataraman S. (2004) 'The economic implications of exaptation', *Journal of Evolutionary Economics*, 14: 69–84

Dierickx, I. and Cool, K. (1989) 'Asset stock accumulation and sustainability of competitive advantage', *Management Science*, 35: 1504–11.

DiMaggio, P. and Powell, W. (1983) 'The iron cage revisited: institutional isomorphism', *American Sociological Review*, 48: 147–60.

Djelic, M-L. and Durand, R. (2003) 'A genealogical contribution to the notion of selection for strategic management', *Academy of Management*, MH division, Seattle, August.

Djelic, M-L. and Quack, S. (eds) (2003) *Globalization and Institutions*. Cheltenham, UK: Edward Elgar.

Dobbin, F. (1994) *Forging Industrial Policy: the United States, Britain and France in the Railway Age*. Cambridge: Cambridge University Press.

Dobbin, F. (1995) 'The origins of economic principles – railway entrepreneurs and public policy in nineteenth-century America', in W.R. Scott and S. Sorensen (eds), *The Institutional Construction of Organizations*. London and California: Sage, pp. 277–301.

Dobrev, S.D. and Carroll, G. (2003) 'Size (and competition) among organizations: modeling scale-based selection among automobile producers in four major countries, 1885–1981', *Strategic Management Journal*, 24: 541–59.

Dobzhansky, T. (1937) *Genetics and the Origin of Species*, New York: Columbia University Press.

Donaldson, L. (2001) *The Contingency Theory of Organizations* London and California: Sage.

Donaldson, L. (2003) 'Organization theory as a positive science', in H. Tsoukas and C. Knudsen (eds), *The Oxford Handbook of Organization Theory*. Oxford: Oxford University Press, pp. 39–62.

Dosi, G. (1988) 'Sources, procedures, and micro-effects of innovation', *Journal of Economic Literature*, 26: 1120–71.

Dosi, G. and Nelson, R. (1994) 'An introduction to evolutionary theories in economics', *Journal of Evolutionary Economics*, 4: 153–72.

Durand, R. (2000) *Entreprise et évolution économique*. Paris: Éditions Belin.

Durand, R. (2001) 'Firm selection: an integrative perspective', *Organization Studies*, 22(3): 393–418.

Durand, R. (2002) 'Competitive advantages exist: a response to Powell', *Strategic Management Journal*, 23(9): 867–72.

Durand, R. (2003) 'Predicting a firm's forecasting ability – the role of organizational illusion of control and organizational attention', *Strategic Management Journal*, 24(9): 821–38.

Durand, R. and Calori, R. (2006) 'Sameness, otherness? Enriching organizational change theories with philosophical considerations on the same and the other', *Academy of Management Review* (forthcoming).

Durand, R. and Coeurderoy, R. (2001) 'Age, order of entry, strategic orientation, and organizational performance', *Journal of Business Venturing*, 16: 471–94.

Durand, R. and McGuire, J. (2005) 'Legitimating agencies facing selection: the case of AACSB', *Organization Studies*, 26(2): 113–42.

Durand, R., Rao, H. and Monin, P. (2004) 'Code-change strategies and external evaluations', *CRECIS Workshop*, Université Catholique de Louvain, Brussels, September 14–15.

Durand, R. and Vaara, E. (2005) 'A true competitive advantage? Reflections on different epistemological approaches to strategy research', Working Paper, HEC School of Management, Paris.

Dutton, J.and Dukerich, J. (1991) 'Keeping an eye on the mirror: image and identity in organizational adaptation', *Academy of Management Journal*, 34: 517–54.

Dyer, J. and Nobeoka, K. (2000) 'Creating and managing a high-performance knowledge-sharing network: the Toyota case', *Strategic Management Journal*, 21: 345–67.

Eisenhardt, E. and Martin, J.A. (2000) 'Dynamic capabilities: what are they', *Strategic Management Journal*, 21: 1105–23.

Eldredge, N. and Gould, S.J. (1972) 'Punctuated equilibria: an alternative to phyletic gradualism', in T.J.M. Shopf (ed.) *Models of Paleobiology*. San Francisco: Freeman and Cooper, pp. 82–115.

Elsbach, K. and Kramer, R. (1996) ''Members' responses to organizational identity threats', *Administrative Science Quarterly*, 41: 442–76.

Feldman, M.S. (2000) 'Organizational routines as a source of continuous change', *Organization Science*, 11: 611–29.

Ferraro, F., Pfeffer, J., and Sutton, R. (2005) 'Economics language and assumptions: how theories can become self-fulfilling', *Academy of Management Review*, 30: 8–25.

Fichman, M. and Levinthal, D. (1991) 'Honeymoon and the liability of adolescence: a new perspective on duration dependence in social and organizational relationships', *Academy of Management Review*, 16: 442–68.

Fisher, R.A. (1930) *The Genetical Theory of Natural Selection*. Oxford: Clarendon Press.

Fiss, P.C. and Zajac, E.J. (2004) 'The diffusion of ideas over contested terrain: the (non)adoption of a shareholder value orientation among German firms', *Administrative Science Quarterly*, 49: 501–34.

Fleetwood, S. (2004) 'An ontology for organization and management studies', in S. Fleetwood and S. Ackroyd (eds), *Critical Realist Applications in Organization and Management Studies*. London: Routledge, pp. 27–54.

Flier, B., Van den Bosch, F.A.J. and Volberda, H. (2003) 'Coevolution in strategic renewal behaviour of British, Dutch, and French financial incumbents: interaction of environmental selection, institutional effects, and managerial intentionality', *Journal of Management Studies*, 40: 2163–87.

Fligstein, N. (1996) 'Markets as politics: a political cultural approach to market institutions', *American Sociological Review*, 61: 656–73.

Foss, N.J. (1996) 'Research in strategy, economics and Michael Porter', *Journal of Management Studies*, 33: 1–24.

Foss, N.J. and Eriksen, B. (1995) 'Competitive advantage and industry capabilities, in resource based and evolutionary theories of the firm: towards a synthesis', in C. Montgomery (ed.), *Resource-Based and Evolutionary Theories of the Firm*. Boston: Kluwer Academic Publishers, pp. 43–70.

Foss, N.J. and Knudsen, T. (2003) 'The resource-based tangle: towards a sustainable explanation of competitive advantage', *Managerial and Decision Economics*, 24: 291–307.

Fox-Wolfgramm, S., Boal, K. and Hunt, J. (1998) 'Organizational adaptation to institutional changes: a comparative study of first-order changes in prospector and defender banks', *Administrative Science Quarterly*, 43: 87–126.

Freeman, J. (1990) 'Organizational life cycles and natural selection processes', in L.L. Cummings and B.M. Staw (eds), *The Evolution and Adaptation of Organizations*. Greenwich, CT: JAI Press Ltd, pp. 1–32.

Freeman, J. (1995) 'Business strategy from the population level', in C. Montgomery (ed.), *Resource-based and Evolutionary Theories of the Firm*. Boston: Kluwer Academic, pp. 219–50.

Freeman, J. and Hannan, M.T. (1983) 'The liability of newness: age dependence in organizational death rates', *American Sociological Review*, 48: 692–710.

Fukuyama, F. (1993) *The End of History and the Last Man*. New York: Free Press.

Futuyuma, D.J. (1998) *Evolutionary Biology*. Sunderland, MA: Sinauer Associates, (third edition).

Garud, R., Jain, S., and Kumaraswamy, A. (2002) 'Orchestrating institutional processes for technology sponsorship: the case of Sun Microsystems and Java', *Academy of Management Journal*, 45: 196–214.

Garud, R. and Rappa, M. (1994) 'A socio-cognitive model of technology evolution: the case of cochlear implants', *Organization Science*, 5(3): 344–62.

Gayon, J. (2003) *Darwin's Struggle for Existence*. Cambridge: Cambridge University Press.

Gersick, C. (1991) 'Revolutionary change theories: a multilevel exploration of the punctuated equilibrium paradigm', *Academy of Management Review*, 16: 10–36.

Ghiselin, M.T. (1974) 'The economy of nature and the evolution of sex', Berkeley and Los Angeles: California University Press.

Gillespie, N.C. (1979) *Charles Darwin and the Problem of Creation*, Chicago: Chicago University Press.

Gimeno, J. and Woo, C. (1999) 'Multimarket contact, economies of scope, and firm performance', *Academy of Management Journal*, 42: 239–59.

Gioia, D. and Thomas J. (1996) 'Identity, image, and issue interpretation: sensemaking during strategic change in academia', *Administrative Science Quarterly*, 41: 370–403.

Gould, S.J. (2002) *The Structure of Evolutionary Theory*. Cambridge, MA: Harvard University Press.

Gould, S.J. and Eldredge, N. (1977) 'Punctuated equilibria: the tempo and mode of evolution reconsidered', *Paleobiology*, 3: 115–51.

Gould, S.J. and Lewontin, R.C. (1979) 'The sprandels of San Marco and the Panglossian paradigm: a critique of the adaptionist programme', *Proceedings of the Royal Society London, Services B*, 205: 581–98.

Grant, B.R. and Grant, P.R. (1995) 'Predicting micro-evolutionary responses to directional selection on heritable variation', *Evolution*, 49: 241–51.

Grant, R.M. (1991) 'The resource-based theory of competitive advantage: implications for strategy reformulation', *California Management Review*, Spring, pp. 114–35.

Grant, R.M. (1996) 'Prospering in dynamically-competitive environments: organizational capability as knowledge integration', *Organization Science*, 7: 375–87.

Grant, R.M. (2005) *Contemporary Strategy Analysis*. Malden; MA: Blackwell Publishing

Greenwood, R. and Hinings, C.R. (1996) 'Understanding radical organizational change: bringing together the old and new institutionalism', *Academy of Management Review*, 21: 1022–54.

Greve, H. (1998) 'Managerial cognition and the mimetic adoption of market positions: what you see is what you do', *Strategic Management Journal*, 19: 967–988.

Greve, H. (1999) 'The effect of core change on performance: inertia and regression toward the mean', *Administrative Science Quarterly*, 44: 590–614.

Greve, H. (2002) 'Interorganizational evolution', in J.A.C. Baum (ed.), *Companion to Organization*. Oxford, UK: Blackwell Publishers, pp. 557–78.

Greve, H. (2003) *Organizational Learning from Performance Feedback*, Cambridge UK: Cambridge University Press.

Grimoult, C. (2001) *L'évolution biologique en France*. Genève-Paris: Librairie Droz.

Gulati, R. (1999) 'Network location and learning: the influence of network resources and firm capabilities on alliance formation', *Strategic Management Journal*, 20: 297–420.

Haines, V. (1988) 'Is Spencer's theory an evolutionary theory?', *American Journal of Sociology*, 93(5): 1200–23.

Hall, P. and Soskice, D. (2001) *Varieties of Capitalism: The Institutional Foundations of Comparative Advantage*. Oxford, UK: Oxford University Press.

Hancké, B. (2001) 'Revisiting the French model: coordination and restructuring in French industry', in P. Hall and D. Soskice (eds), *Varieties of Capitalism*. Oxford: Oxford University Press, pp. 307–37.

Hannan, M.T. and Carroll, G.R. (1992) *Dynamics of Organizational Populations: Density, Legitimation, and Competition*. New York: Oxford University Press.

Hannan, M.T., Carroll, G.R., Dundon, E.A. and Torres, J.C. (1995) 'Organizational evolution in a multinational: entries of automobile manufacturers in Belgium, Britain, France, and Germany', *American Sociological Review*, 60: 509–28.

Hannan, M.T. and Freeman, J. (1977) 'The population ecology of organizations', *American Journal of Sociology*, 82: 929–64.

Hannan, M.T. and Freeman, J. (1984), 'Structural inertia and organizational change', *American Sociological Review*, 49: 149.

Hannan, M.T. and Freeman, J. (1989) *Organizational Ecology*. Cambridge, MA: Harvard University Press.

Hannan, M.T., Polos, L. and Carroll, G.R., (2003) 'Cascading organizational change', *Organization Science*, 14: 463–82.

Hargadon, A.B. and Douglas, Y. (2001) 'When innovations meet institutions : Edison and the design of electric light', *Administrative Science Quarterly*, 46: 476–501.

Hartl, D.L. and Clark, A.G. (1997) *Principles of Population Genetics*. Sunderland, MA: Sinauer Associates.

Haveman, H.A. (1992) 'Between a rock and a hard place: organizational change and performance under conditions of fundamental environment transformation', *Administrative Science Quarterly*, 37, 48.

Haveman, H.A. (1993) 'Organizational size and change: diversification in the savings and loan industry after deregulation', *Administrative Science Quarterly*, 38: 20–50.

Hayward, M.L. and Hambrick, D.C. (1997) 'Explaining premium paid for large acquisitions: evidence of CEO hubris', *Administrative Science Quarterly*, 42: 103–27.

Hayward, M.L., Rindova, V. and Pollock, T. (2004) 'Believing one's own press: the causes and consequences of CEO celebrity', *Strategic Management Journal*, 25: 637–51.

Hegel, G.W. (1807) (1977 edition) *The Phenomenology of Spirit*. Oxford: Oxford University Press.

Helfat, C. and Peteraf, M. (2003) 'The dynamic resource-based view: capability life-cycles', *Strategic Management Journal*, 24: 997–1010.

Henderson, A. and Stern, I. (2004) 'Selection-based learning: the coevolution of internal and external selection in high-velocity environments', *Administrative Science Quarterly*, 49: 39–75.

Henderson, R. and Clark, K.B. (1990) 'Architectural innovation: the reconfiguration of existing product technologies and the failure of established firms', *Administrative Science Quarterly*, 35: 9–30.

Henderson, R. and Mitchell, W. (1997) 'The interactions of organizational and competitive influences on strategy and performance', *Strategic Management Journal*, 18: 5–14.

Hendrick, M. (1999) 'What can management researchers learn from D.T. Campbell, the philosopher? An exercise in hermeneutics', in J.A.C. Baum and B. McKelvey (eds), *Variations in Organization Science*. Thousand Oaks, CA: Sage, pp. 339–82.

Hendry, A.P. and Kinnison, M.T. (2001) 'An introduction to micro-evolution: rate, pattern, process', *Genetica*, 112–13: 1–8.

Hinings, C.R. and Greenwood, R. (2002) 'Disconnects and consequences in organization theory?', *Administrative Science Quarterly*, 47: 411–21.

Hitt, M.A., Ireland, R.D. and Hoskisson R.E. (2005) *Strategic Management-Competitiveness and Globalization*. London: Thomson Learning.

Hodgson, G. (1993) *Economics and Evolution – Bringing back Life into Economics*. Cambridge: Polity Press.

Hodgson, G. and Knudsen T. (2004) 'The firm as an interactor: firms as vehicles for habits and routines', *Journal of Evolutionary Economics*, 14: 281–307.

Hofstader, R. (1959) 'Social Darwinism in American thought', New York: George Braziller.

Hoskisson, R.E., Cannella, A.A., Tihanyi, L. and Faraci, R. (2004) 'Asset restructuring and business group affiliation in French civil law countries', *Strategic Management Journal*, 25: 525–43.

Hrebeniak, L.G. and Joyce, W.F. (1985) Organizational adaptation, strategic choice and environmental determinism', *Administrative Science Quarterly*, 30: 336–56.

Huber, J. and Mirowsky J. (1997) 'On facts and fables: reply to Denzin', *American Journal of Sociology*, 102: 1423–28.

Hull, D. (1976) 'Are species really individuals?', *Systematic Zoology*, 25: 174–91.

Hull, D. (2001) *Science and Selection*. Cambridge: Cambridge University Press.

Hull, D., Langman, R. and Glenn, S. (2001) 'A general account of selection: biology, immunology, and behavior', *Behavioral and Brain Sciences,* 24: 511–28 (reprinted in Hull, 2001, pp. 49–93).

Huy, Q. (2001) 'Time, temporal capability, and planned change', *Academy of Management Review*, 26: 601–23.

Huygens, M., Baden-Fuller C., Van den Bosch F. and Volberda, H. (2001) 'Coevolution of firm capabilities and industry competition: investigating the music industry', *Organization Studies*, 22: 971–1011.

Iansiti, M. and Khanna, T. (1995) 'Technological evolution, system architecture and the obsolescence of firm capabilities', *Industrial and Corporate Change*, 4: 333–61.

Ingram, P. and Baum, J.A.C. (1997) 'Opportunity and constraint: organization's learning from the operating and competitive experience of industries', *Strategic Management Journal*, 17: 85–98.

Iwai, K. (1984) 'Schumpeterian dynamics', *Journal of Economic Behavior and Organization*, 5: 321–51.

Jacobides, M.G. and Winter, S.G. (2005) 'The co-evolution of capabilities and transaction costs: explaining the institutional structure of production', *Strategic Management Journal*, 26: 395–414.

Jensen, M. and Zajac, E.J. (2004) 'Corporate elites and corporate strategy: how demographic preferences and structural position shape the scope of the firm', *Strategic Management Journal*, 25: 507–24.

Johnson, N.A. and Porter, A.H. (2001) 'Toward a new synthesis: population genetics and evolutionary development biology', *Genetica,* 112–13: 45–58.

Kelly, D. and Amburgey, T. (1991) 'Organizational inertia and momentum: a dynamic model of strategic change', *Academy of Management Journal,* 34: 591–612.

Kim, W.C. and Mauborgne, R. (1997) 'Value innovation: the strategic logic of high growth', *Harvard Business Review*, 75 Jan–Feb: 102–12.

Kimura, M. (1983) *The Neutral Theory of Molecular Evolution*. Cambridge: Cambridge University Press.

Kingsolver, J.G., Hoekstra, H., Hoekstra, J., Berrigan, D., Vignieri, S., Hill, C., Hoang, A., Gibert, P. and Beerli, P. (2001) 'The strength of phenotypic selection in natural populations', *The American Naturalist*, 157: 245–61.

Klepper, S. and Simons, K.L. (2000) 'Dominance by birthright: entry of prior radio producers and competitive ramifications in the U.S. television receiver industry', *Strategic Management Journal*, 21: 1017–42.

Kogut, B. and Walker, G., (2001) 'The small world of Germany and the durability of national networks', *American Sociological Review*, 66: 317–35.

Kogut, B., Walker, G. and Anand, J. (2002) 'Agency and institutions: organizational form and national divergence in diversification behaviour', *Organization Science*, 13/2: 162–78.

Kondra, A. and Hinings, C.R. (1998) 'Organizational diversity and change in institutional theory', *Organization Studies* 19(5): 743–67.

Kraatz, M.S. and Zajac, E.J. (1996) 'Exploring the limits of the new institutionalism: the causes and consequences of illegitimate organizational change', *American Sociological Review*, 61: 812–36.

Kraatz, M.S. and Zajac E.J. (2001) 'How do organizational resources affect strategic change and performance in turbulent environments: theory and evidence', *Organization Science*, 12: 632–57.

Kwan, K.M. and Tsang, E.W.K. (2001) 'Realism and constructivism in strategy research: a critical realist response to Mir and Watson', *Strategic Management Journal*, 22(12): 1163–68.

Lamarck, J.B. (1809) *Philosophie Zoologique*, (English version translated by H. Elliot, 1914 'Zoological Philosophy', London).

Langton, J. (1979) 'Darwinism and the behavioral theory of sociocultural evolution: an analysis', *American Journal of Sociology*, 85: 288–309.

Lawrence, P. and Lorsch, J. (1967) *Organization and Environment: Managing Differentiation and Integration*. Boston, MA: Harvard University.

Levinthal, D.A. (1991) 'Organizational adaptation and environmental selection-interrelated proceses of change', *Organization Science*, 2: 140–5.

Levinthal, D.A. (1995) 'Strategic management and the exploration of diversity', in C. Montgomery (ed.), *Resource-Based and Evolutionary Theories of the Firm*: Boston: Kluwer Academic Publishers: 20–42.

Levinthal, D.A. (1997) 'Adaptation on rugged landscape', *Management Science*, 43: 934–50.

Levinthal, D.A. and March, J.G. (1993) 'The myopia of learning', *Strategic Management Journal*, 14: 95–112.

Levinthal, D.A. and Myatt, J. (1994) 'Co-evolution of capabilities and industry: the evolution of mutual fund processing', *Strategic Management Journal*, 15: 45–62.

Lewin, A., Long C., and Carroll, T. (1999) 'The coevolution of new organizational forms', *Organization Science*, 10: 535–50.

Lewin, A. and Volberda, H. (1999) 'Prolegomena on coevolution: a framework for research on strategy and new organizational forms', *Organization Science*, 10: 519–34.

Lewontin, R. (1974) *The Genetic Basis of Evolutionary Change*, New York: Columbia University Press.

Lomi, A. and Larsen, E.R. (2001) *Dynamics of Organizations*, Menlo Park, California: AAAI Press-MIT Press.

Lounsbury, M. (2002) 'Institutional transformation and status mobility: the professionalization of the field of finance', *Academy of Management Journal*, 45: 255–66.

Lounsbury, M. (2004) 'Instituting expertise in the American mutual fund industry', Working Paper, Edmonton, Alberta: University of Alberta.

Lounsbury, M. and Glynn, M.A. (2001) 'Cultural entrepreneurship:stories, legitimacy and the acquisition of resources', *Strategic Management Journal*, 22: 545–64.

Lovas, B. and Ghoshal, S. (2000) 'Strategy as guided evolution', *Strategic Management Journal*, 21: 875–96.

Lubatkin, M., Schulze, W., Mainkar, A. and Cotterill, R. (2001) 'Ecological investigation of firm effects in horizontal mergers', *Strategic Management Journal*, 22: 335–57.

MacKay, T.F.C. (1996) 'The nature of quantitative genetic variation revisited: lessons from Drosophilia bristles', *BioEssays,* 18: 113–21.

MacKenzie, D. and Millo, Y. (2003) 'Constructing a market, performing theory: the historical sociology of a financial derivatives exchange', *American Journal of Sociology,* 109: 107–45.

Makadok, R. (1999) 'Interim differences in scale economies and the evolution of market shares', *Strategic Management Journal*, 20: 935–52.

Makadok, R. and Barney J.B. (2001) 'Strategic factor market intelligence: an application of information economics to strategy formulation and competitor intelligence', *Management Science*, 47: 1621–38.

March, J.G. (1994), 'The evolution of evolution', in J.A.C. Baum and J. Singh (eds), *Evolutionary Dynamics of Organizations*. Oxford: Oxford University Press, pp. 39–49.

Maritan, C. and Brush, T. (2003) 'Heterogeneity and transferring practices: implementing flow manufacturing in multiple plants', *Strategic Management Journal*, 24: 945–59.

Matthen, M. and Ariew, A. (2002) 'Two ways of thinking about fitness and natural selection', *The Journal of Philosophy*, XCIX (2): 55–83.

Mayr, E. (1942) 'Systematics and the origin of species', New York: Columbia University Press.

Mayr, E. (1982) 'The growth of biological thought', Cambridge, MA: Harvard University Press.

Mayr, E. (1991) *One Long Argument – Charles Darwin and the Genesis of Modern Evolutionary Thought*. Cambridge?, MA: Harvard University Press.

Mayr, E. (2001) *What Evolution Is*. New York: Basic Books.

McGrath, M.G., McMillan, I. and Venkataraman, S. (1995) 'Defining and developing competence: a strategic process paradigm', *Strategic Management Journal*, 16: 251–75.

McKelvey, B. (1982) *Organizational Systematics*, Berkeley and Los Angeles, California: University of California Press.

McKelvey, B. (1997) 'Quasi-natural organization science', *Organization Science,* 8: 352–80.

McKendrick, D.G. and Carroll, G.R. (2001) 'On the genesis of organizational forms: evidence from the market of disk arrays', *Organization Science*, 12: 661–82.

Metcalfe, J. (1994) 'Evolutionary economics and technological policy', *Economic Journal,* 104: 931–43.

Michael, S. (2000) 'Investments to create bargaining power: the case of franchising', *Strategic Management Journal*, 21: 497–514.

Miner, A.S. (1994) 'Seeking adaptive advantage', in J.A.C. Baum and J. Singh (eds), *Evolutionary Dynamics of Organizations*. Oxford: Oxford University Press, pp. 76–89.

Miner, A.S., Amburgey, T.L. and Stearns, T.M. (1990) 'Interorganizational linkages and population dynamics: buffering and transformational shields', *Administrative Science Quarterly,* 35: 689–713.

Miner, A.S. and Raghavan, S. (1999) 'Interorganizational imitation: a hidden engine of selection', in J.A.C. Baum and B. McKelvey (eds), *Variations in Organizational Science*. London and California: Sage, pp. 35–63.

Mitchell, T.R. and James, L.R. (2001) 'Building better theory: time and the specification of when things happen', *Academy of Management Review*, 26(4): 530–48.

Mitchell, W. (1991) 'Dual clocks: entry order influences on incumbent and newcomer market share and survival when specialized assets retain their value', *Strategic Management Journal*, 12: 85–100.

Montgomery, C. (1995) *Resource-Based and Evolutionary Theories of the Firm*. Boston, MA: Kluwer Academic Publishers.

Moorman, C. and Miner, S. (1998) 'Organizational improvisation and organizational memory', *Academy of Management Review*, 23: 698–723.

Moran, P. and Ghoshal, S. (1999) 'Markets, firms, and the process of economic development', *Academy of Management Review*, 24: 390–413.

Murmann, J.P. (2003) 'Knowledge and competitive advantage'. Cambridge: Cambridge University Press.

Murtha, T.P. and Lenway, S.A. (1994) 'Country capabilities and the strategic state: how national political institutions affect multinational corporations' strategies', *Strategic Management Journal*, Special issue, 15: 113–29.

Nelson, R. (1990) 'Capitalism as an engine of progress', *Research Policy,* 19: 193–214.

Nelson, R. (1995) 'Recent evolutionary theorizing about economic change', *Journal of Economic Literature*, 33: 45–90.

Nelson, R. and Winter, S. (1977) 'In search on a useful theory of innovation', *Research Policy*, 7: 36–76.

Nelson, R. and Winter, S. (1982), *An Evolutionary Theory of Economic Change*, Cambridge, MA: Harvard University Press.

Nickerson, J.A. and Silverman, B.S. (2003) 'Why firms want to organize efficiently and what keeps them from doing so: inappropriate governance, performance, and adaptation in a deregulated industry', *Administrative Science Quarterly*, 48(3): 433–65.

Nietszche, F. (1885) *Thus Spoke Zarathustra*. Harmondsworth: Penguin Classics.

Ocasio, W. (1997) 'Towards an attention-based view of the firm', *Strategic Management Journal*, 18: 187–206.

Oliver C. (1997) 'Sustainable competitive advantage: combining institutional and resource-based views', *Strategic Management Journal*, 18: 697–713.

Orr, H.A. (1998) 'The population genetic of adaptation: the distribution of factors fixed during adaptive evolution', *Evolution,* 52: 935–49.

Palich, L. Cardinal, L. and Miller, C.C. (2000): 'Curvilinearity in the diversification-linkage : an examination of over three decades of research', *Strategic Management Journal*, 21: 155–74.

Palmer, D.A., Pennings, P.D., and Zhou, X. (1993) 'Late adoption of the multidivisional form by large US corporations: institutional, political, and economic accounts', *Administrative Science Quarterly*, 38: 100–31.

Peel, J.D. (1971) *Herbert Spencer, The Evolution of a Sociologist*. New York: Basic Books Publishers.

Penrose, E. (1952) 'Biological analogies in the theory of the firm', *American Economic Review*, 42: 804–19.

Penrose, E. (1959) *The Theory of the Growth of the Firm*. Oxford: Basil Blackwell.

Pentland, B. and Reuter, H. (1994) 'Organizational routines as grammars of action', *Administrative Science Quarterly*, 39: 484–510.

Perrin, R. (1976) 'Herbert Spencer's four theories of social evolution', *American Journal of Sociology*, 81: 1339–59.

Peteraf, M. (1993) 'The cornerstones of competitive advantage: a resource-based view', *Strategic Management Journal*, 14: 179–91.

Peteraf, M. and Barney, J. (2003) 'Unraveling the resource-based tangle', *Managerial and Decision Economics*, 24: 309–23.

Phillips, D. and Zuckerman, E. (2001) 'Middle status conformity: theoretical restatement and evidence from two markets', *American Journal of Sociology*, 107: 379–429.

Polos, L., Hannan, M.T., and Carroll, G.R. (2002) 'Foundations of a theory of social forms', *Industrial and Corporate Change*, 11: 85–115.

Poole, M.S., Van de Ven, A., Dooley, K., and Holmes, M.E. (2000) *Organizational Change and Innovation Processes*. New York: Oxford University Press.

Poppo, L. and Zenger, T. (1998) 'Testing alternative theories of the firm: transaction cost, knowledge-based, and measurement explanations for make-or-buy decisions in information services', *Strategic Management Journal*, 19: 853–77.

Porter, M. (1996) 'What is strategy?', *Harvard Business Review*, November–December: 61–78.

Porter, M.E. (1991) 'Towards a dynamics theory of strategy', *Strategic Management Journal*, 12: 95–117.

Powell, T. (1992) 'Organizational alignment as competitive advantage', *Strategic Management Journal*, 13: 119–34.

Powell, T. (2001) 'Competitive advantage: logical and philosophical considerations', *Strategic Management Journal*, 22: 875–88.

Priem, R.L. and Butler, J.E. (2001) 'Tautology in the resource-based view and the implications of externally determined resource value: further comments', *Academy of Management Review*, 26: 57–66.

Raff, D.M.G. (2000) 'Superstores and the evolution of firm capabilities in American bookselling', *Strategic Management Journal*, 21: 1043–60.

Ranger-Moore, J. (1997) 'Bigger may be better but is older wiser? Organizational age and size in the New York life insurance industry', *American Sociological Review*, 62: 903–20.

Rao, H. (1998) 'Caveat emptor: the construction of nonprofit consumer watchdog organizations', *American Journal of Sociology*, 103: 912–61.

Rao, H., Greve, H., and Davis, G. (2001) 'Fool's gold: social proof in the initiation and abandonment of coverage by Wall Street analysts', *Administrative Science Quarterly*, 46: 502–26.

Rao, H., Monin, P., and Durand, R. (2003) 'Institutional change in Toque Ville: nouvelle cuisine as an identity movement in French gastronomy', *American Journal of Sociology*, 108: 795–843.

Rindova, V.P. and Fombrun, C.J. (1999) 'Constructing competitive advantage: the role of firm-constituents interactions', *Strategic Management Journal*, 20: 691–720.

Romanelli, E. (1999) 'Blind (but not unconditioned) variation – problems of copying in sociocultural evolution', in J.A.C. Baum and B. McKelvey (eds), *Variations in Organization Science: in Honor of Donald Campbell*. Newbury Park, CA: Sage, pp. 79–91.

Rosenberg, N. (1982) *Inside the Black Box, Technology and Economics*, Cambridge University Press.

Rosenbloom, R. and Christensen, C. (1994) 'Technological discontinuities organizational capabilities, and strategic commitments', *Industrial and Corporate Change*, 3: 655–86.

Rumelt, R. (1991) 'How much does industry matter?', *Strategic Management Journal*, 12: 167–85.

Rumelt, R. (1995) 'Inertia and transformation', in C. Montgomery (eds) *Resource-Based and Evolutionary Theories of the Firm*. Boston, MA: Kluwer Academic Publishers, pp. 101–32.

Sandberg, J. (2000) 'Understanding human competence at work: an interpretative approach', *Academy of Management Journal*, 43: 9–25.

Sastry, M.A. (1997) 'Problems and paradoxes in a model of punctuated organizational change', *Administrative Science Quarterly*, 42: 237–75.

Saviotti, P.P. and Mani, G. (1994) 'Competition, variety and technological evolution a replicator dynamics model', *Journal of Evolutionary Economics*, 5: 365–92.

Schluter, D. (1996) 'Adaptive radiation along genetic lines of least resistance', *Evolution*, 50: 1766–74.

Schluter, D. (2000) *The Ecology of Adaptive Radiation*. Oxford: Oxford University Press.

Schmalensee, R. (1985) 'Do markets differ much', *American Economic Review*, 75: 341–51.

Scott, R. (2001) *Institutions and Organizations*, Thousand Oaks, CA: Sage Publications.

Scott, S.G. and Lane, V.R. (2000) 'A stakeholder approach to organizational identity', *Academy of Management Review*, 25: 43–62.

Shane, S. (2000) 'Prior knowledge and the discovery of entrepreneurial opportunity', *Organization Science*, 11(4): 449–69.

Siggelkow, N. (2001) 'Change in the presence of fit: the rise, fall, and renaissance of Liz Claiborne', *Academy of Management Journal*, 44(4): 838–57.

Silverberg, G., Dosi, G. and Orsenigo, L. (1988) 'Innovation, diversity and diffusion: a self-organisation model', *The Economic Journal*, 98: 1032–54.

Silverman, B.S., Nickerson, J.A. and Freeman, J. (1997) 'Profitability, transactional alignment, and organizational mortality in the U.S. trucking industry', *Strategic Management Journal*, 18: 31–52.

Simpson, G.G. (1944) 'Tempo and mode in evolution', New York: Columbia University Press.

Singh, J.V. and Lumsden, C.J. (1990) 'Theory and research in organizational ecology', *Annual Review of Sociology*, 16: 161–95.

Sober, E. (1984) *The Nature of Selection: Evolutionary Theory in Philosophical Focus*. Cambridge MA: Bradford Books.

Spencer, H. (1850) *Social Statics*. London: Williams and Norgate.

Spencer, H. (1852) 'The development hypothesis', *Leader*: March.

Spencer, H. (1857) 'Progress: its law and cause', *Westminter Review*: April.

Spencer, H. (1862) *First Principles*. London: Williams and Norgate.

Spencer, H. (1883) *Essays Scientific, Political, and Speculative*, 3 vols. London: Williams and Norgate.

Spencer, H. (1892) *Social Statics Together with the Man versus the State*. London: Williams and Norgate.

Stabell, C. and Fjeldstad, O. (1998) 'Configuring value for competitive advantage: on chains, shops, and networks', *Strategic Management Journal*, 19: 413–37.

Stern, R. and Barley, S. (1996) 'Organizations and social systems: organization theory's neglected mandate', *Administrative Science Quarterly*, 41: 146–62.

Stinchcombe, A. (1965) 'Social structure and organizations', in J.G. March (ed.), *Handbook of Organizations'*. Chicago: Rand McNally, pp. 153–93.

Stuart, T.E. (1998) 'Network positions and propensities to collaborate: an investigation of strategic alliance formation in a high technology industry', *Administrative Science Quarterly*, 43: 668–98.

Stuart, T.R. and Podolny, J.M. (1996) 'Local search and the evolution of technological capabilities', *Strategic Management Journal*, 17(7): 21–38.

Suarez, F. and Utterback, J. (1995) 'Dominant designs and the survival of firms', *Strategic Management Journal,* 16: 415–30.

Szulanski, G. (1996) 'Exploring internal stickiness: impediments to the transfer of best practice within the firm', *Strategic Management Journal,* 17 Winter Special Issue: 27–43.

Teece, D. and Pisano, G. (1994) 'The dynamic capabilities of firms: an introduction', *Industrial and Corporate Change,* 3: 537–56.

Teece, D., Pisano, G. and Schuen, A. (1997) 'Dynamic capabilities and strategic management', *Strategic Management Journal,* 18: 509–35.

Tegarden, L., Hartfield, D.E. and Echols, A. (1999) 'Doomed from the start: what is the value of selecting a future dominant design', *Strategic Management Journal,* 20: 495–518.

Thompson, P. (2003) 'Selection and firm survival – evidence from the shipbuilding industry, 1825–1914', Working Paper, Carnegie Mellon University.

Tomiuk, J., Guldbrandsten, B. and Loeschcke, V. (1998) 'Population differentiation though mutation and drift – a comparison of genetic identity measures', *Genetica,* 102–3: 545–58.

Tripsas, M. and Gavetti, G. (2000), 'Capabilities, cognition, and inertia: evidence from digital imaging', *Strategic Management Journal,* 21: 1147–61.

Tsang, E.W.K. and Kwan, K.M.(1999) 'Replication and theory development in organizational science: a critical realist perspective', *Academy of Management Review,* 24: 759–80.

Tushman, M. and Anderson, P. (1986) 'Technological discontinuities and organizational environments', *Administrative Science Quarterly,* 31: 439–65.

Tushman, M. and Romanelli, E. (1985) 'Organizational evolution: a metamorphosis model of convergence and reorientation', in B.M. Staw and L.L. Cummings (eds), *Research in Organizational Behavior,* Greenwich, CT: JAI Press, Vol. 7: pp. 171–222.

Tushman, M. and Romanelli, E. (1994) 'Organizational transformation as punctuated equilibrium: an empirical test', *Academy of Management Journal,* 37: 1141–68.

Tushman, M. and Rosenkopf, L. (1992) 'Organizational determinants of technological change: towards a sociology of technological evolution', *Research in Organization Behavior,* 14: 311–47.

Utterback, J.M. (1994) *Mastering the Dynamics of Innovation,* Cambridge, MA: Harvard Business Press.

Uzzi, B. (1999) 'Embeddedness in the making of financial capital: how social relations and networks benefit firms seeking finance', *American Sociological Review,* 64: 481–505.

Van de Ven, A. and Grazman, D.N. (1999) 'Evolution in a nested hierarchy, a genealogy of twin cities health care organizations, 1853–1995', in J.A.C. Baum and B. McKelvey (eds), *Variations in Organization Science.* Thousand Oaks, CA: Sage, pp. 185–212.

Van de Ven, A. and Poole, M.S. (1995) 'Explaining development and change in organizations', *Academy of Management Review,* 20: 510–40.

Van de Ven, A. and Poole, M.S. (2001) 'Field research on processes of organizational change', in Joel A.C. Baum (eds), *Companion to Organizations.* London: Blackwell.

Van den Bosch, F.A.J., Volberda, H. and de Boer, M. (1999) 'Coevolution of firm absorptive capacity and knowledge environment: organizational forms and combinative capabilities', *Organization Science,* 10: 551–68.

Venkataraman, N. (1989) 'The concept of fit in strategy research: toward verbal and statistical correspondence', *Academy of Management Review,* 14: 423–44.

Vermeulen, F. and Barkema, H. (2002) 'Pace, rhythm, and scope: process dependence in building a profitable multinational corporation', *Strategic Management Journal*, 23: 637–53.

Volberda, H. and Lewin, A. (2003) 'Co-evolutionary dynamics within and between firms: from evolution to co-evolution', *Journal of Management Studies*, 40: 2111–36.

Walsh, J., Weber, K., and Margolis, J. (2003) 'Social issues and management: our lost cause found', *Journal of Management*, 29(6): 859–81.

Warglien, M. (2002) 'Intraorganizational evolution', in J.A.C. Baum (eds), *Companion to Organization*. Oxford, UK: Blackwell Publishers, pp. 98–118.

Washington, M. and Zajac, E. (2005) 'Status evolution and competition: theory and evidence', *Academy of Management Journal*, 48: 281–97.

Weick, K. (1979) *The Social Psychology of Organizing*. Reading, MA: Addison-Wesley.

Weismann, A. (1883) *Studies in the Theory of Descent*. New York: AMS Press.

Weeks, J. and Galunic, C. (2003) 'A theory of the cultural evolution of the firm: the intra-organizational ecology of memes', *Organization Studies*, 24(8): 1309–52.

Wernerfelt, B. (1984) 'A resource-based view of the firm', *Strategic Management Journal*, 5 (April–June): 171–80.

Westphal, J.D., and Zajac, E.J. (2001) 'Decoupling policy from practice: the case of stock repurchase programs', *Administrative Science Quarterly*, 46: 202–28.

Whittington, R. (2001) 'What is strategy – and does it matter?'. London: UK: Thomson Learning.

Wholley, D.R. and Brittain, J.W. (1989) 'Characterizing environmental change', *Academy of Management Journal*, 32: 867–82.

Wiggins R. and Ruefli T. (2002) 'Sustained competitive advantage: temporal dynamics and the incidence and persistence of superior economic performance', *Organization Science*, 13: 82–106.

Williams, G.C. (1966) *Adaptation and Natural Selection*. Princeton: Princeton University Press.

Williamson, O. (1985) *The Economic Institutions of Capitalism'*. New York: New York Free Press.

Williamson, O. (1999) 'Strategy research governance and competence perspectives', *Strategic Management Journal*, 20: 1087–109.

Wiltshire, D. (1971) *The Social and Political Thought of Herbert Spencer*. Oxford: Oxford University Press.

Winter, S. (1995) 'Four Rs of profitability: rents, resources, routines and replication', in C. Montgomery (ed.), *Resource-based and Evolutionary Theories of the Firm*. Boston: Kluwer Academic Publishers, pp. 147–78.

Winter, S. (2003) 'Understanding dynamic capabilities', *Strategic Management Journal*, 24: 991–5.

Winter, S.G. and Szulanski, G. (2001) 'Replication as strategy', *Organization Science*, 12: 730–43.

Zollo, M. and Winter, S. (2002) 'Deliberate learning and the evolution of dynamic capabilities', *Organization Science*, 13: 339–51.

Zott, C. (2003) 'Dynamic capabilities and the emergence of intra-industry differential firm performance: insights from a simulation', *Strategic Management Journal*, 24: 97–127.

Zucker, L.G. (1989) 'Combining institutional theory and population ecology: No legitimacy, no history', *American Sociological Review*, 54: 542–45.

Zuckerman, E.W. (1999) 'The categorical imperative: securities analysts and the illegitimacy discount', *American Journal of Sociology*, 104: 1398–438.

INDEX